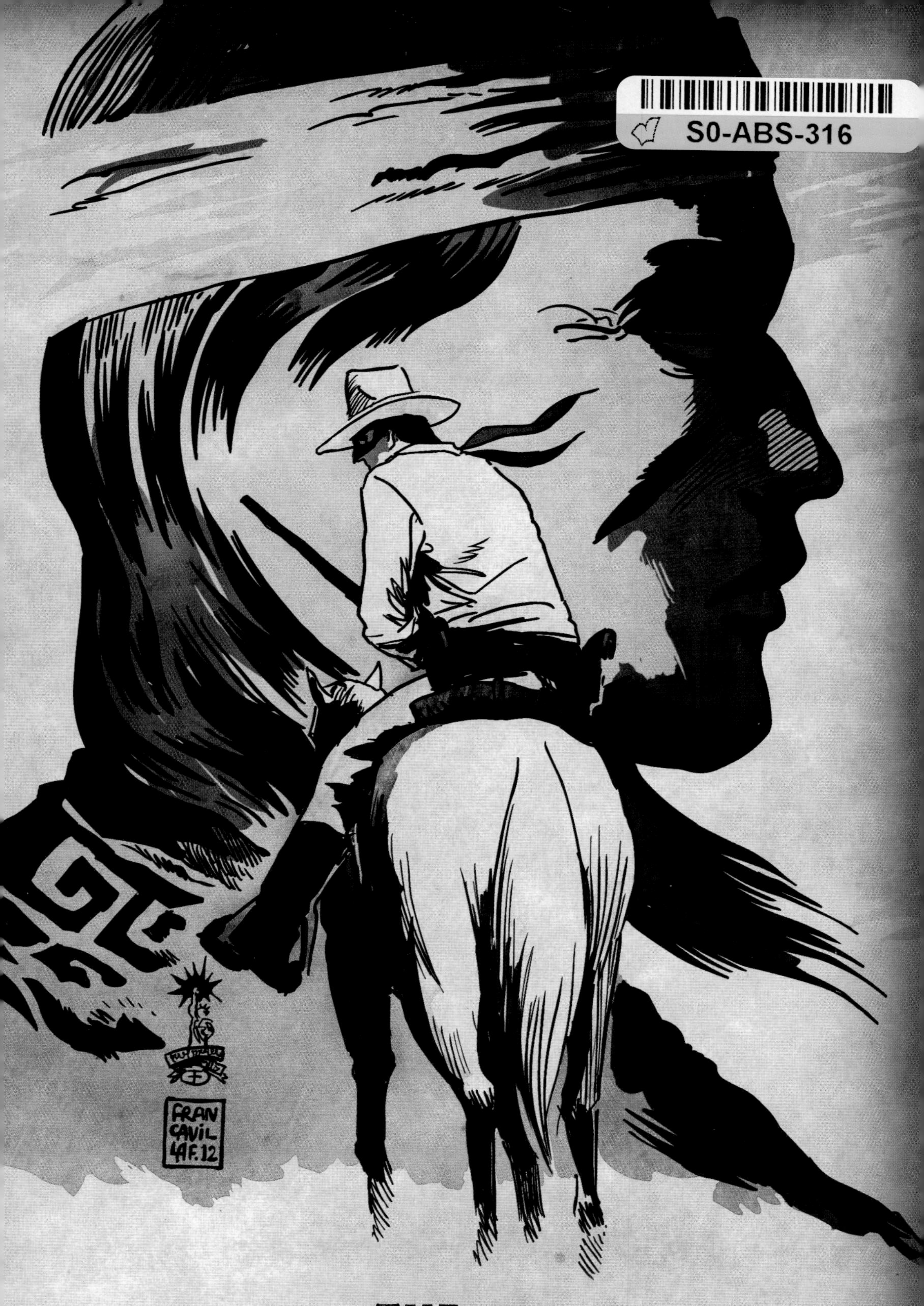
FRAN
CAVIL

THE
LONE RANGER®

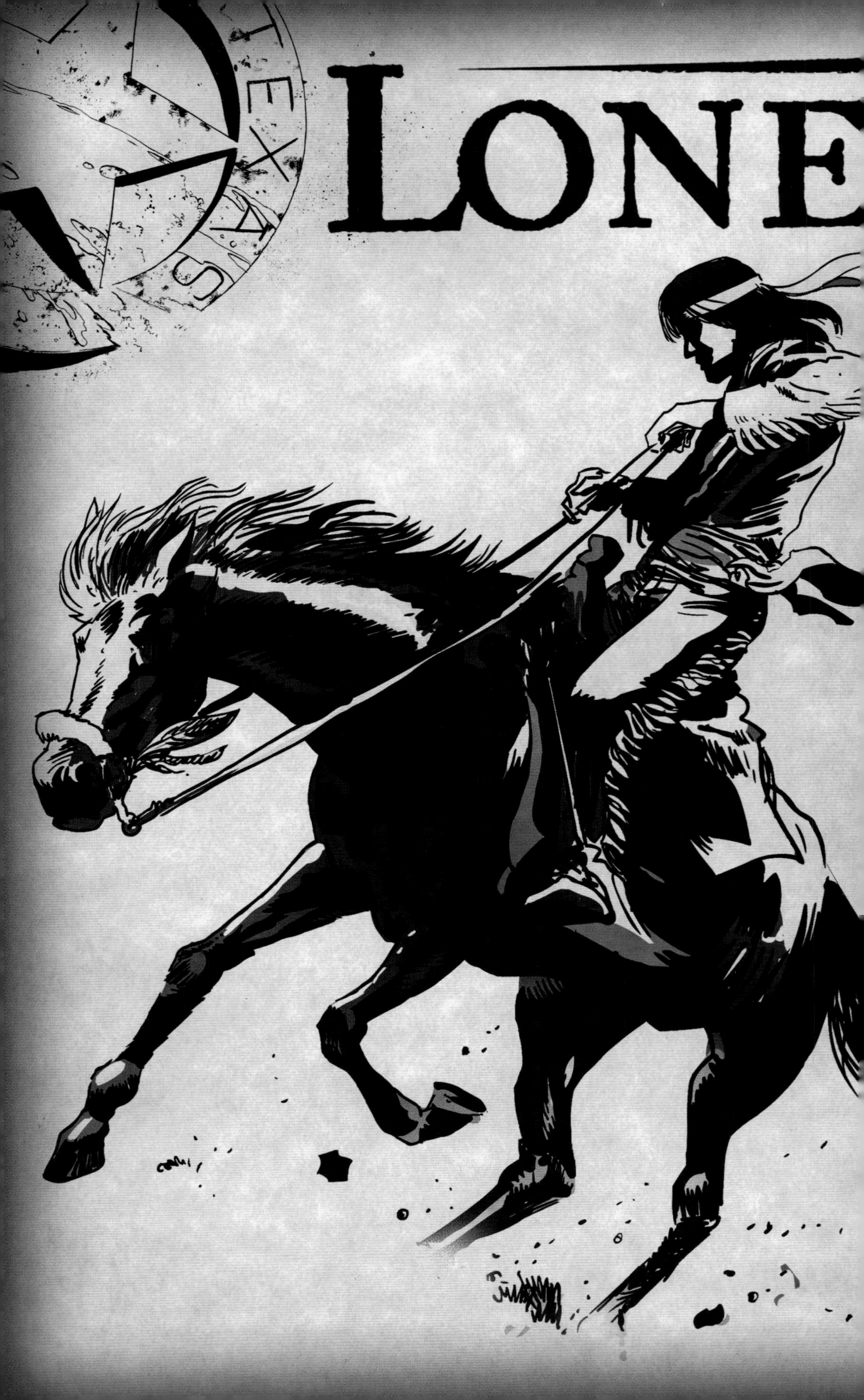
TEXAS
LONE

THE RANGER

★ VOLUME VI: NATIVE GROUND ★

WRITER:
ANDE PARKS

ARTIST:
ESTEVE POLLS

COLORIST:
MARCELO PINTO
OF IMPACTO STUDIO

COVER ARTIST:
FRANCESCO FRANCAVILLA

COLLECTION DESIGN:
JASON ULLMEYER

SPECIAL THANKS TO:
SCOTT SHILLET
COLIN MCLAUGHLIN
DAMIEN TROMEL

THIS VOLUME COLLECTS THE LONE RANGER VOLUME 2 ISSUES 7-12
BY DYNAMITE ENTERTAINMENT

DYNAMITE ®

Visit us online at www.DYNAMITE.com
Follow us on Twitter @dynamitecomics
Like us on Facebook /Dynamitecomics
Watch us on YouTube /Dynamitecomics

Nick Barrucci, CEO / Publisher
Juan Collado, President / COO
Joe Rybandt, Senior Editor
Josh Johnson, Art Director
Rich Young, Director Business Development
Jason Ullmeyer, Senior Graphic Designer
Keith Davidsen, Marketing Manager
Josh Green, Traffic Coordinator
Chris Caniano, Production Assistant

COMIC SHOP LOCATOR SERVICE
888-COMIC-BOOK
comicshoplocator.com

First Printing
ISBN-10: 1-60690-401-9
ISBN-13: 978-1-60690-401-5
10 9 8 7 6 5 4 3 2 1

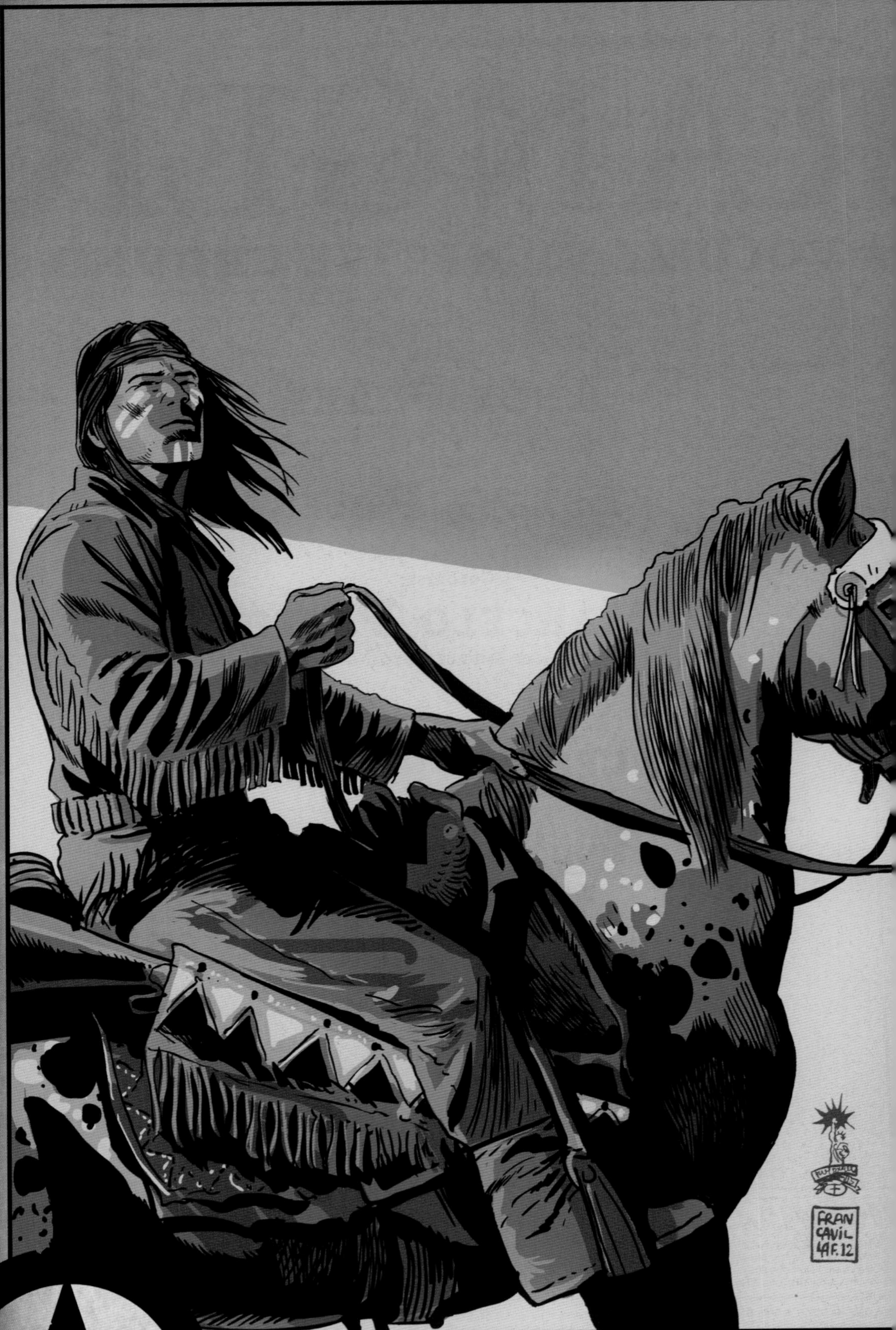
FRAN
CAVIL
LAF. 12

7

COVER BY FRANCESCO FRANCAVILLA

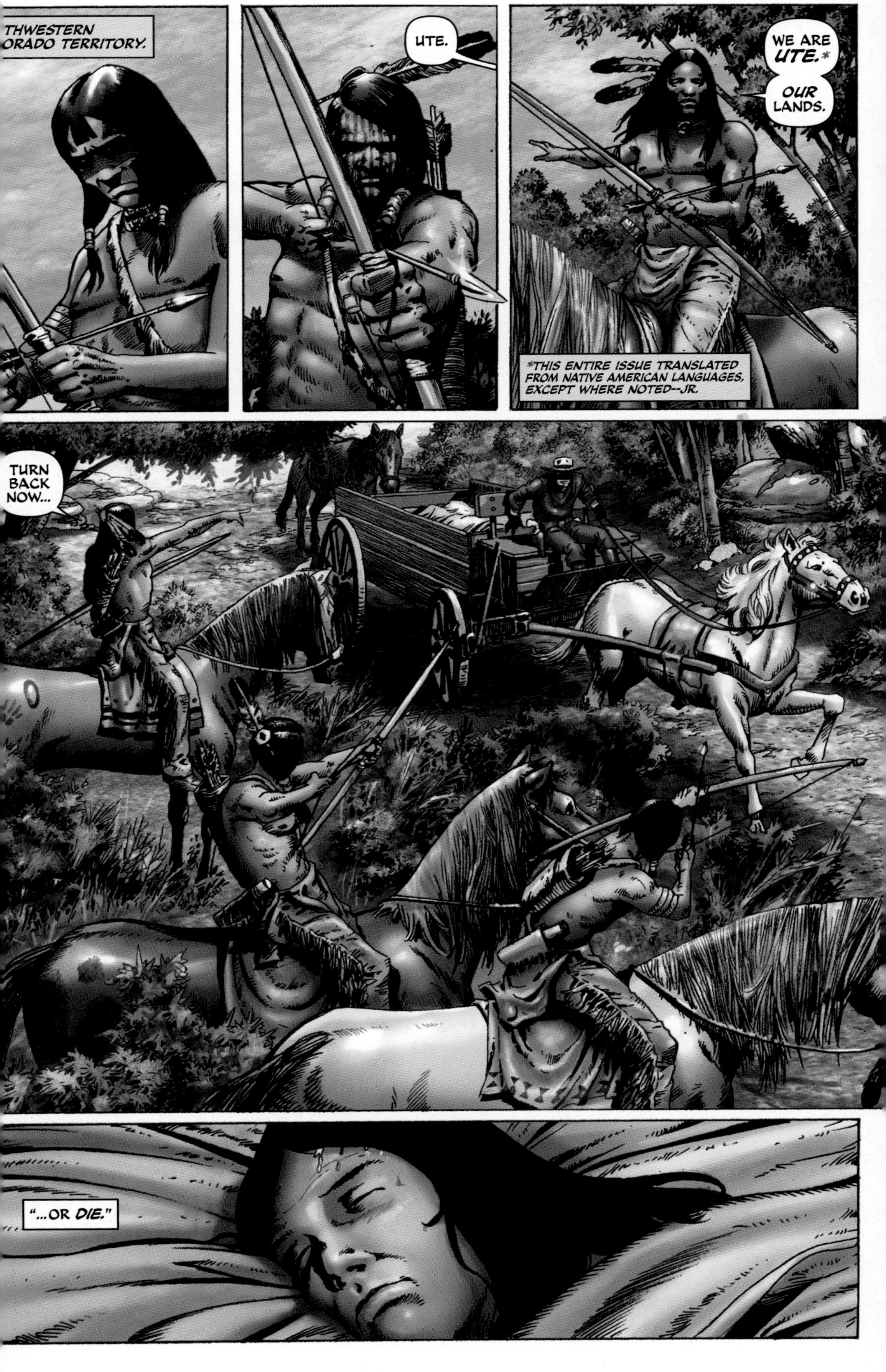
THWESTERN
ORADO TERRITORY.
UTE.
WE ARE UTE.*
OUR LANDS.
*THIS ENTIRE ISSUE TRANSLATED FROM NATIVE AMERICAN LANGUAGES, EXCEPT WHERE NOTED--JR.
TURN BACK NOW...
"...OR DIE."

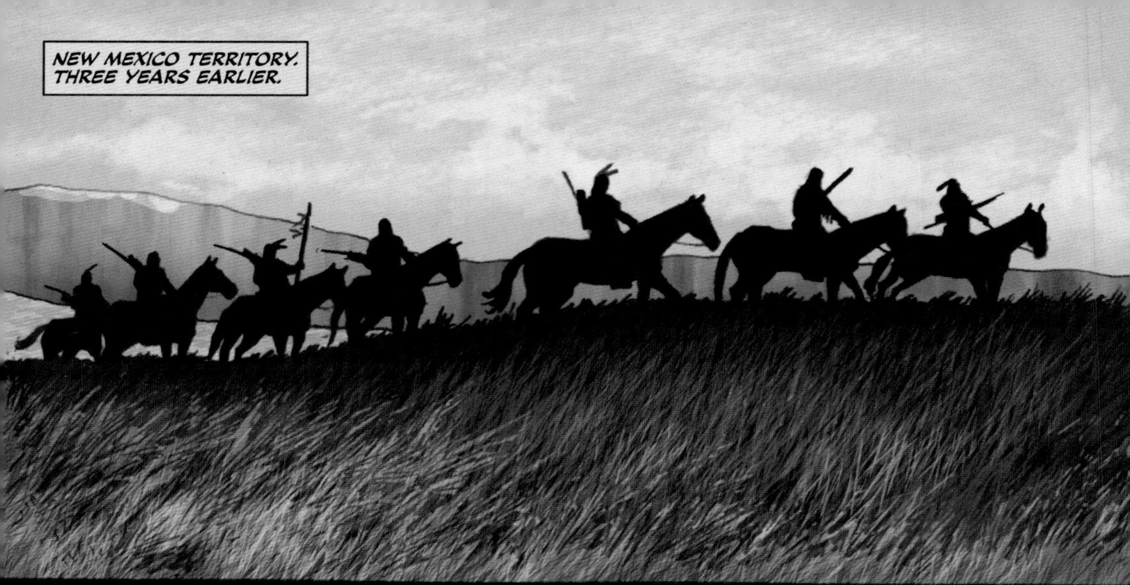
NEW MEXICO TERRITORY.
THREE YEARS EARLIER.

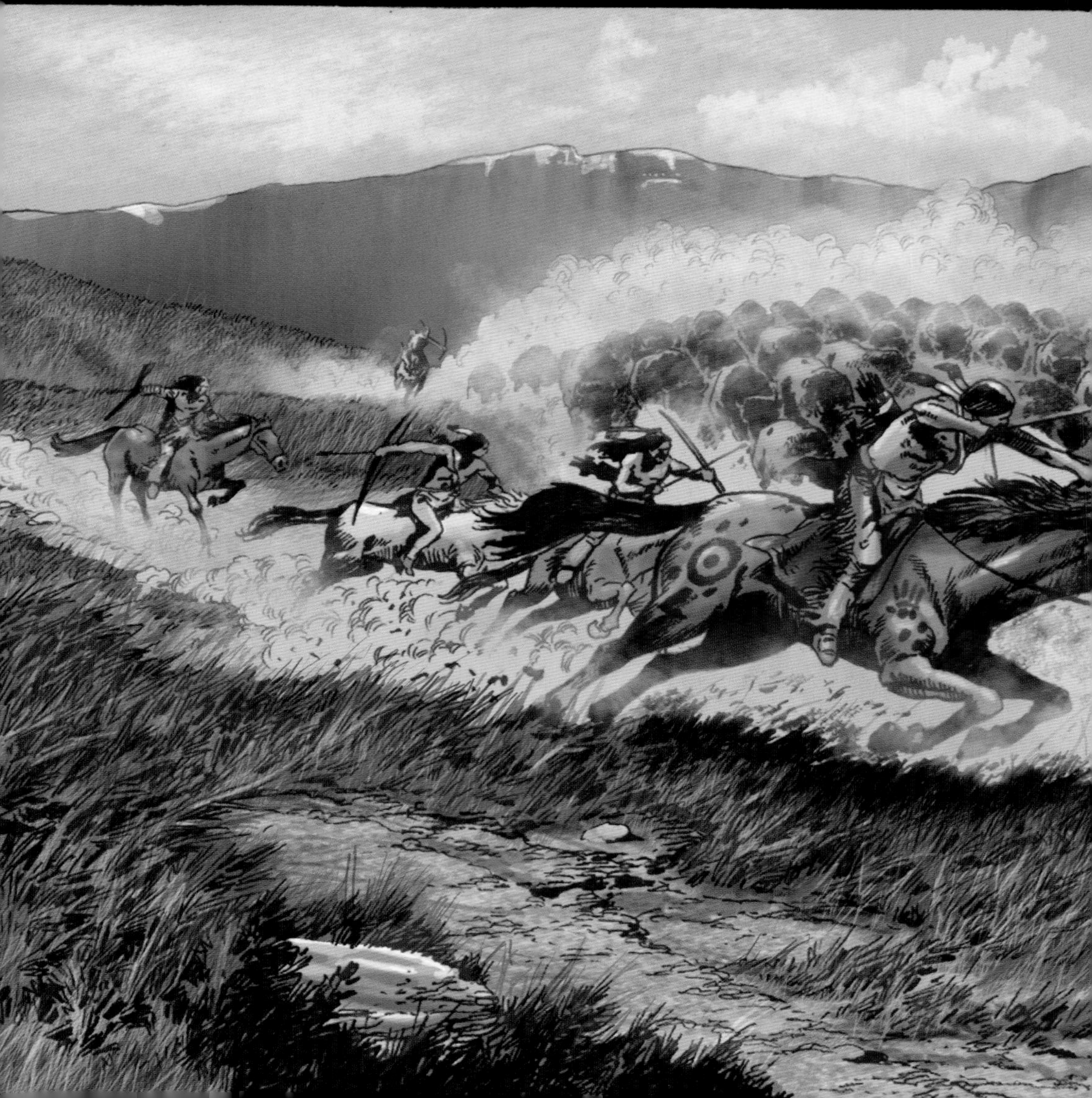

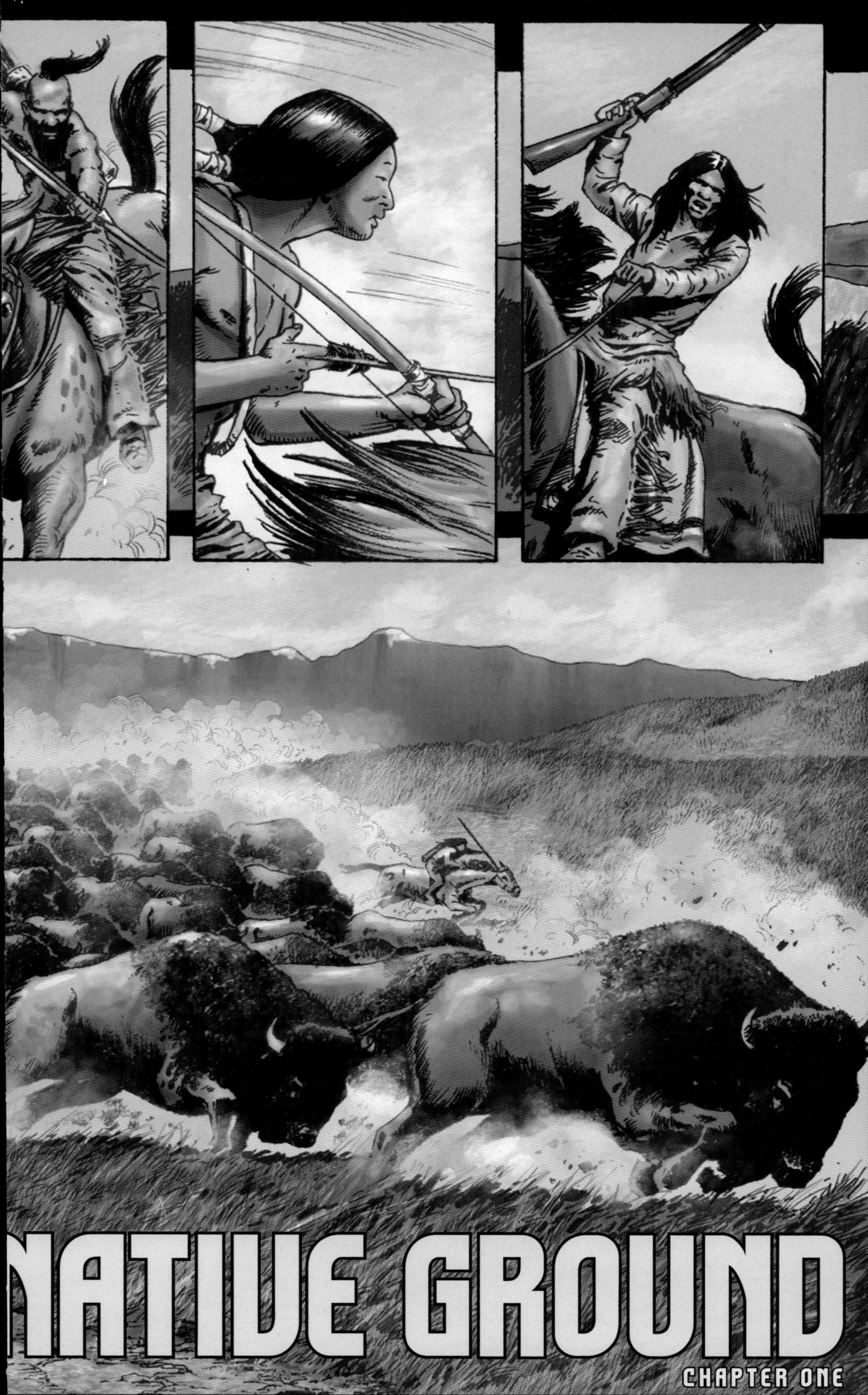
NATIVE GROUND
CHAPTER ONE

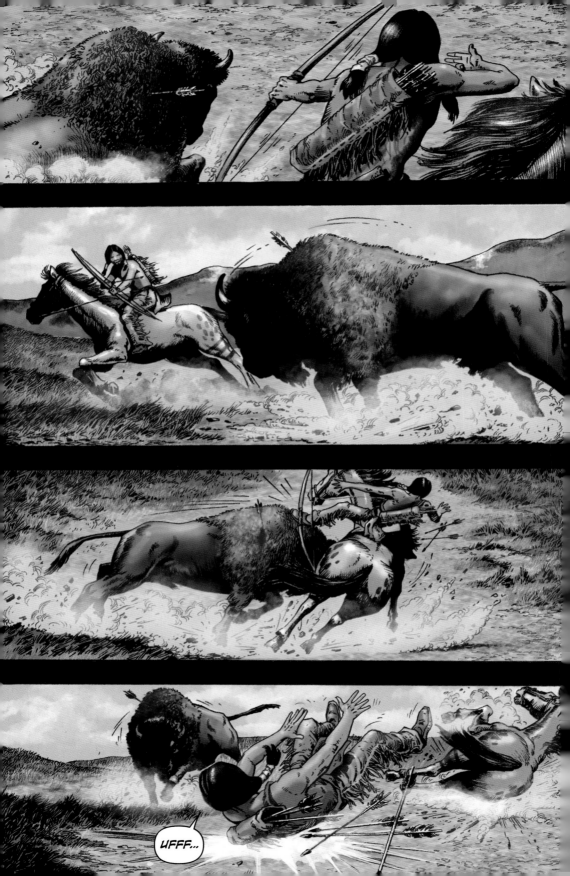

UFFF...

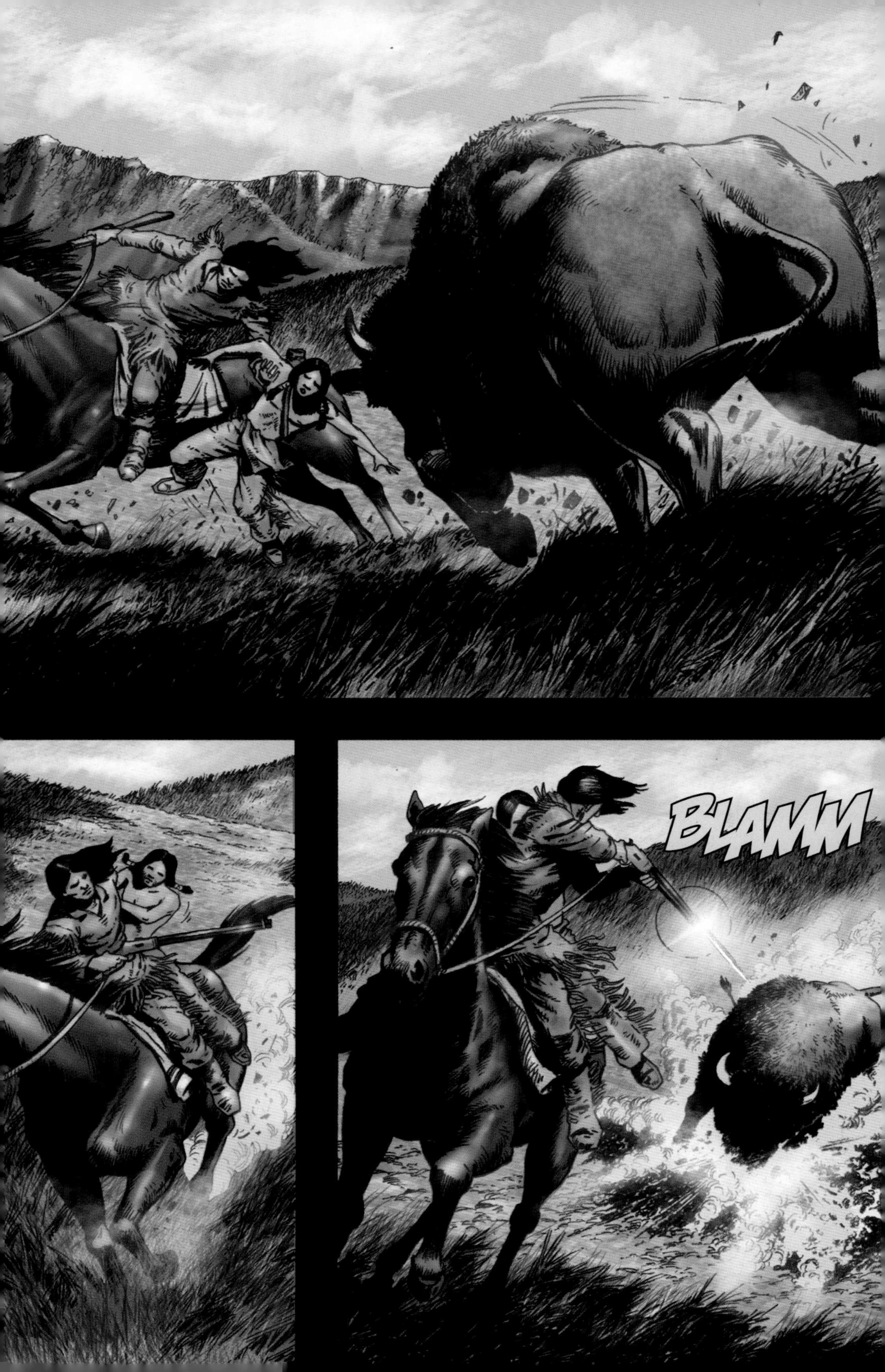
BLAMM

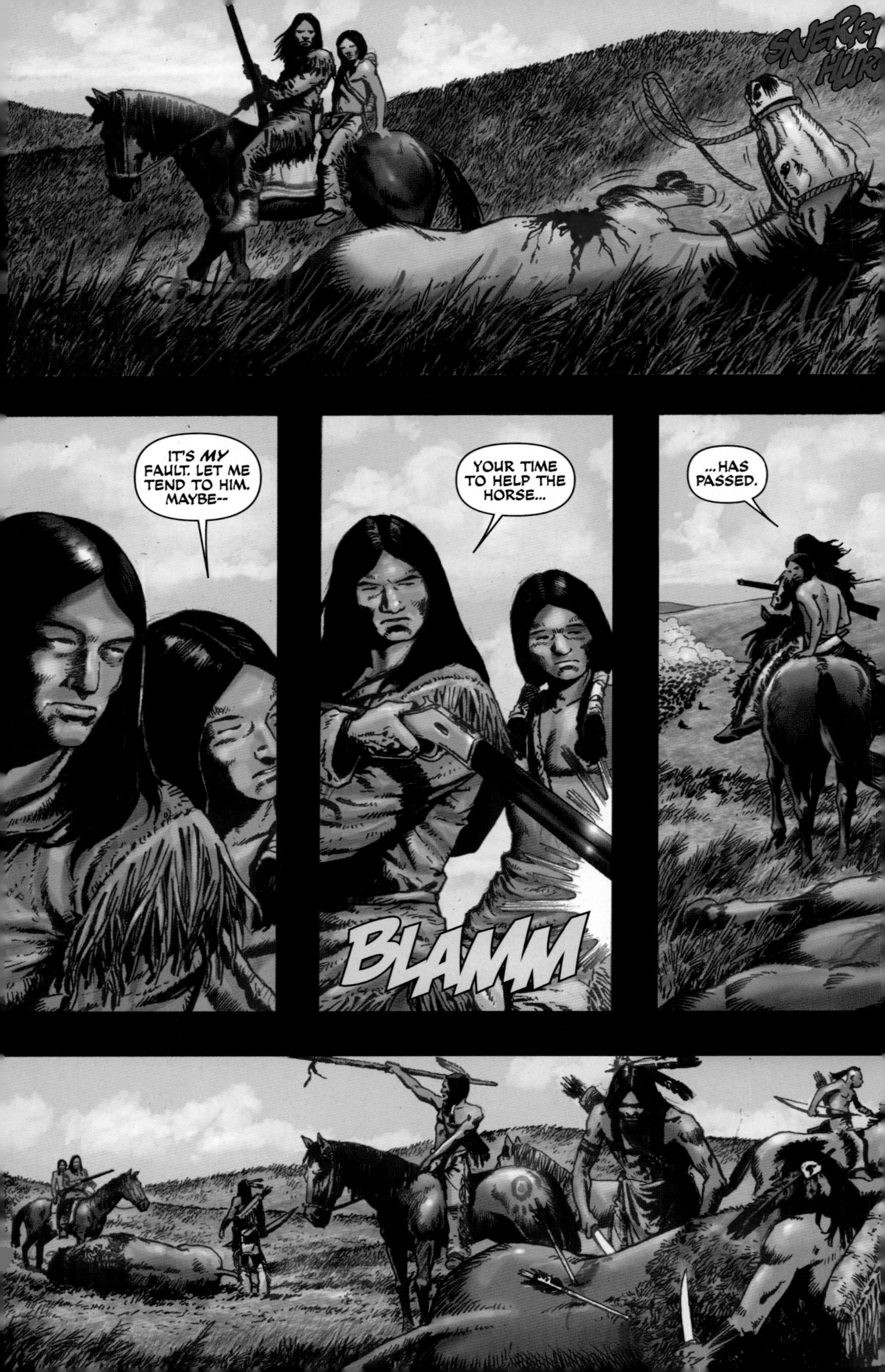
IT'S *MY* FAULT. LET ME TEND TO HIM. MAYBE--
YOUR TIME TO HELP THE HORSE...
BLAMM
...HAS PASSED.

IT'S NOT *RIGHT*, TONTO. YOU *KNOW* THIS! THE BOY DID NOTHING MORE THAN *ANGER* THE BISON AND GET HIS HORSE KILLED.

YOU FELLED THE BISON...NOT THE BOY. ALLOWING HIM TO EAT THE LIVER WAS AN *INSULT* TO THE REST OF US.

HE HAS NO FATHER OF HIS OWN, SO YOU *CODDLE* HIM.

THE BOY WILL *NEVER*--

KAHNAKA WENT THROUGH HIS VISION QUEST LIKE EVERY BRAVE IN THE TRIBE. HE IS AS MUCH A MAN AS ANY OF US.

NONE OF US WERE *ALWAYS* GREAT HUNTERS.

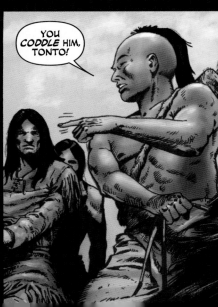

MAYBE, SHKNO, YOU COULD TELL US THE GLORY OF *OUR* FIRST HUNT?

YOU *CODDLE* HIM, TONTO!

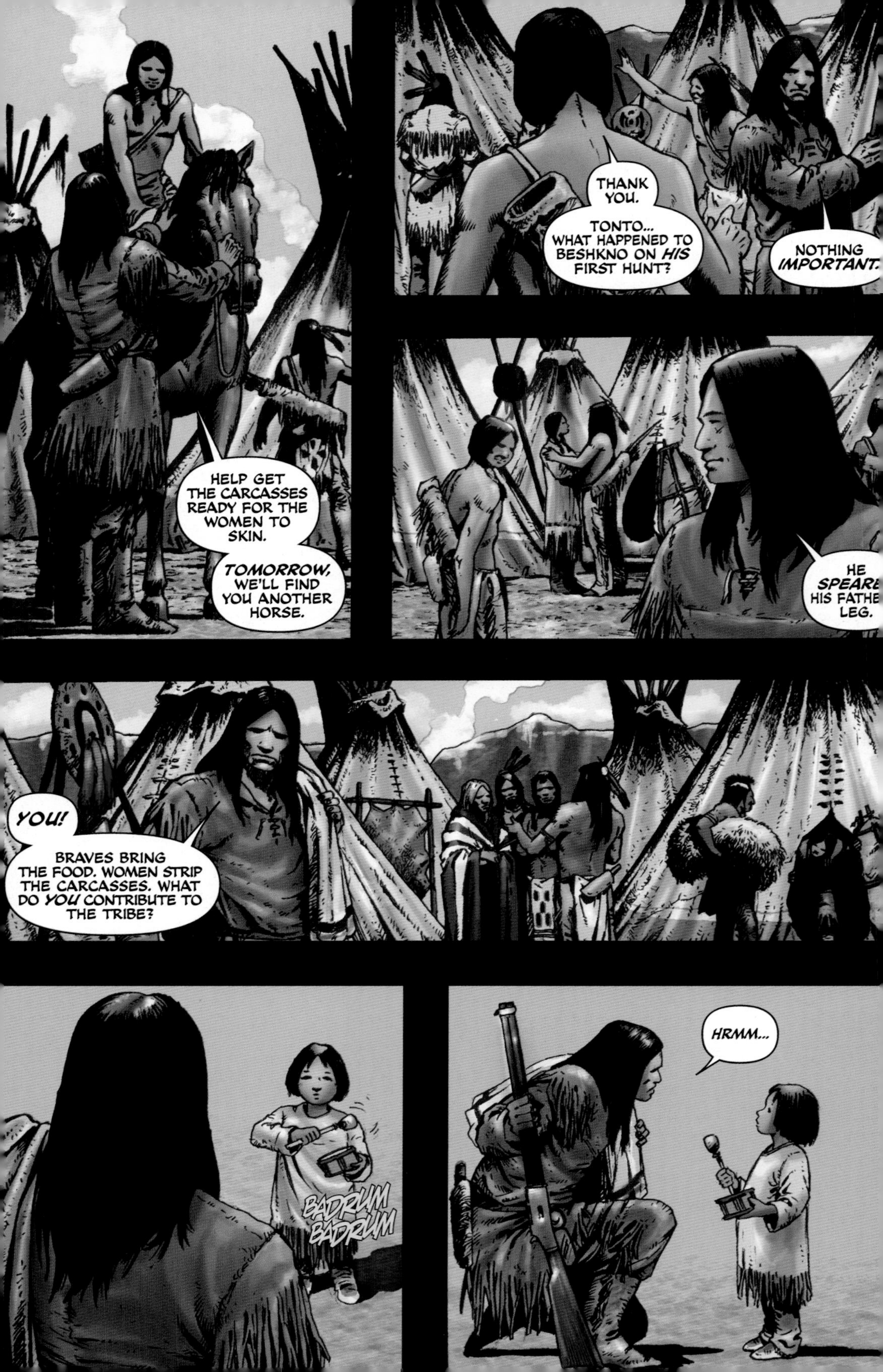

HELP GET THE CARCASSES READY FOR THE WOMEN TO SKIN.
TOMORROW, WE'LL FIND YOU ANOTHER HORSE.
THANK YOU.
TONTO... WHAT HAPPENED TO BESHKNO ON HIS FIRST HUNT?
NOTHING IMPORTANT.
HE SPEARE HIS FATHE LEG.
YOU!
BRAVES BRING THE FOOD. WOMEN STRIP THE CARCASSES. WHAT DO YOU CONTRIBUTE TO THE TRIBE?
BADRUM BADRUM
HRMM...

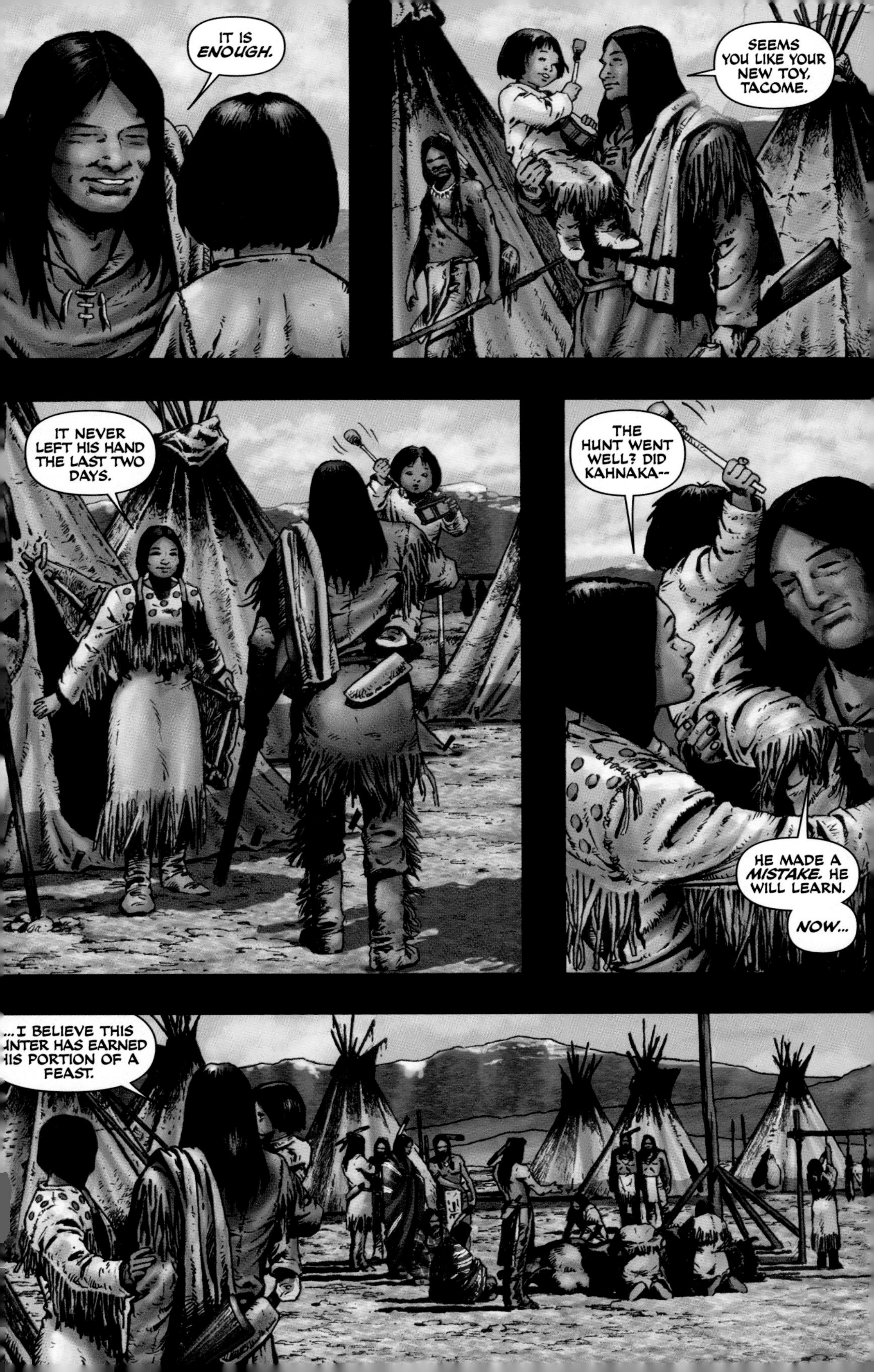
IT IS ENOUGH.
SEEMS YOU LIKE YOUR NEW TOY, TACOME.
IT NEVER LEFT HIS HAND THE LAST TWO DAYS.
THE HUNT WENT WELL? DID KAHNAKA--
HE MADE A MISTAKE. HE WILL LEARN.
NOW...
...I BELIEVE THIS
INTER HAS EARNED
IIS PORTION OF A
FEAST.

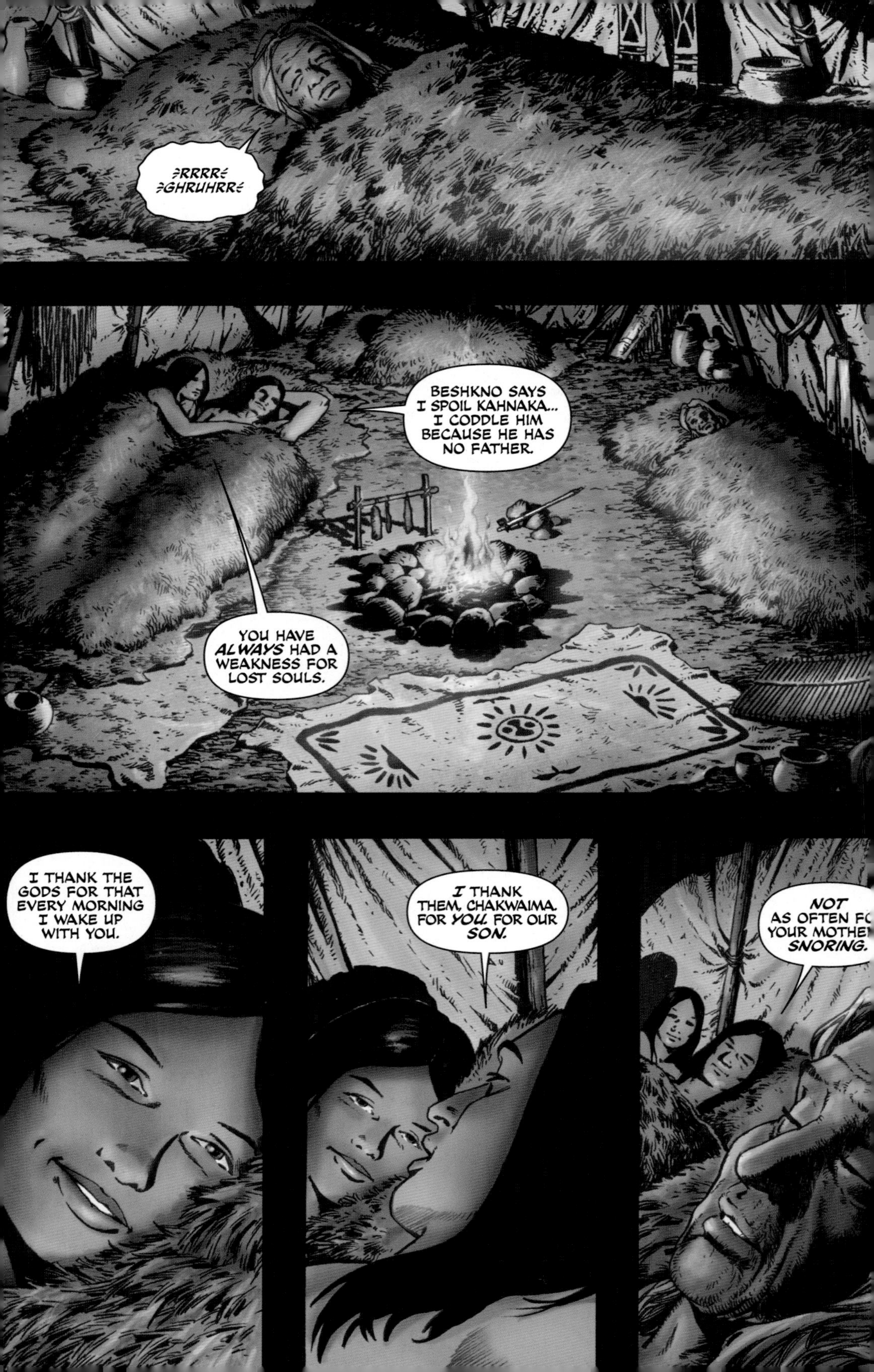

≈RRRR≈ ≈GHRUHRR≈
BESHKNO SAYS I SPOIL KAHNAKA... I CODDLE HIM BECAUSE HE HAS NO FATHER.
YOU HAVE ALWAYS HAD A WEAKNESS FOR LOST SOULS.
I THANK THE GODS FOR THAT EVERY MORNING I WAKE UP WITH YOU.
I THANK THEM, CHAKWAIMA. FOR YOU. FOR OUR SON.

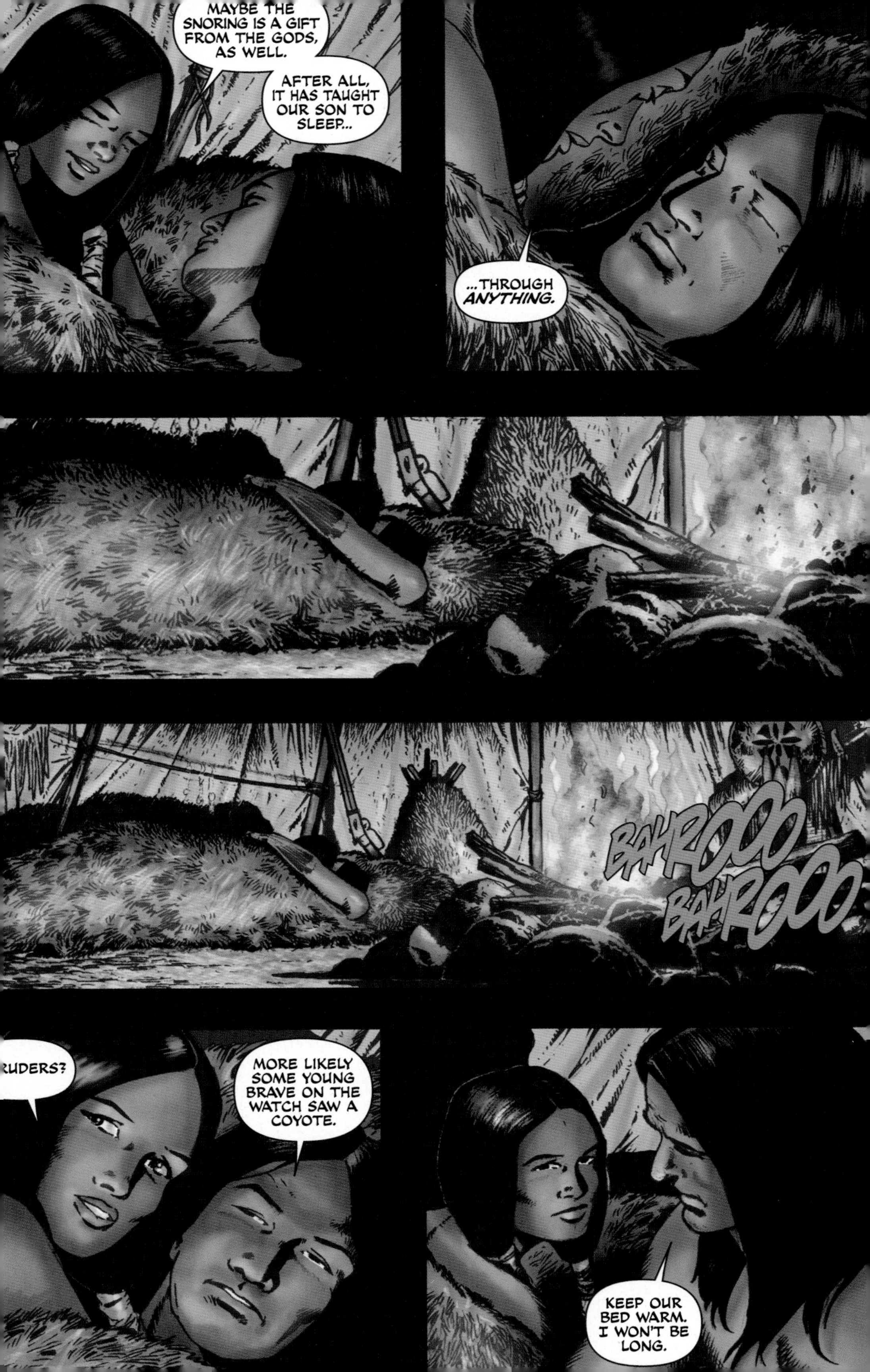
MAYBE THE SNORING IS A GIFT FROM THE GODS, AS WELL.
AFTER ALL, IT HAS TAUGHT OUR SON TO SLEEP...
...THROUGH *ANYTHING.*
BAHROOO
BAHROOO
RUDERS?
MORE LIKELY SOME YOUNG BRAVE ON THE WATCH SAW A COYOTE.
KEEP OUR BED WARM. I WON'T BE LONG.

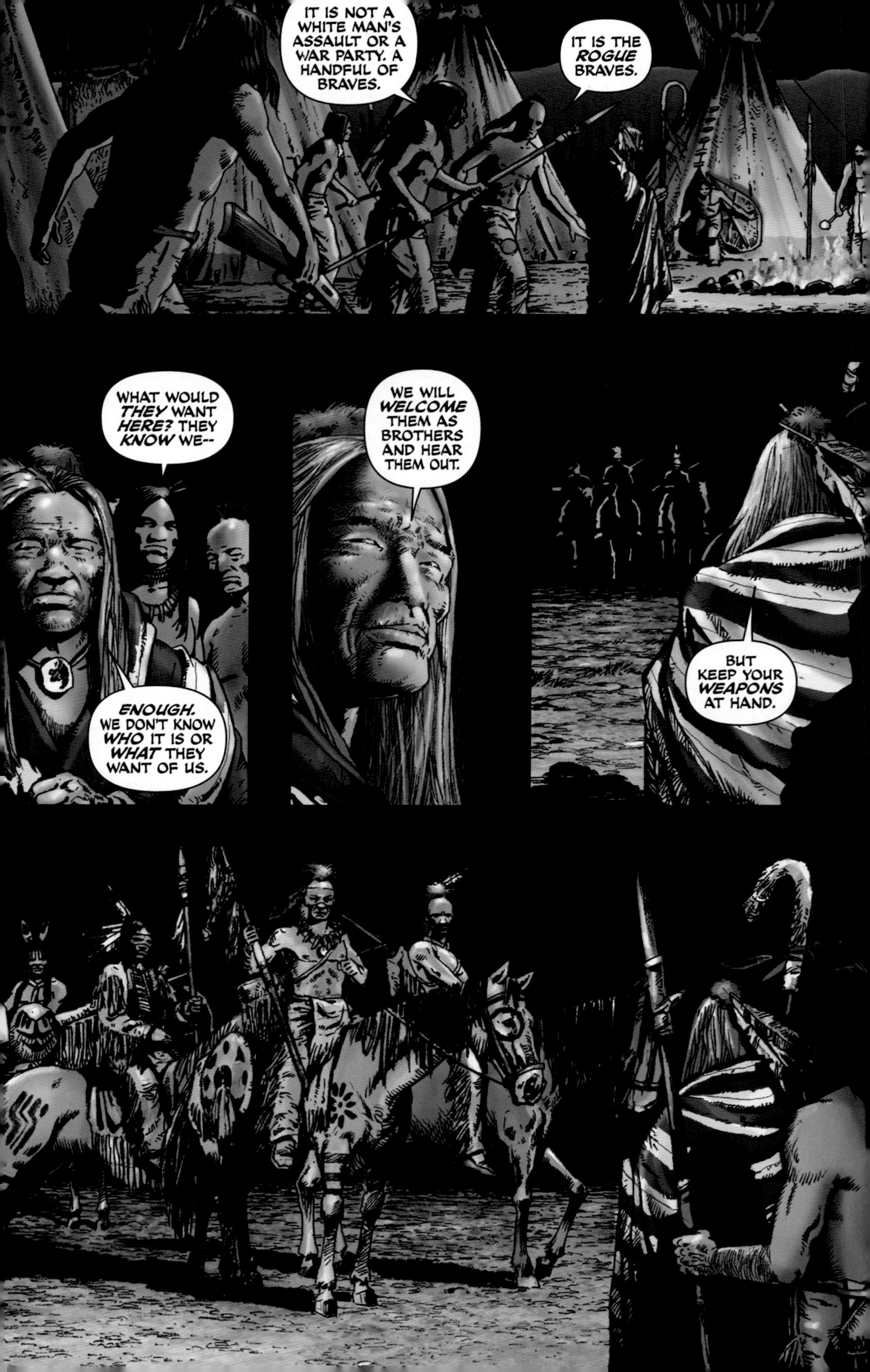
IT IS NOT A WHITE MAN'S ASSAULT OR A WAR PARTY. A HANDFUL OF BRAVES.
IT IS THE *ROGUE* BRAVES.
WHAT WOULD *THEY* WANT *HERE?* THEY *KNOW* WE--
ENOUGH. WE DON'T KNOW *WHO* IT IS OR *WHAT* THEY WANT OF US.
WE WILL *WELCOME* THEM AS BROTHERS AND HEAR THEM OUT.
BUT KEEP YOUR *WEAPONS* AT HAND.

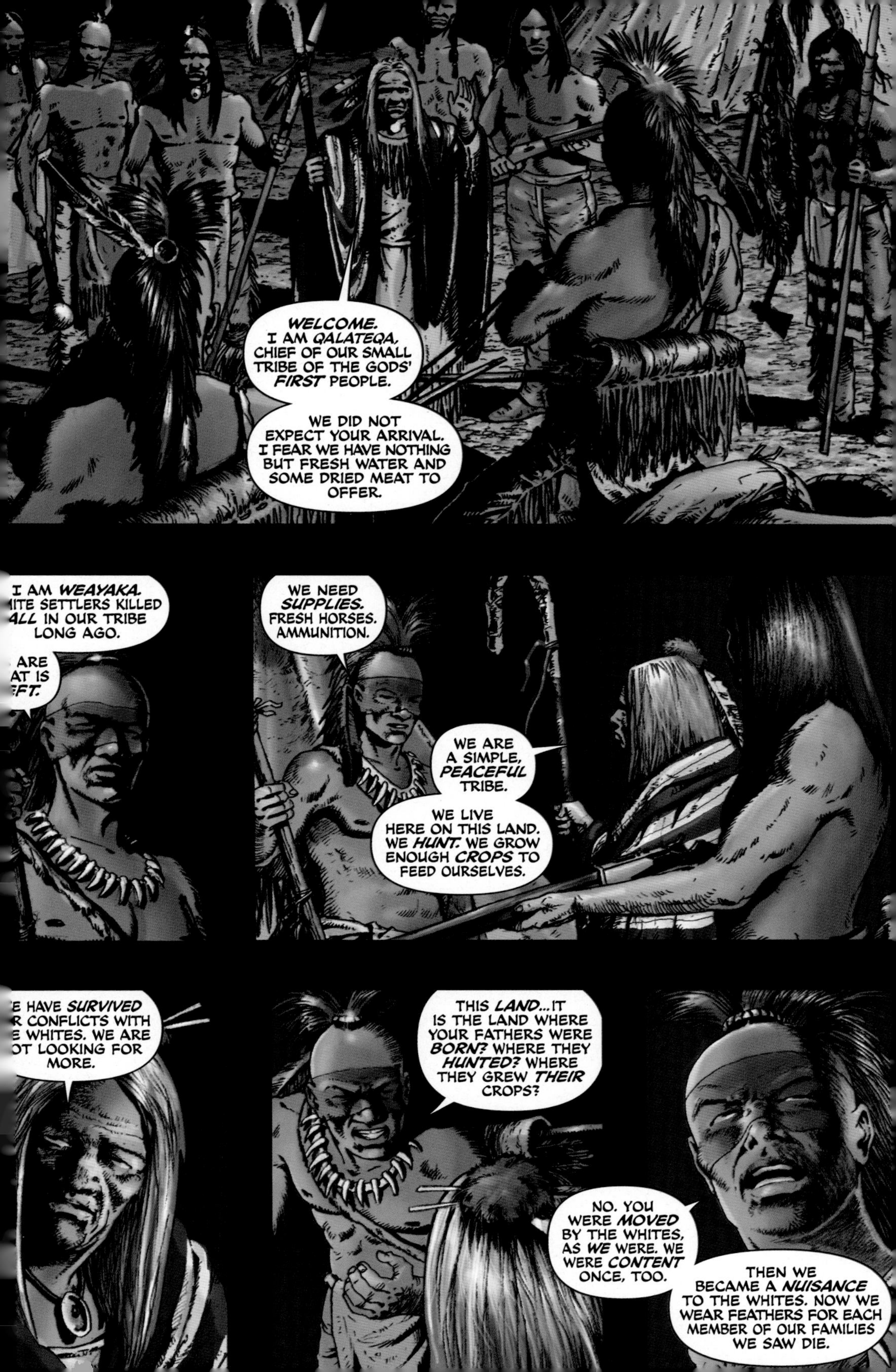
WELCOME. I AM QALATEQA, CHIEF OF OUR SMALL TRIBE OF THE GODS' FIRST PEOPLE.
WE DID NOT EXPECT YOUR ARRIVAL. I FEAR WE HAVE NOTHING BUT FRESH WATER AND SOME DRIED MEAT TO OFFER.
I AM WEAYAKA. ITE SETTLERS KILLED ALL IN OUR TRIBE LONG AGO.
ARE AT IS FT.
WE NEED SUPPLIES. FRESH HORSES. AMMUNITION.
WE ARE A SIMPLE, PEACEFUL TRIBE.
WE LIVE HERE ON THIS LAND. WE HUNT. WE GROW ENOUGH CROPS TO FEED OURSELVES.
E HAVE SURVIVED R CONFLICTS WITH E WHITES. WE ARE OT LOOKING FOR MORE.
THIS LAND...IT IS THE LAND WHERE YOUR FATHERS WERE BORN? WHERE THEY HUNTED? WHERE THEY GREW THEIR CROPS?
NO. YOU WERE MOVED BY THE WHITES, AS WE WERE. WE WERE CONTENT ONCE, TOO.
THEN WE BECAME A NUISANCE TO THE WHITES. NOW WE WEAR FEATHERS FOR EACH MEMBER OF OUR FAMILIES WE SAW DIE.

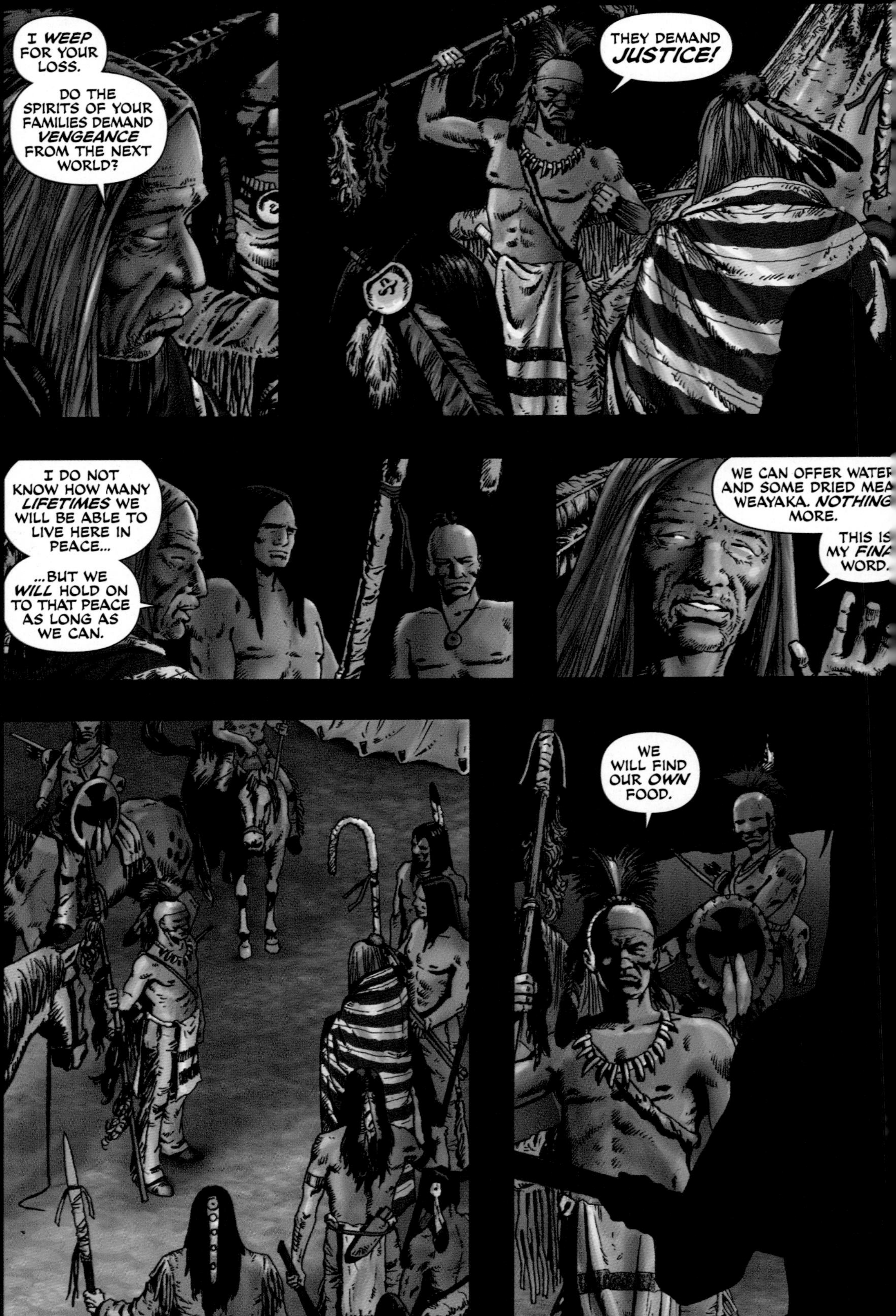
I WEEP FOR YOUR LOSS.
DO THE SPIRITS OF YOUR FAMILIES DEMAND VENGEANCE FROM THE NEXT WORLD?
THEY DEMAND JUSTICE!
I DO NOT KNOW HOW MANY LIFETIMES WE WILL BE ABLE TO LIVE HERE IN PEACE...
...BUT WE WILL HOLD ON TO THAT PEACE AS LONG AS WE CAN.
WE CAN OFFER WATE AND SOME DRIED MEA WEAYAKA. NOTHING MORE.
THIS IS MY FINA WORD.
WE WILL FIND OUR OWN FOOD.

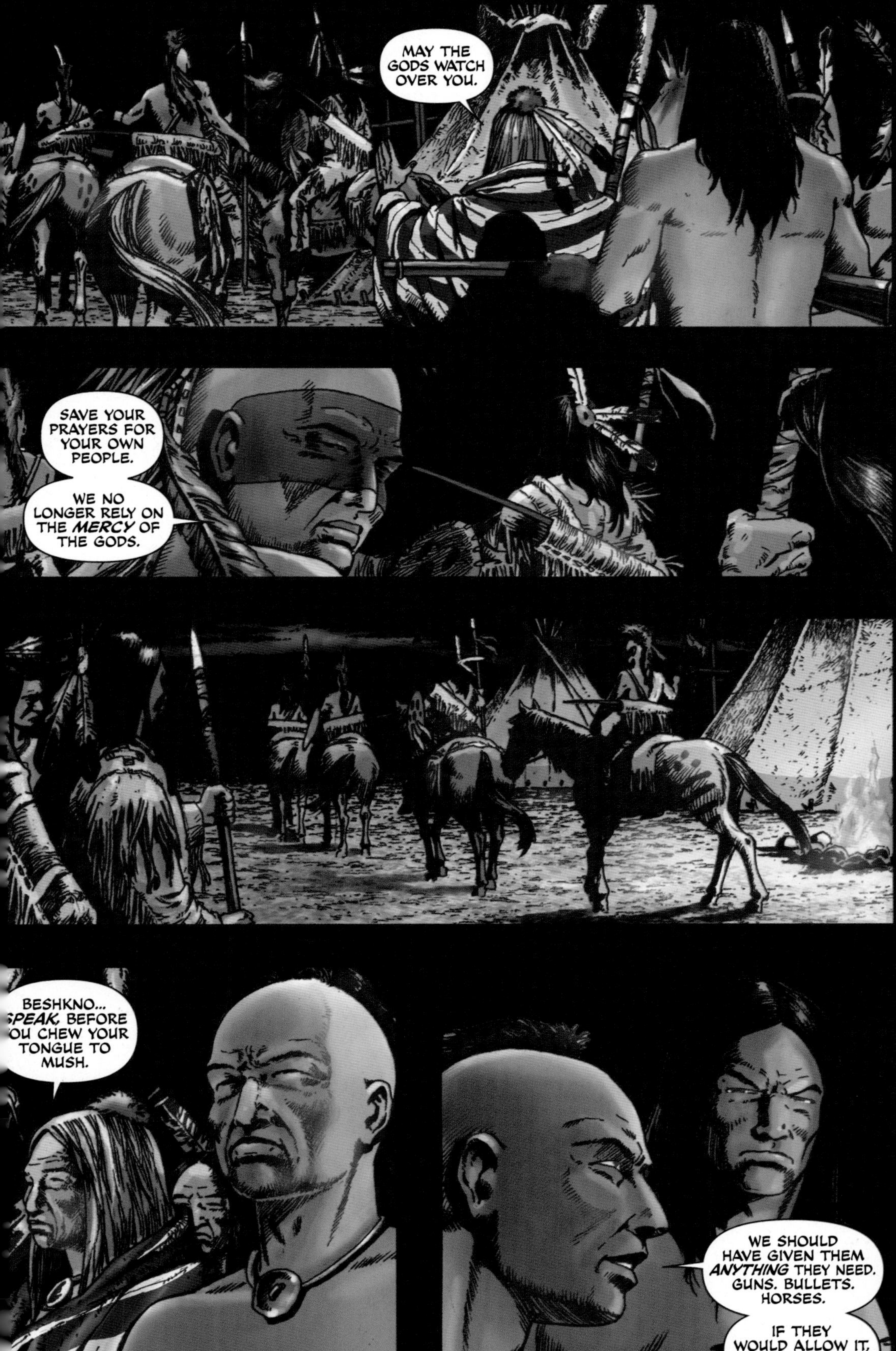
MAY THE GODS WATCH OVER YOU.
SAVE YOUR PRAYERS FOR YOUR OWN PEOPLE.
WE NO LONGER RELY ON THE *MERCY* OF THE GODS.
BESHKNO... *SPEAK*, BEFORE YOU CHEW YOUR TONGUE TO MUSH.
WE SHOULD HAVE GIVEN THEM *ANYTHING* THEY NEED. GUNS. BULLETS. HORSES.
IF THEY WOULD ALLOW IT, WE SHOULD RIDE *WITH* THEM!

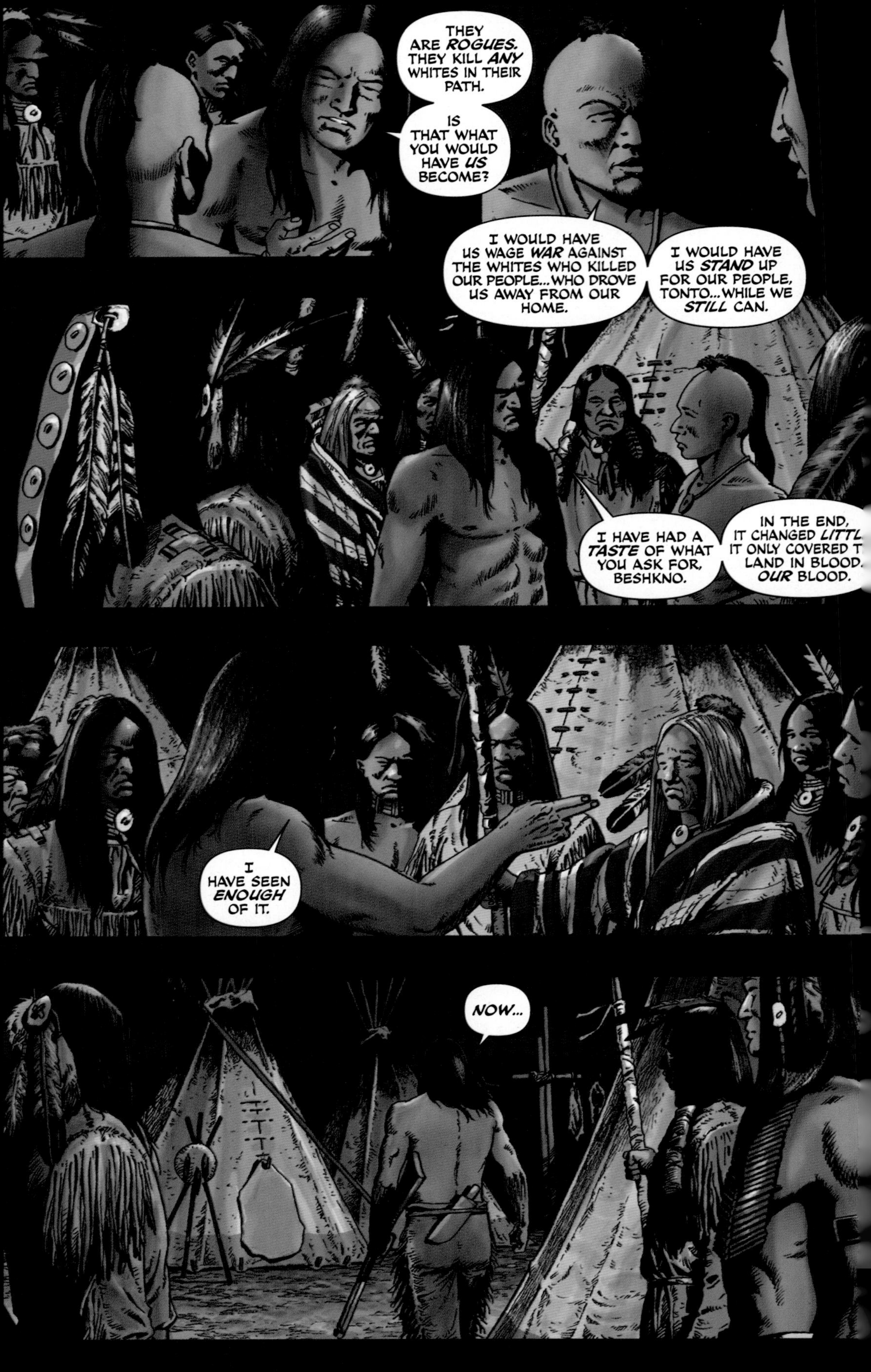
THEY ARE ROGUES. THEY KILL ANY WHITES IN THEIR PATH.
IS THAT WHAT YOU WOULD HAVE US BECOME?
I WOULD HAVE US WAGE WAR AGAINST THE WHITES WHO KILLED OUR PEOPLE...WHO DROVE US AWAY FROM OUR HOME.
I WOULD HAVE US STAND UP FOR OUR PEOPLE, TONTO...WHILE WE STILL CAN.
I HAVE HAD A TASTE OF WHAT YOU ASK FOR, BESHKNO.
IN THE END, IT CHANGED LITTL IT ONLY COVERED T LAND IN BLOOD. OUR BLOOD.
I HAVE SEEN ENOUGH OF IT.
NOW...

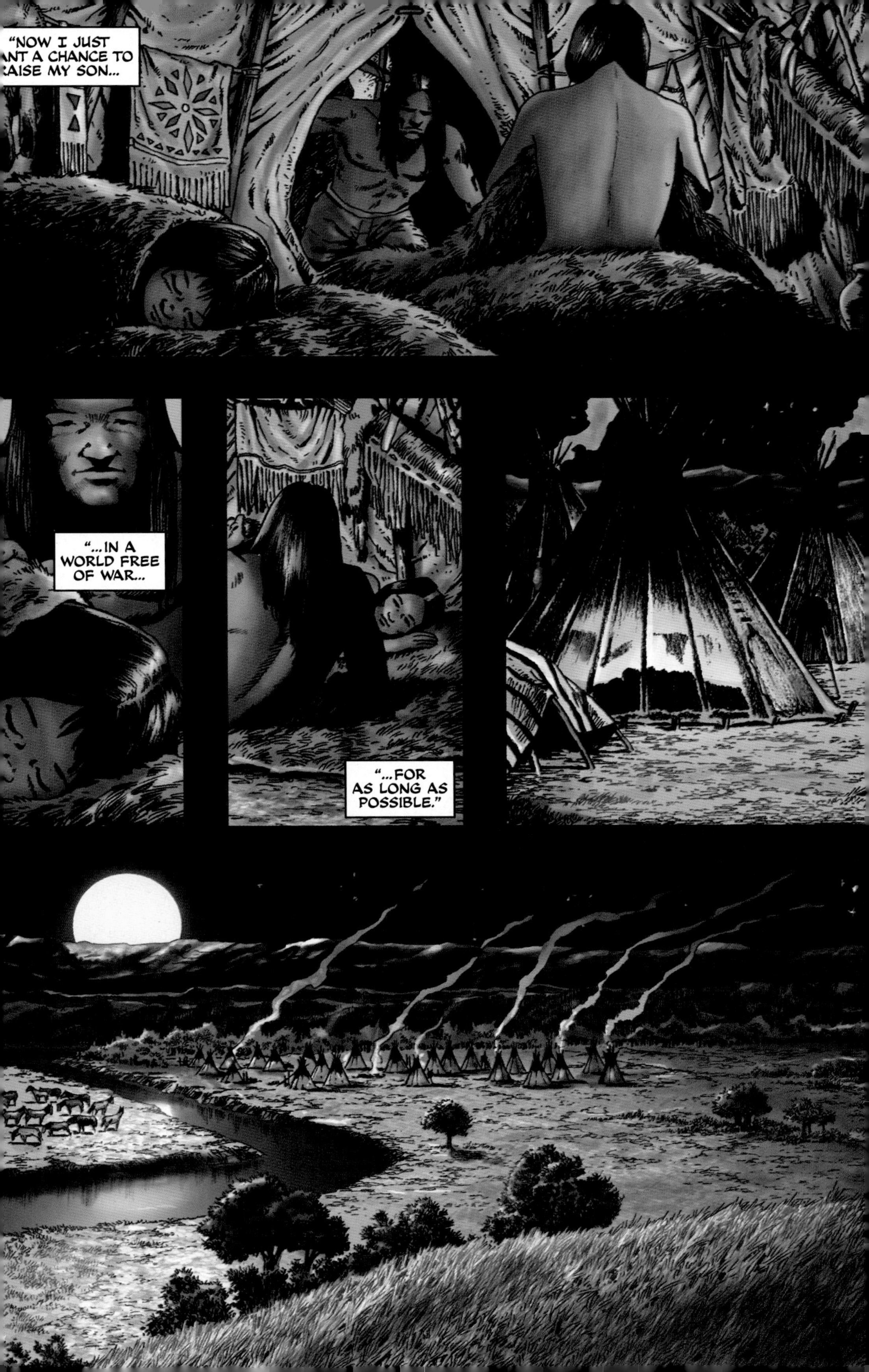
"NOW I JUST
ANT A CHANCE TO
RAISE MY SON...
"...IN A WORLD FREE OF WAR...
"...FOR AS LONG AS POSSIBLE."

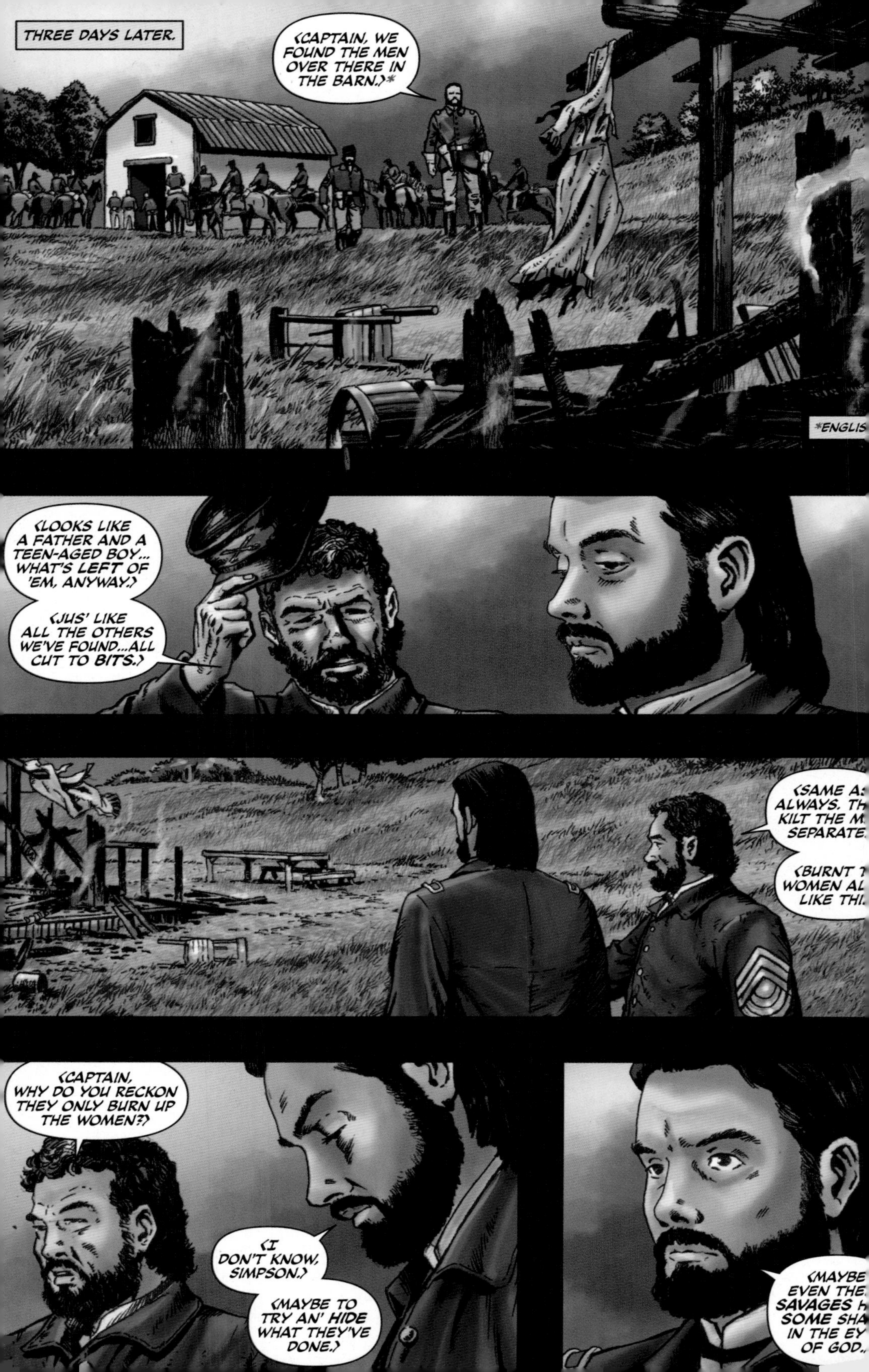
THREE DAYS LATER.
‹CAPTAIN, WE FOUND THE MEN OVER THERE IN THE BARN.›*
*ENGLIS
‹LOOKS LIKE A FATHER AND A TEEN-AGED BOY... WHAT'S LEFT OF 'EM, ANYWAY.›
‹JUS' LIKE ALL THE OTHERS WE'VE FOUND...ALL CUT TO BITS.›
‹SAME A ALWAYS. TH KILT THE M SEPARATE
‹BURNT T WOMEN AL LIKE THI
‹CAPTAIN, WHY DO YOU RECKON THEY ONLY BURN UP THE WOMEN?›
‹I DON'T KNOW, SIMPSON.›
‹MAYBE TO TRY AN' HIDE WHAT THEY'VE DONE.›
‹MAYBE EVEN THE SAVAGES H SOME SHA IN THE EY OF GOD.

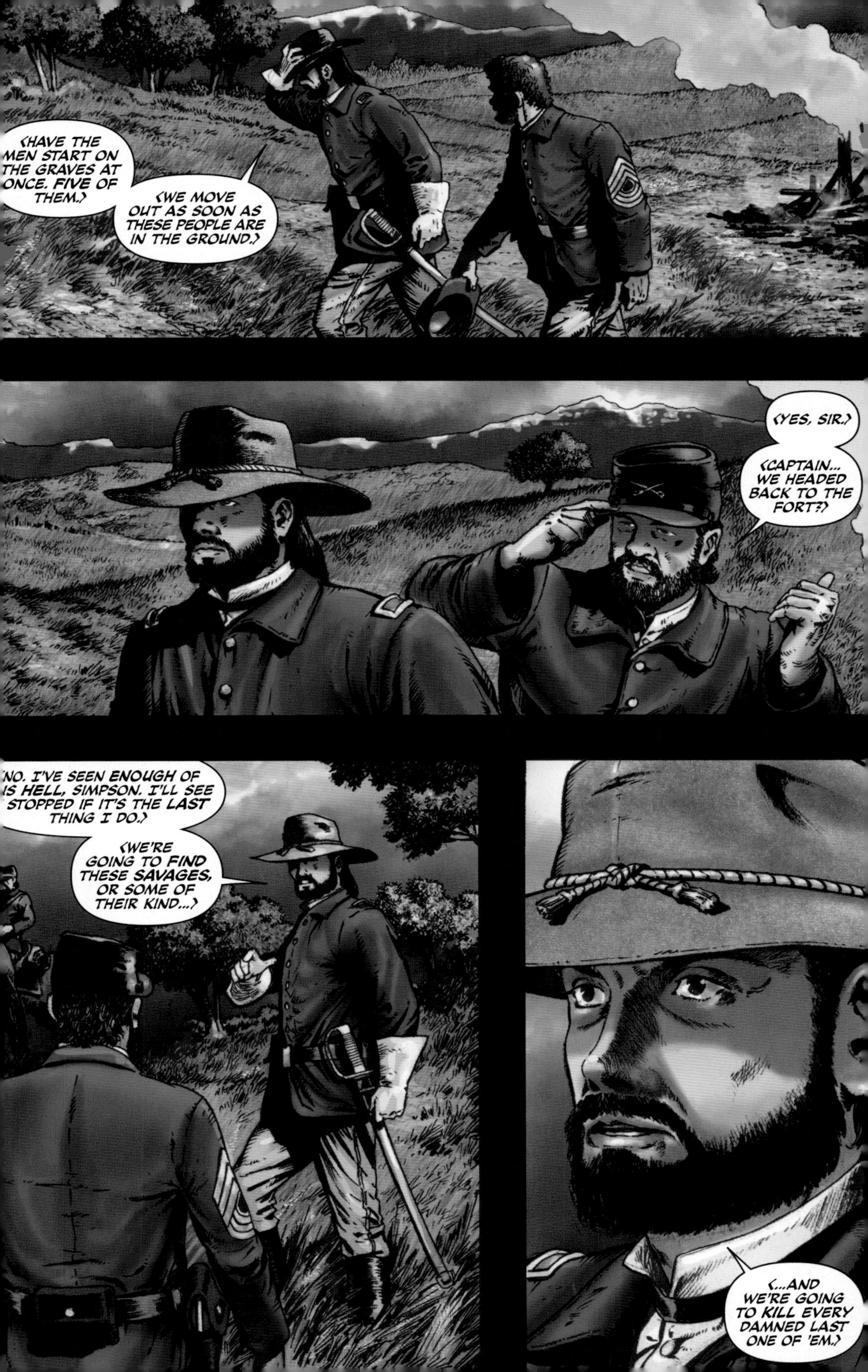
‹HAVE THE MEN START ON THE GRAVES AT ONCE. FIVE OF THEM.›
‹WE MOVE OUT AS SOON AS THESE PEOPLE ARE IN THE GROUND.›
‹YES, SIR.›
‹CAPTAIN... WE HEADED BACK TO THE FORT?›
NO. I'VE SEEN ENOUGH OF IS HELL, SIMPSON. I'LL SEE STOPPED IF IT'S THE LAST THING I DO.›
‹WE'RE GOING TO FIND THESE SAVAGES, OR SOME OF THEIR KIND...›
‹...AND WE'RE GOING TO KILL EVERY DAMNED LAST ONE OF 'EM.›

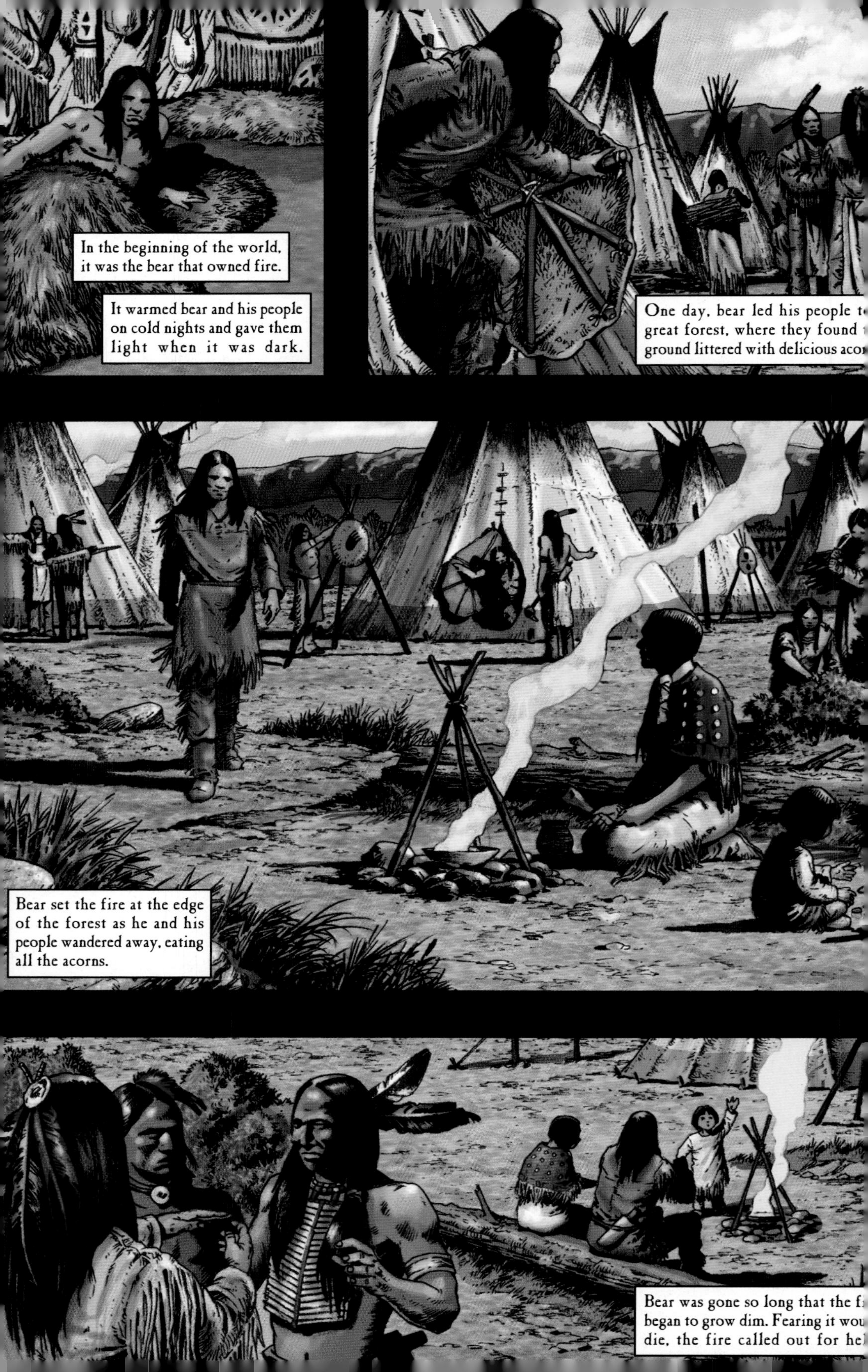
In the beginning of the world, it was the bear that owned fire.
It warmed bear and his people on cold nights and gave them light when it was dark.
One day, bear led his people t
great forest, where they found
ground littered with delicious aco
Bear set the fire at the edge of the forest as he and his people wandered away, eating all the acorns.
Bear was gone so long that the f
began to grow dim. Fearing it wou
die, the fire called out for he

Man came walking through the forest and found fire, just barely flickering and calling for help. Fire begged for man to feed it.

Man asked fire what he could feed it. Fire explained that he ate sticks and logs.

Man laid sticks on the fire until fire was leaping and dancing in delight.

Man warmed himself by the fire. Man and fire were happy together, and man fed fire sticks whenever it grew hungry.

When bear and his people returned from the forest fire raged at bear in white hot anger.

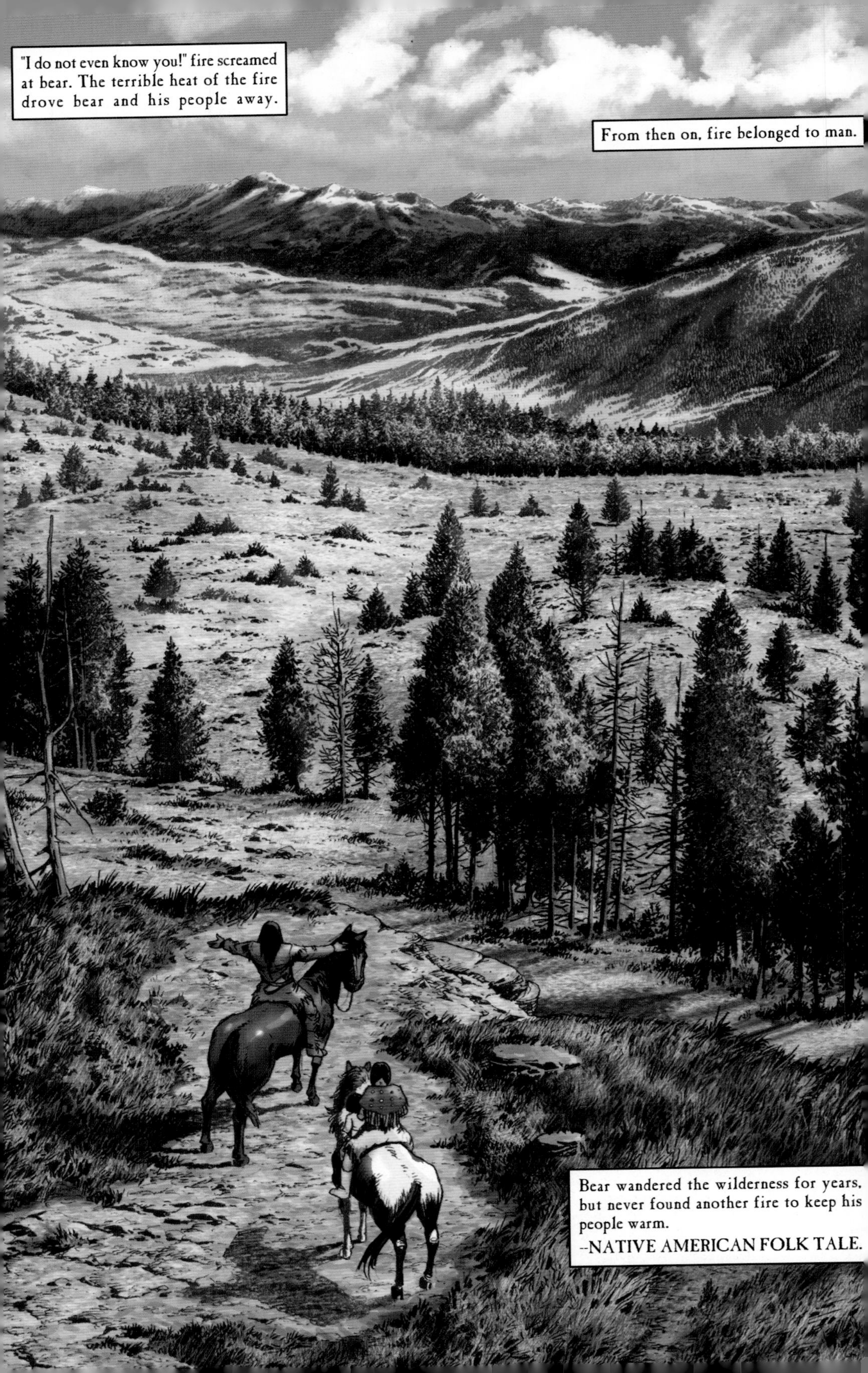
"I do not even know you!" fire screamed at bear. The terrible heat of the fire drove bear and his people away.
From then on, fire belonged to man.
Bear wandered the wilderness for years, but never found another fire to keep his people warm.
--NATIVE AMERICAN FOLK TALE.

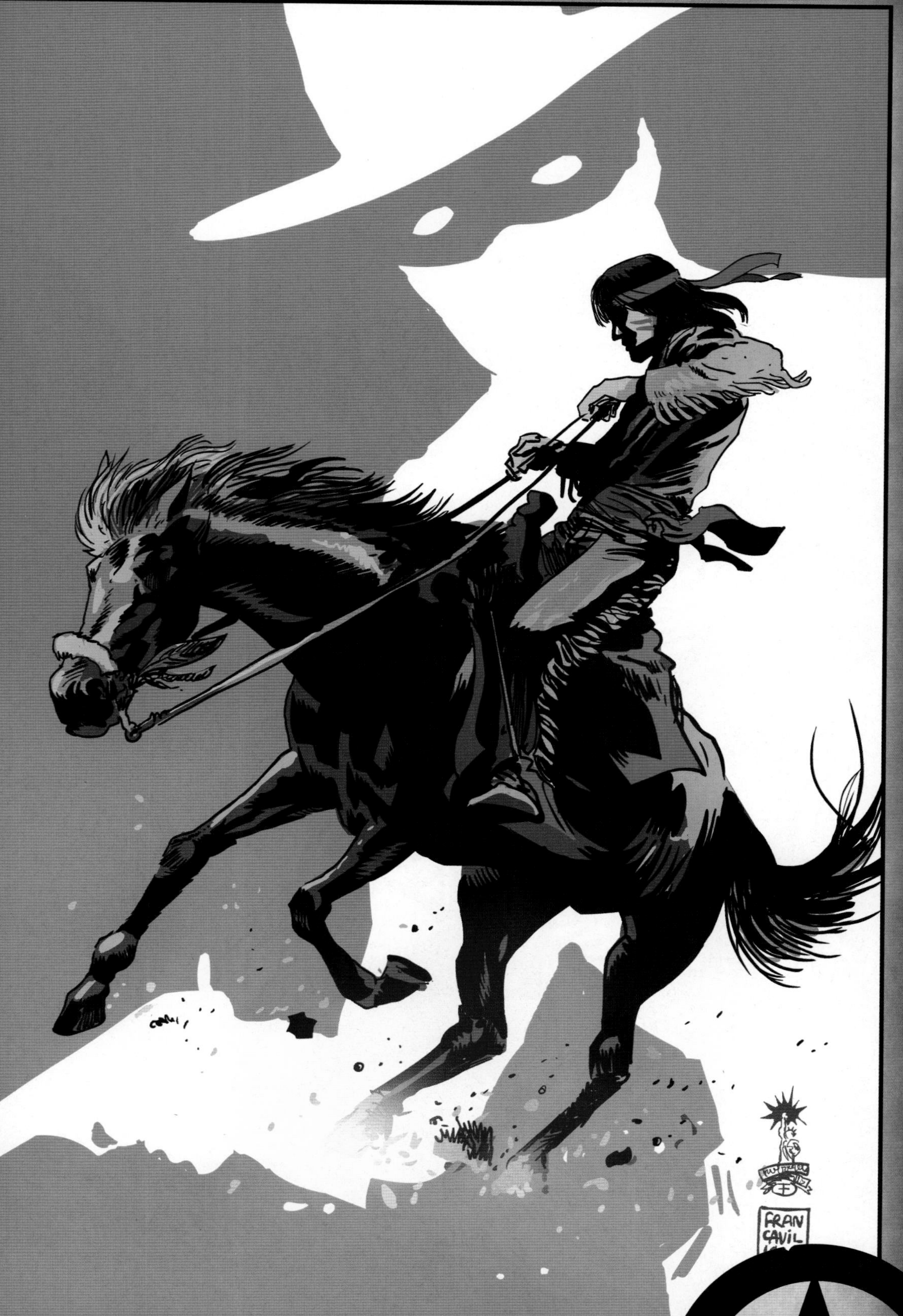

COVER BY **FRANCESCO FRANCAVILLA**

8

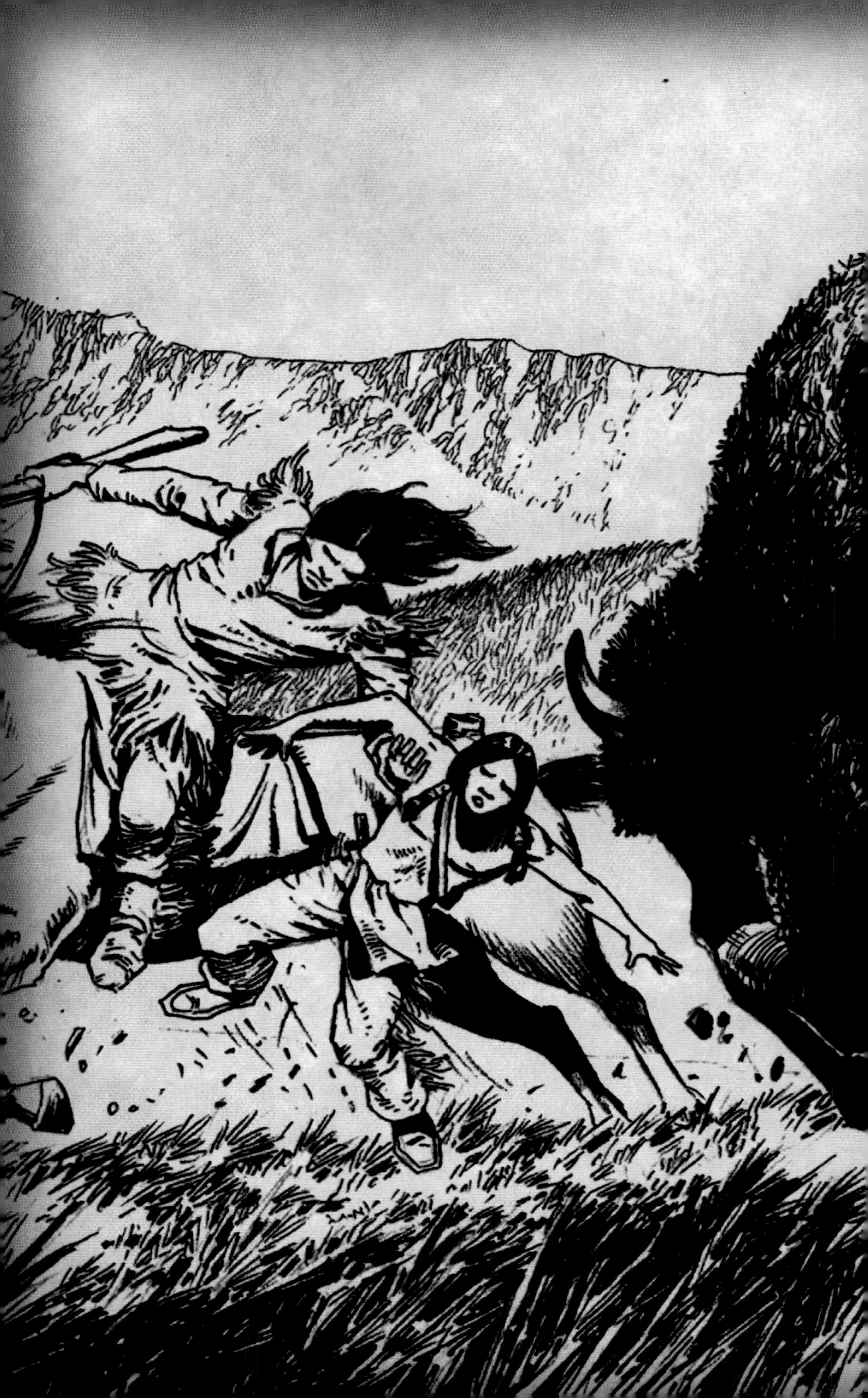

SOUTHWESTERN COLORADO TERRITORY.

⟨OUR LAND, UTE.⟩*

NO WANT...

⟨TRANSLATED FROM NATIVE AMERICAN TRIBAL LANGUAGE--JR.⟩

...WHITE.

I RESPECT UTE LANDS. I WOULD NOT HAVE COME...

...BUT MY FRIEND NEEDS--

THUNNG

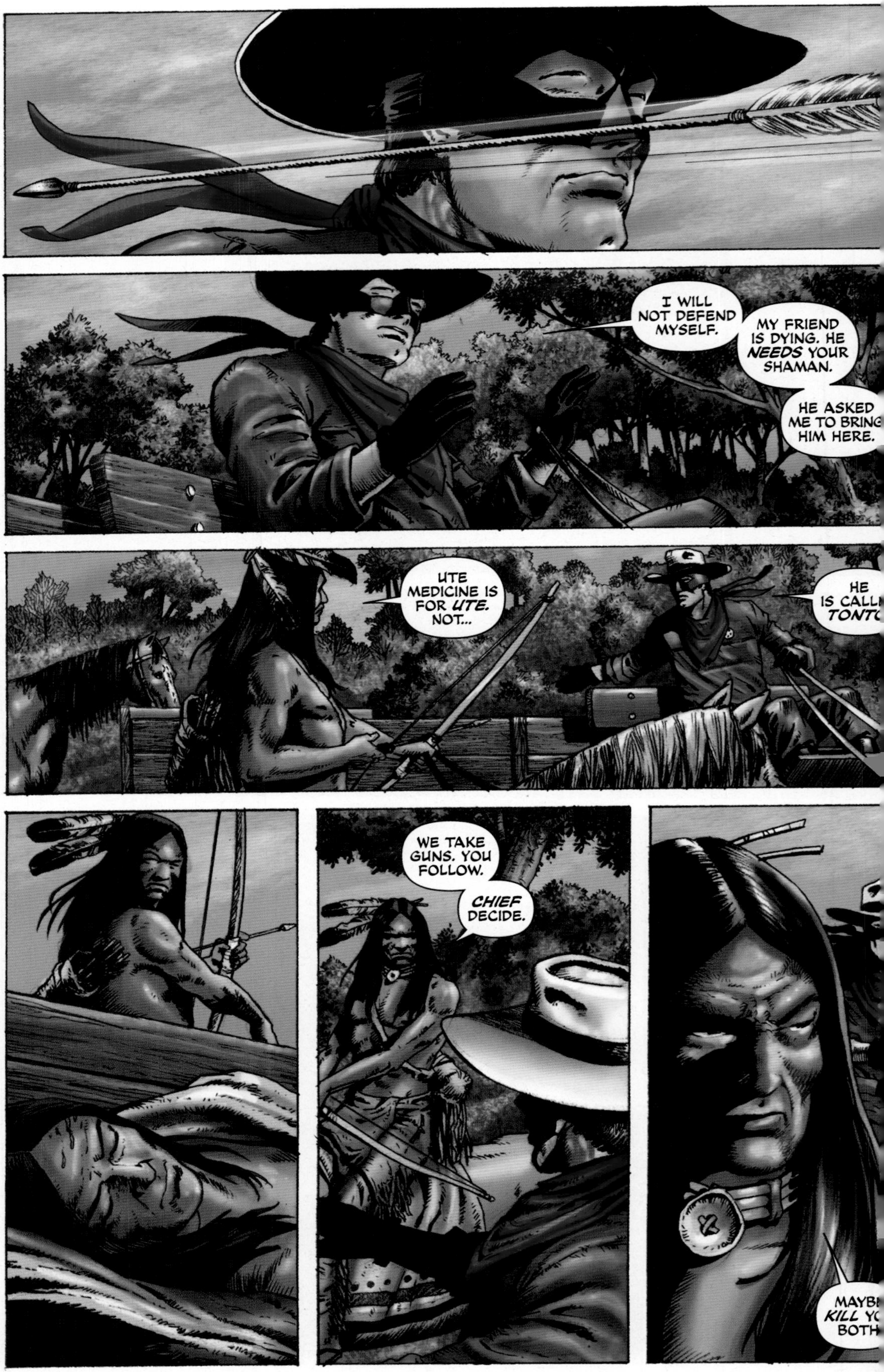
I WILL NOT DEFEND MYSELF.
MY FRIEND IS DYING. HE *NEEDS* YOUR SHAMAN.
HE ASKED ME TO BRING HIM HERE.
UTE MEDICINE IS FOR *UTE.* NOT...
HE IS CALL
TONT
WE TAKE GUNS. YOU FOLLOW.
CHIEF DECIDE.
MAYB
KILL Y
BOTH

THREE YEARS EARLIER.
NEW MEXICO TERRITORY.

‹THEY WERE HERE.›

NATIVE GROUND

CHAPTER TWO

‹THE ROGUE BRAVES RODE THROUGH HERE FAST...A DAY AND A HALF AGO.›

‹DO WE FOLLOW THEM?›

‹THEY ARE NO CONCERN OF OURS. BESIDES....›

‹...I'M NOT SURE YOU COULD STAY ON THAT HORSE AT A GALLOP.›

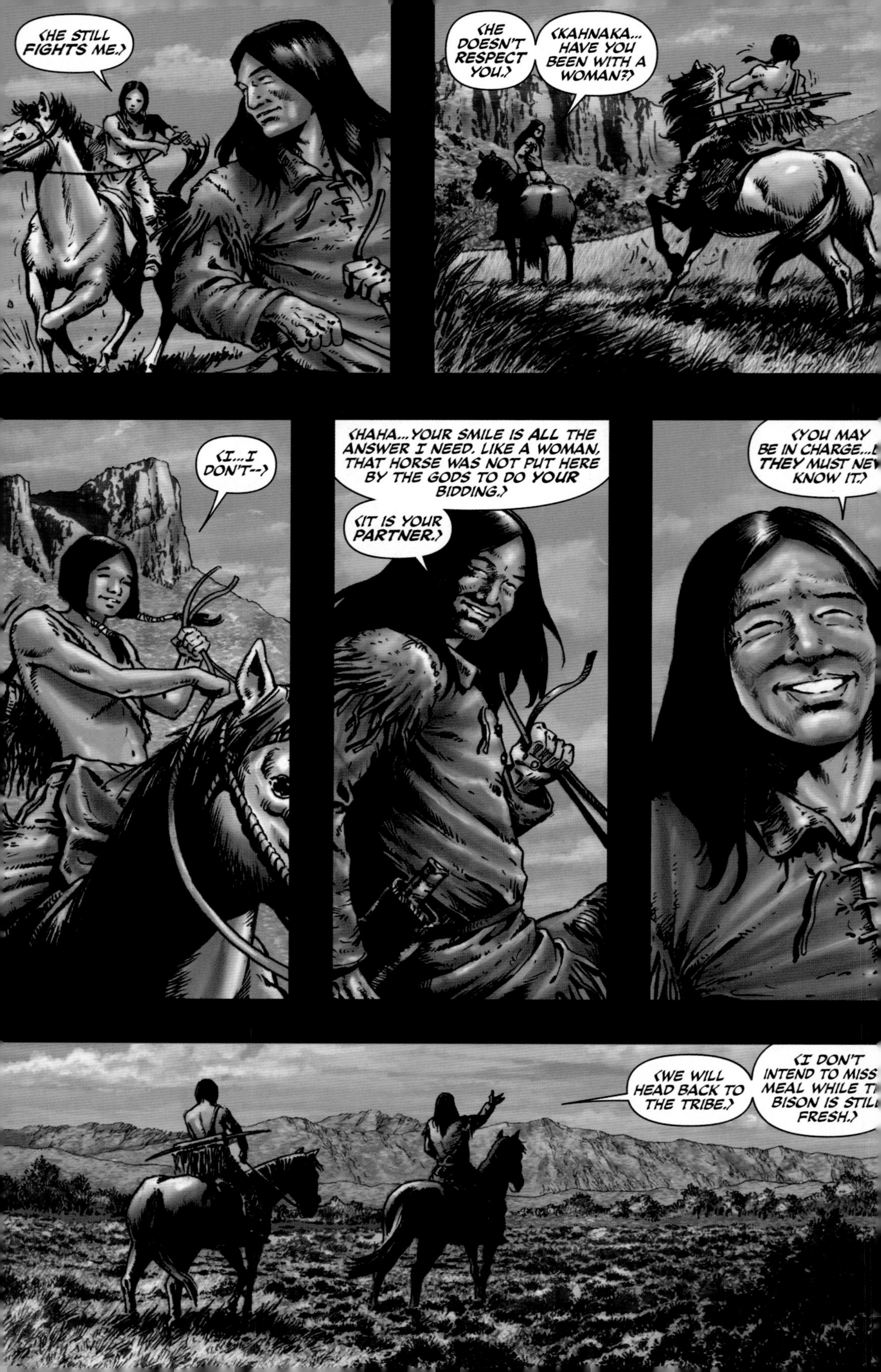
‹HE STILL FIGHTS ME.›
‹HE DOESN'T RESPECT YOU.›
‹KAHNAKA... HAVE YOU BEEN WITH A WOMAN?›
‹I...I DON'T--›
‹HAHA...YOUR SMILE IS ALL THE ANSWER I NEED. LIKE A WOMAN, THAT HORSE WAS NOT PUT HERE BY THE GODS TO DO YOUR BIDDING.›
‹IT IS YOUR PARTNER.›
‹YOU MAY BE IN CHARGE...
THEY MUST NE
KNOW IT.›
‹WE WILL HEAD BACK TO THE TRIBE.›
‹I DON'T INTEND TO MISS
MEAL WHILE T
BISON IS STIL
FRESH.›

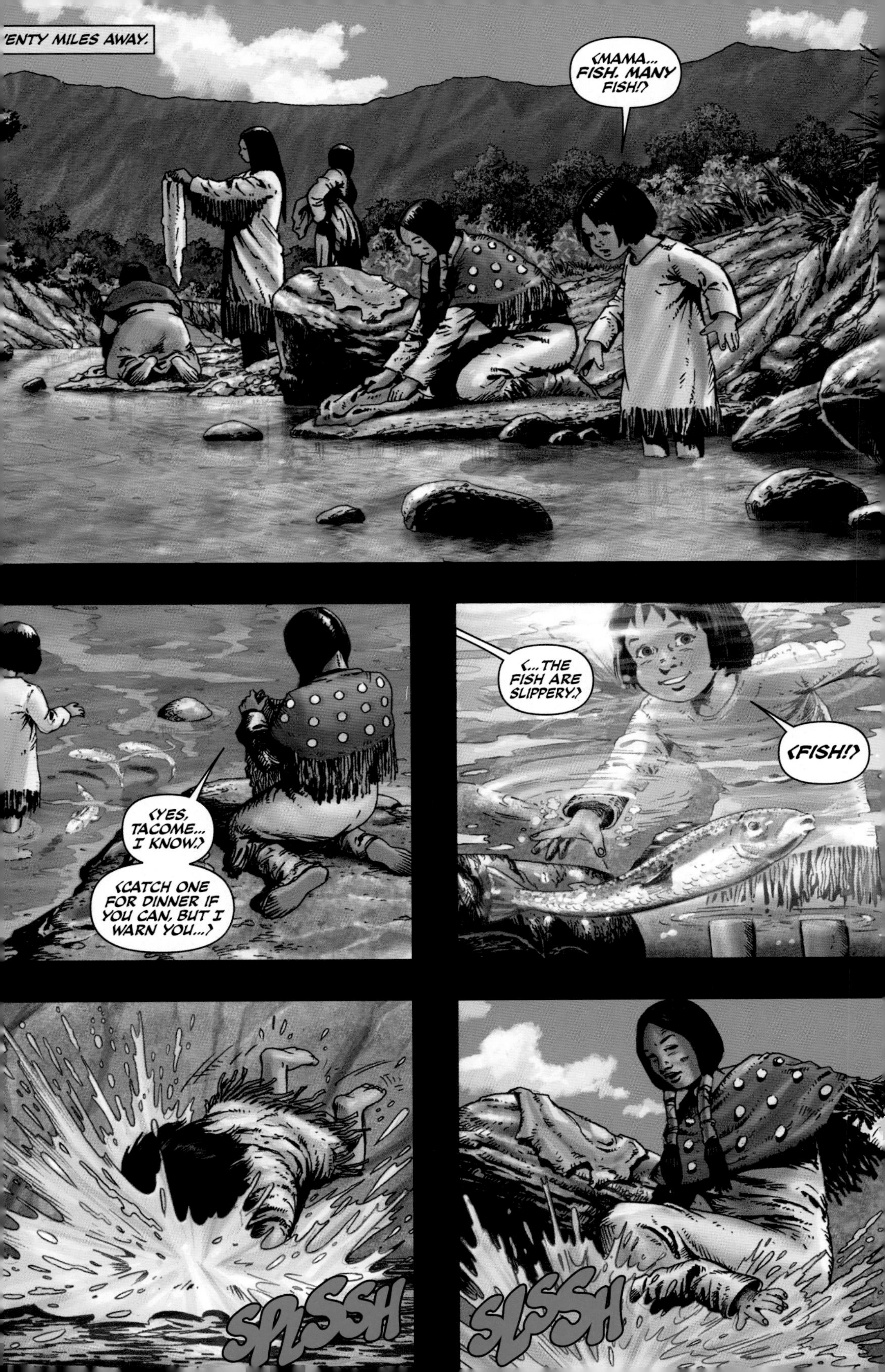

ENTY MILES AWAY.
<MAMA... FISH. MANY FISH!>
<YES, TACOME... I KNOW.>
<CATCH ONE FOR DINNER IF YOU CAN, BUT I WARN YOU...>
<...THE FISH ARE SLIPPERY.>
<FISH!>
SPLSSH
SLSSH

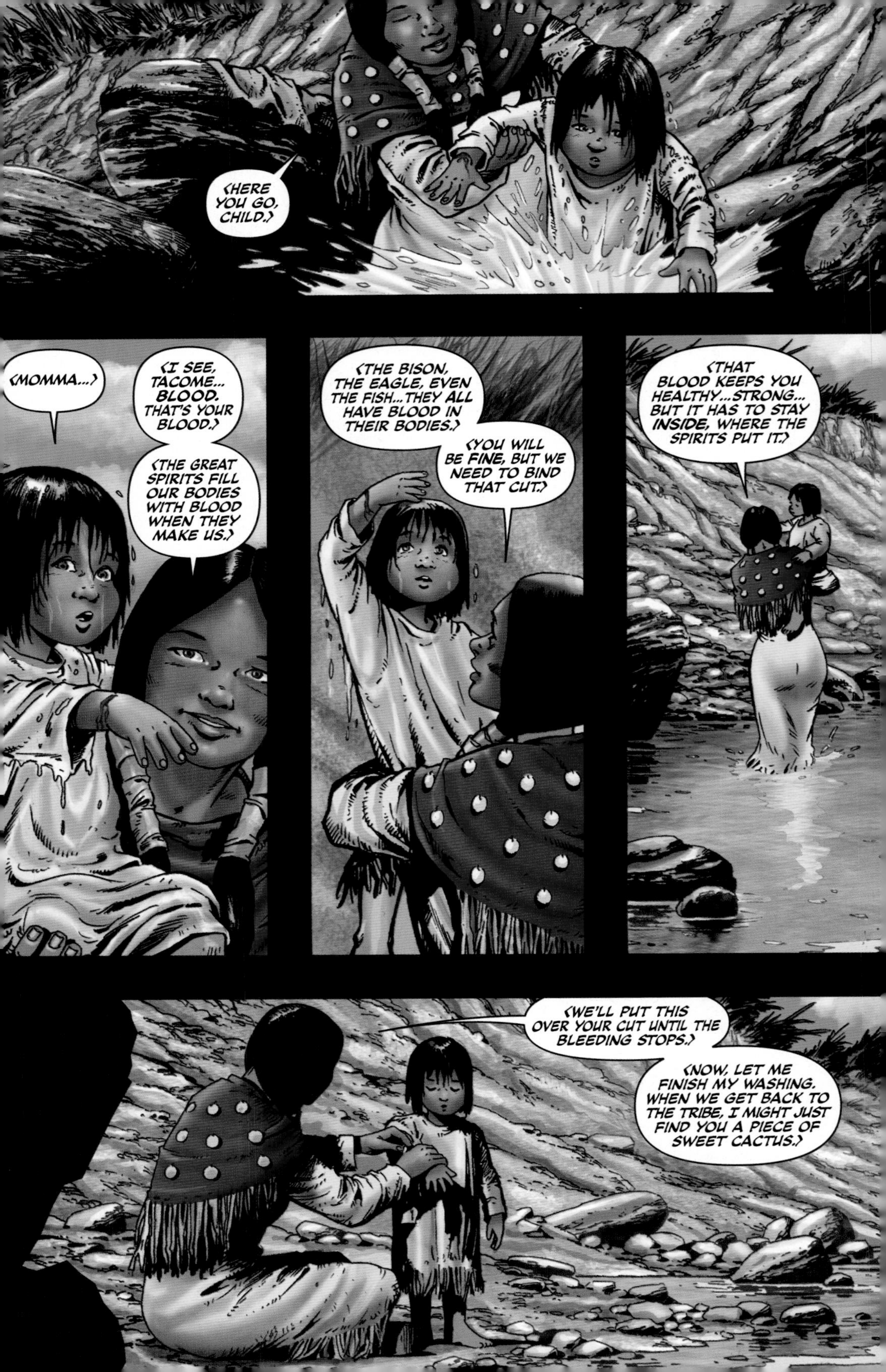
‹HERE YOU GO, CHILD.›
‹MOMMA...›
‹I SEE, TACOME... BLOOD. THAT'S YOUR BLOOD.›
‹THE GREAT SPIRITS FILL OUR BODIES WITH BLOOD WHEN THEY MAKE US.›
‹THE BISON, THE EAGLE, EVEN THE FISH...THEY ALL HAVE BLOOD IN THEIR BODIES.›
‹YOU WILL BE FINE, BUT WE NEED TO BIND THAT CUT.›
‹THAT BLOOD KEEPS YOU HEALTHY...STRONG... BUT IT HAS TO STAY INSIDE, WHERE THE SPIRITS PUT IT.›
‹WE'LL PUT THIS OVER YOUR CUT UNTIL THE BLEEDING STOPS.›
‹NOW, LET ME FINISH MY WASHING. WHEN WE GET BACK TO THE TRIBE, I MIGHT JUST FIND YOU A PIECE OF SWEET CACTUS.›

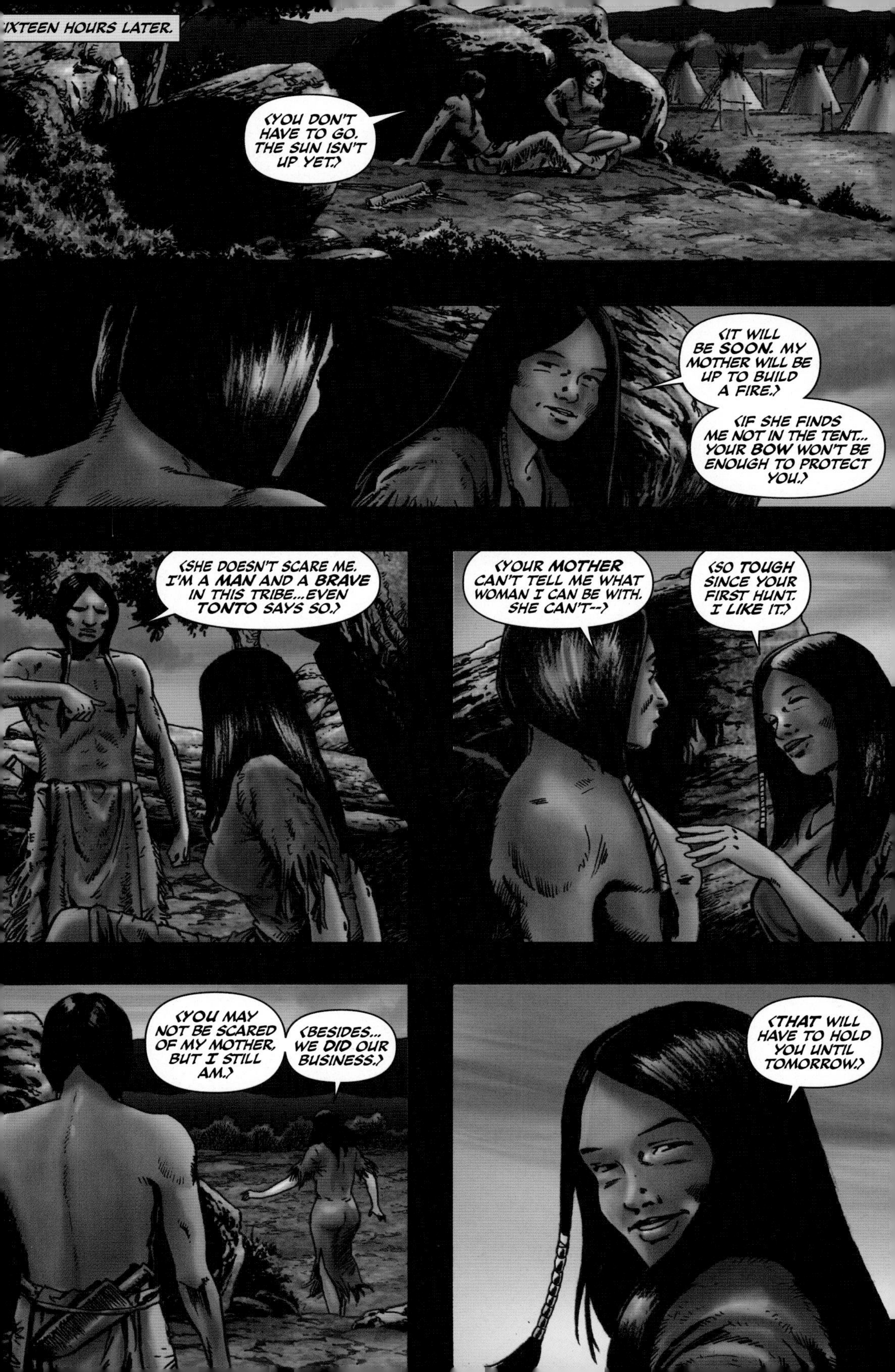
IXTEEN HOURS LATER.
<YOU DON'T HAVE TO GO. THE SUN ISN'T UP YET.>
<IT WILL BE SOON. MY MOTHER WILL BE UP TO BUILD A FIRE.>
<IF SHE FINDS ME NOT IN THE TENT... YOUR BOW WON'T BE ENOUGH TO PROTECT YOU.>
<SHE DOESN'T SCARE ME. I'M A MAN AND A BRAVE IN THIS TRIBE...EVEN TONTO SAYS SO.>
<YOUR MOTHER CAN'T TELL ME WHAT WOMAN I CAN BE WITH. SHE CAN'T-->
<SO TOUGH SINCE YOUR FIRST HUNT. I LIKE IT.>
<YOU MAY NOT BE SCARED OF MY MOTHER, BUT I STILL AM.>
<BESIDES... WE DID OUR BUSINESS.>
<THAT WILL HAVE TO HOLD YOU UNTIL TOMORROW.>

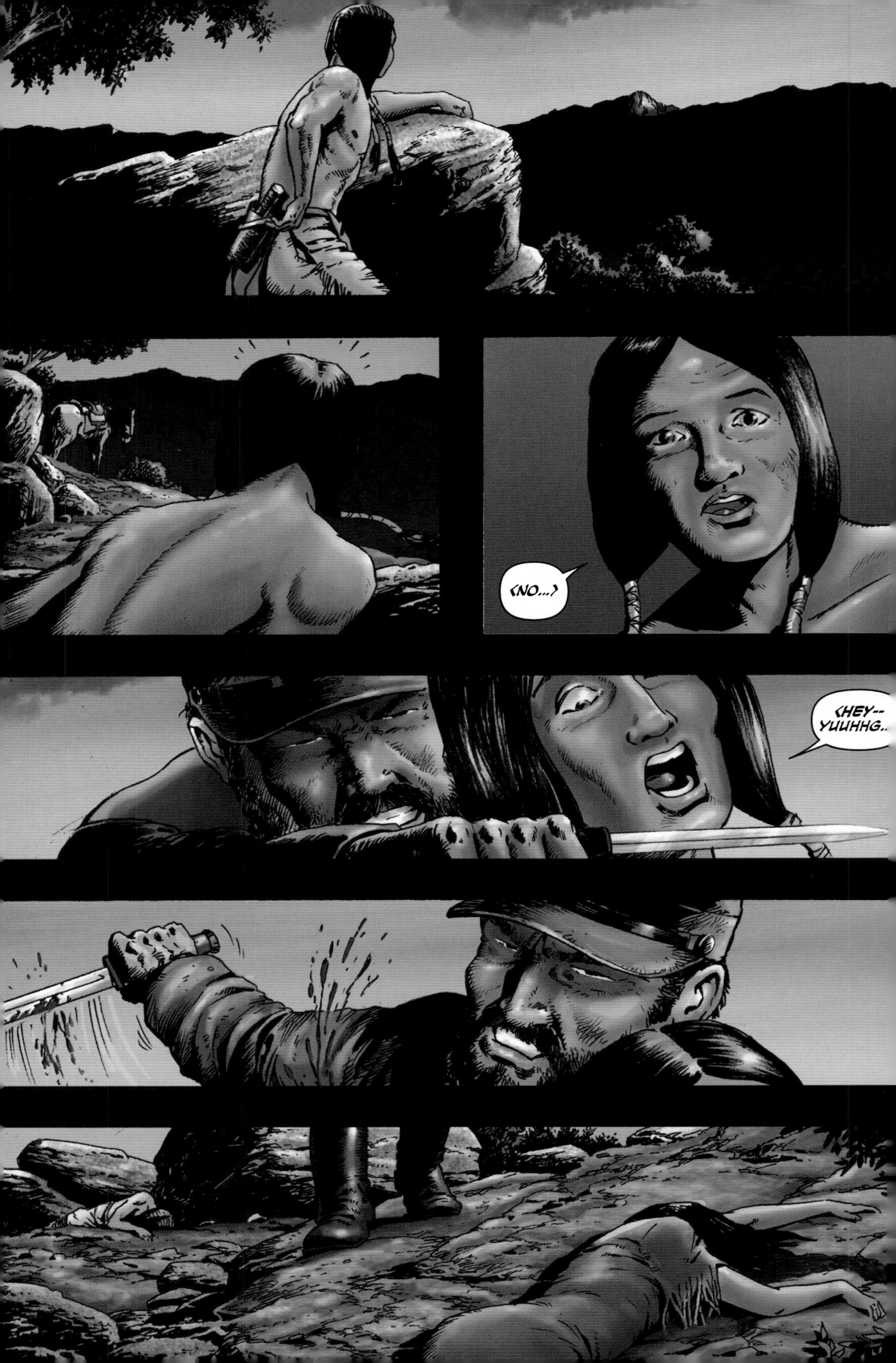
<NO...>
<HEY-- YUUHHG..

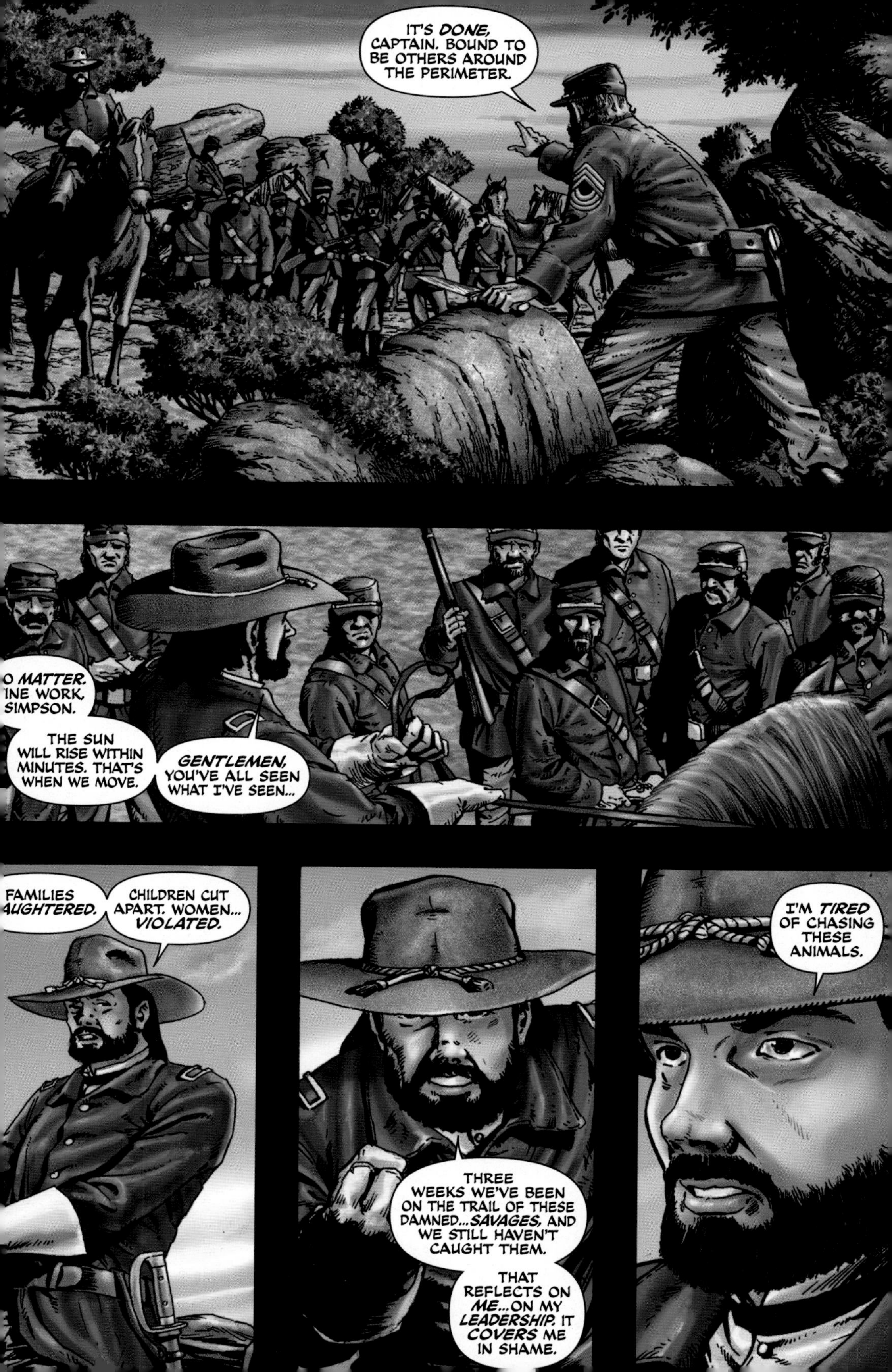
IT'S DONE, CAPTAIN. BOUND TO BE OTHERS AROUND THE PERIMETER.
O MATTER. INE WORK, SIMPSON.
THE SUN WILL RISE WITHIN MINUTES. THAT'S WHEN WE MOVE.
GENTLEMEN, YOU'VE ALL SEEN WHAT I'VE SEEN...
FAMILIES AUGHTERED.
CHILDREN CUT APART. WOMEN... VIOLATED.
THREE WEEKS WE'VE BEEN ON THE TRAIL OF THESE DAMNED...SAVAGES, AND WE STILL HAVEN'T CAUGHT THEM.
THAT REFLECTS ON ME...ON MY LEADERSHIP. IT COVERS ME IN SHAME.
I'M TIRED OF CHASING THESE ANIMALS.

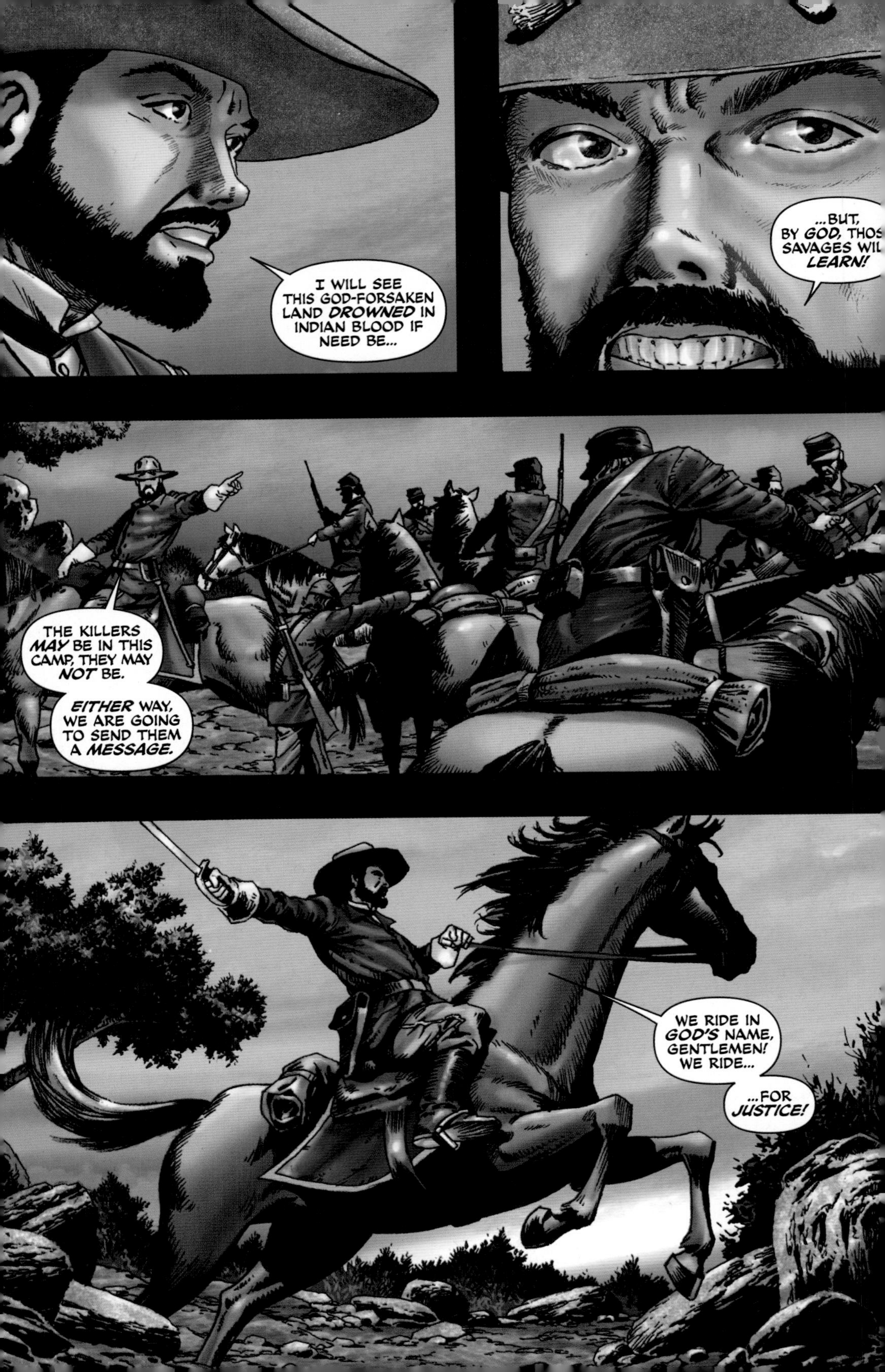
I WILL SEE THIS GOD-FORSAKEN LAND DROWNED IN INDIAN BLOOD IF NEED BE...
...BUT, BY GOD, THOS SAVAGES WIL LEARN!
THE KILLERS MAY BE IN THIS CAMP, THEY MAY NOT BE.
EITHER WAY, WE ARE GOING TO SEND THEM A MESSAGE.
WE RIDE IN GOD'S NAME, GENTLEMEN! WE RIDE...
...FOR JUSTICE!

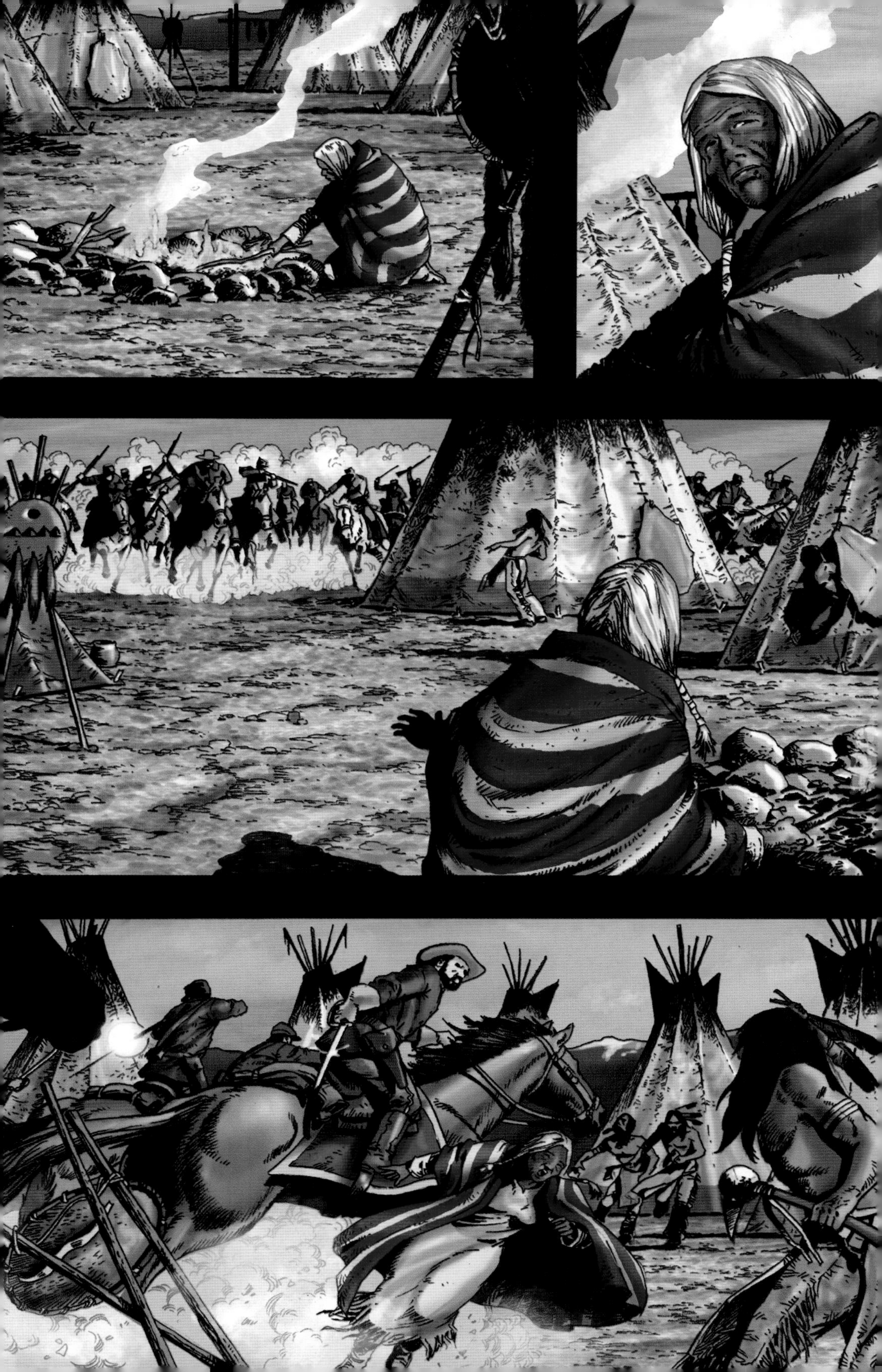

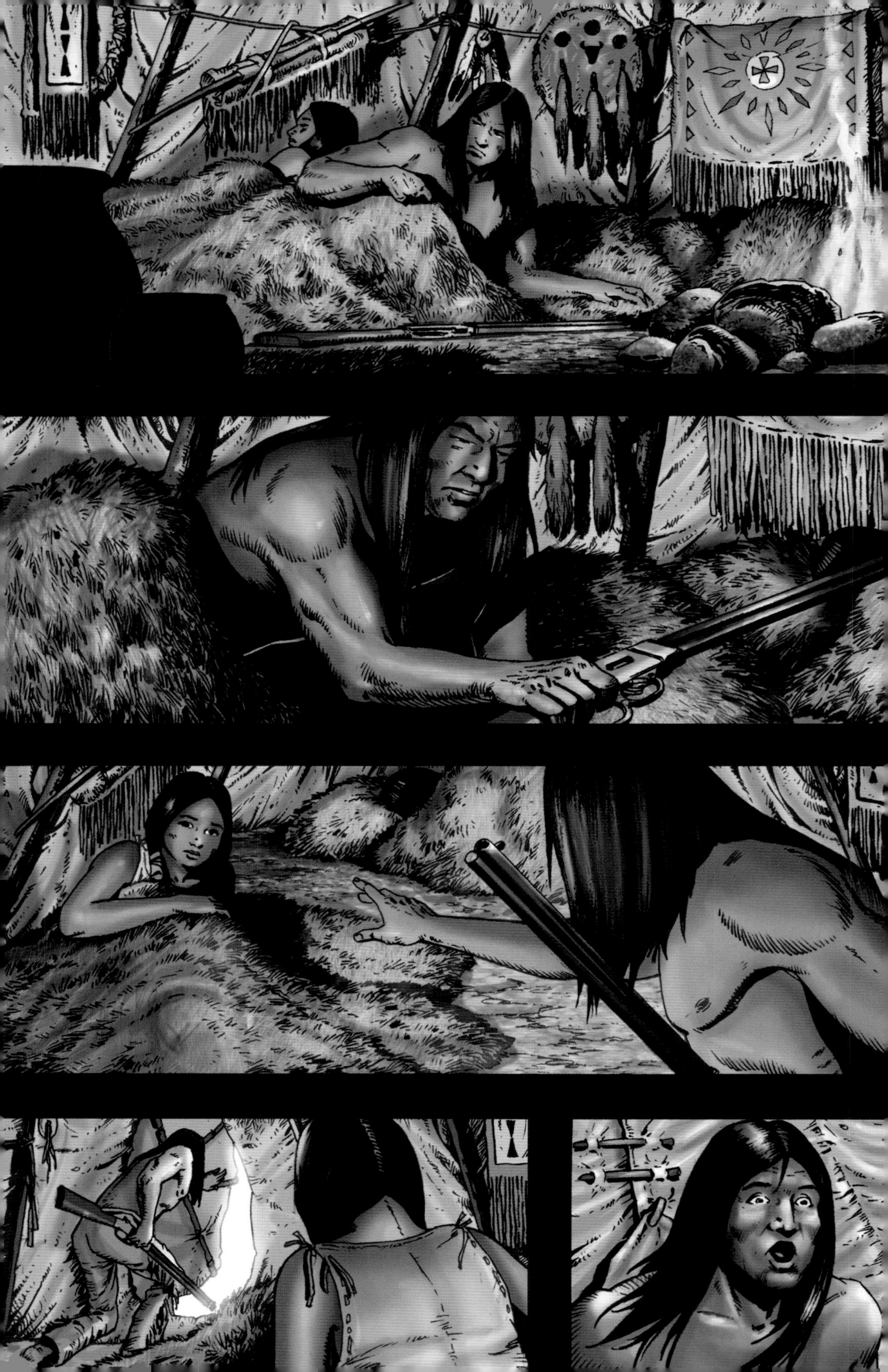

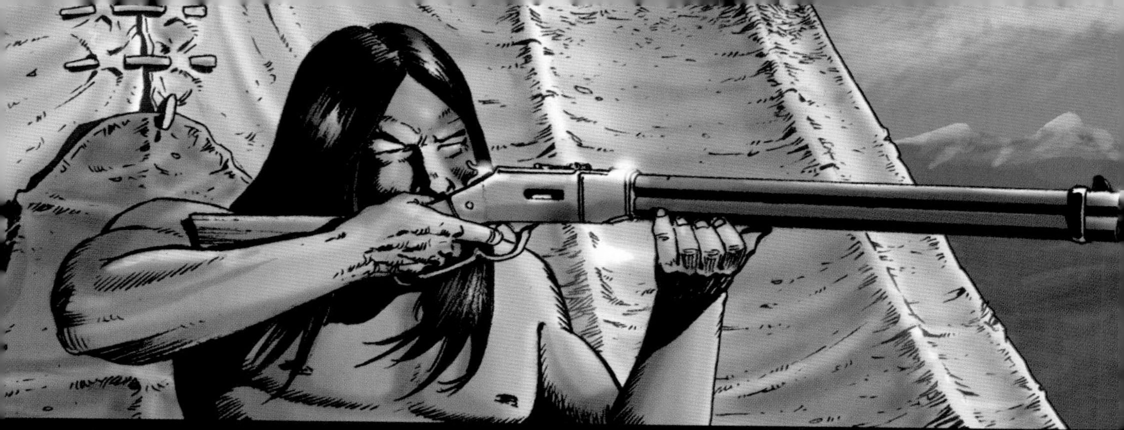

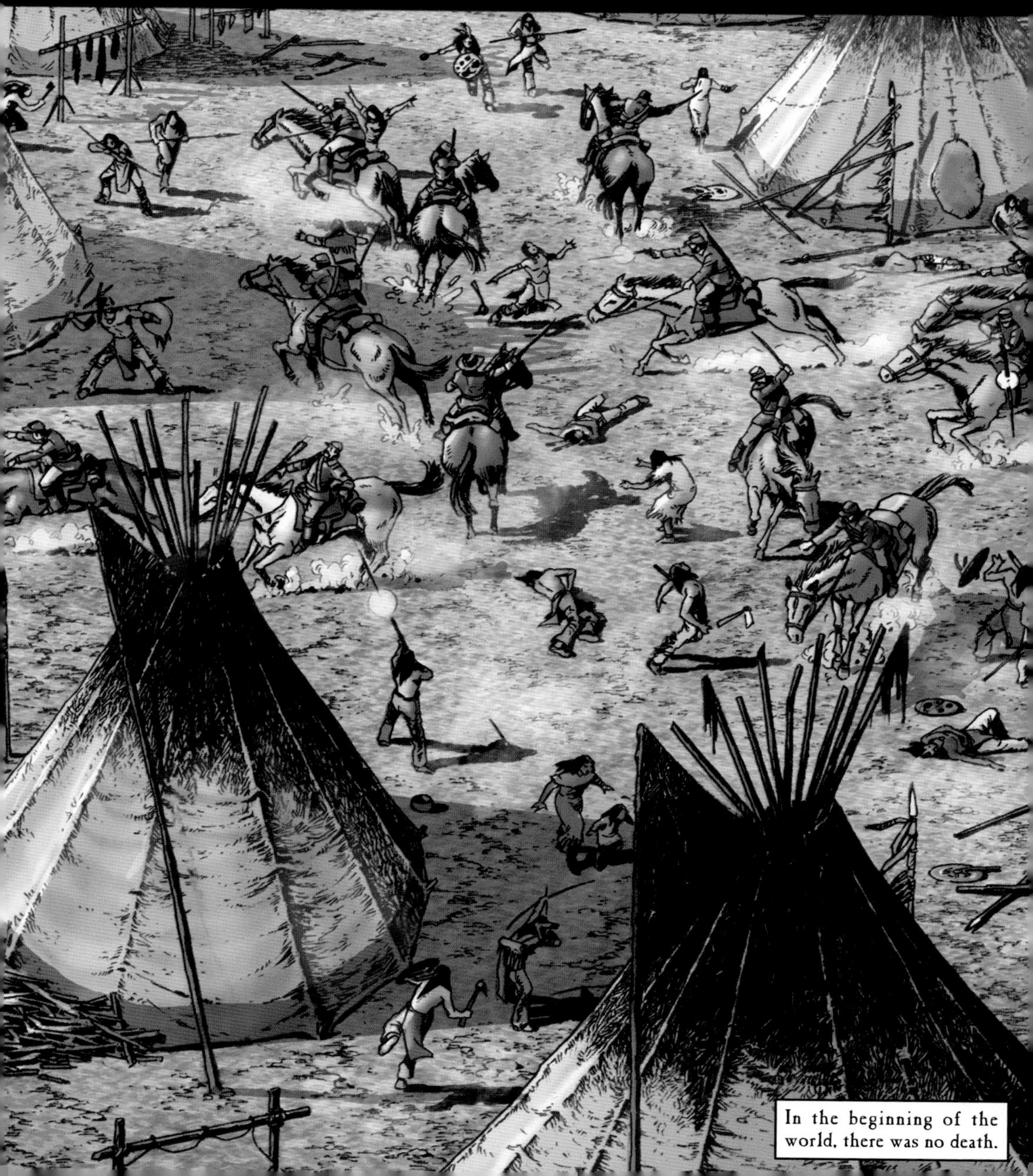
In the beginning of the world, there was no death.

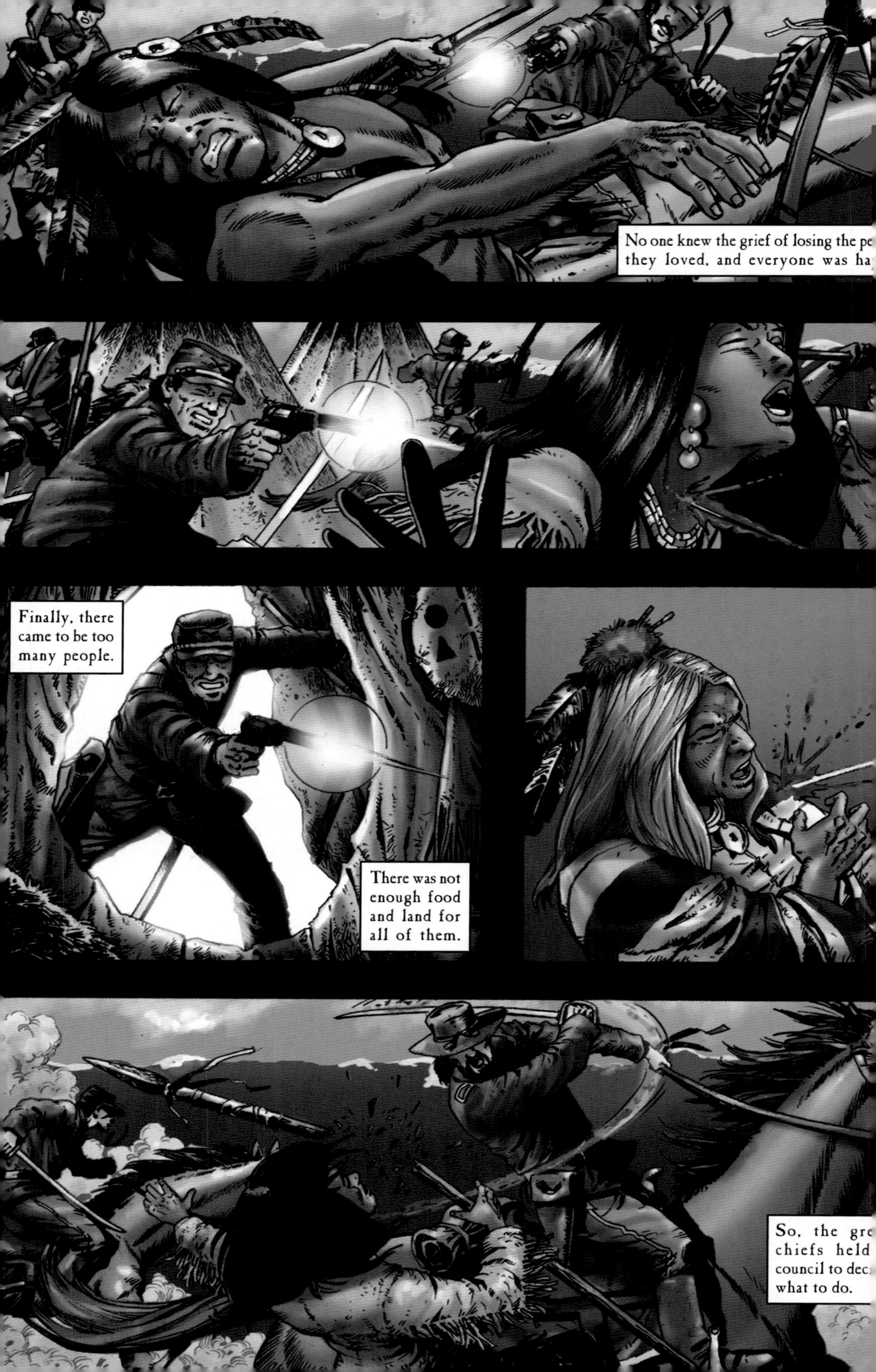
No one knew the grief of losing the pe
they loved, and everyone was ha
Finally, there came to be too many people.
There was not enough food and land for all of them.
So, the gre
chiefs held
council to dec
what to do.

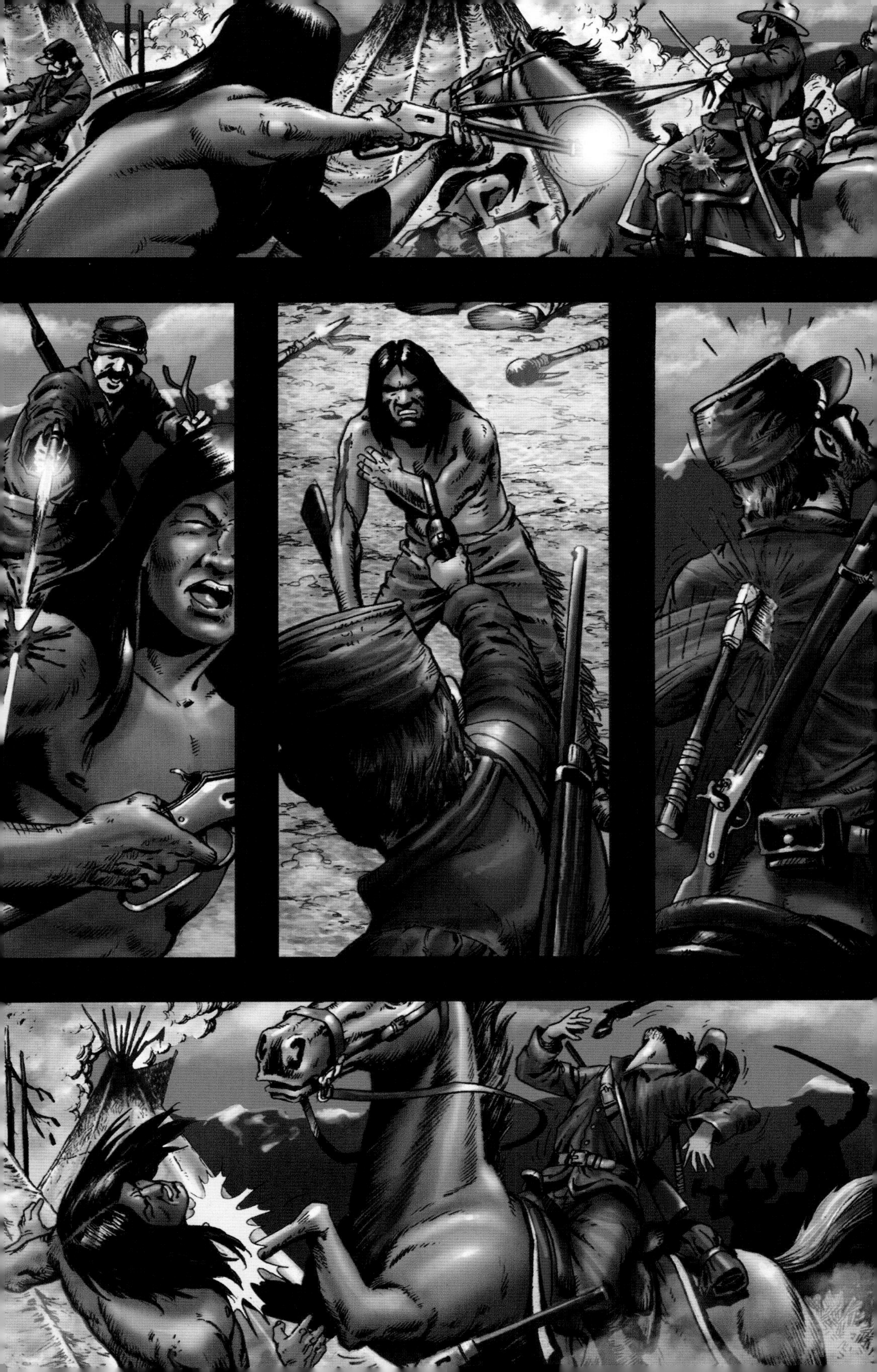

The chiefs decided that people should die and leave the world for awhile before coming back to life again.

The medicine n built a grass house the spirits of the d to return to.

When the first man died he was gone for many moons...

...and then the medicine men gathered in the house to call his spirit back.

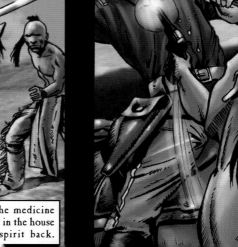

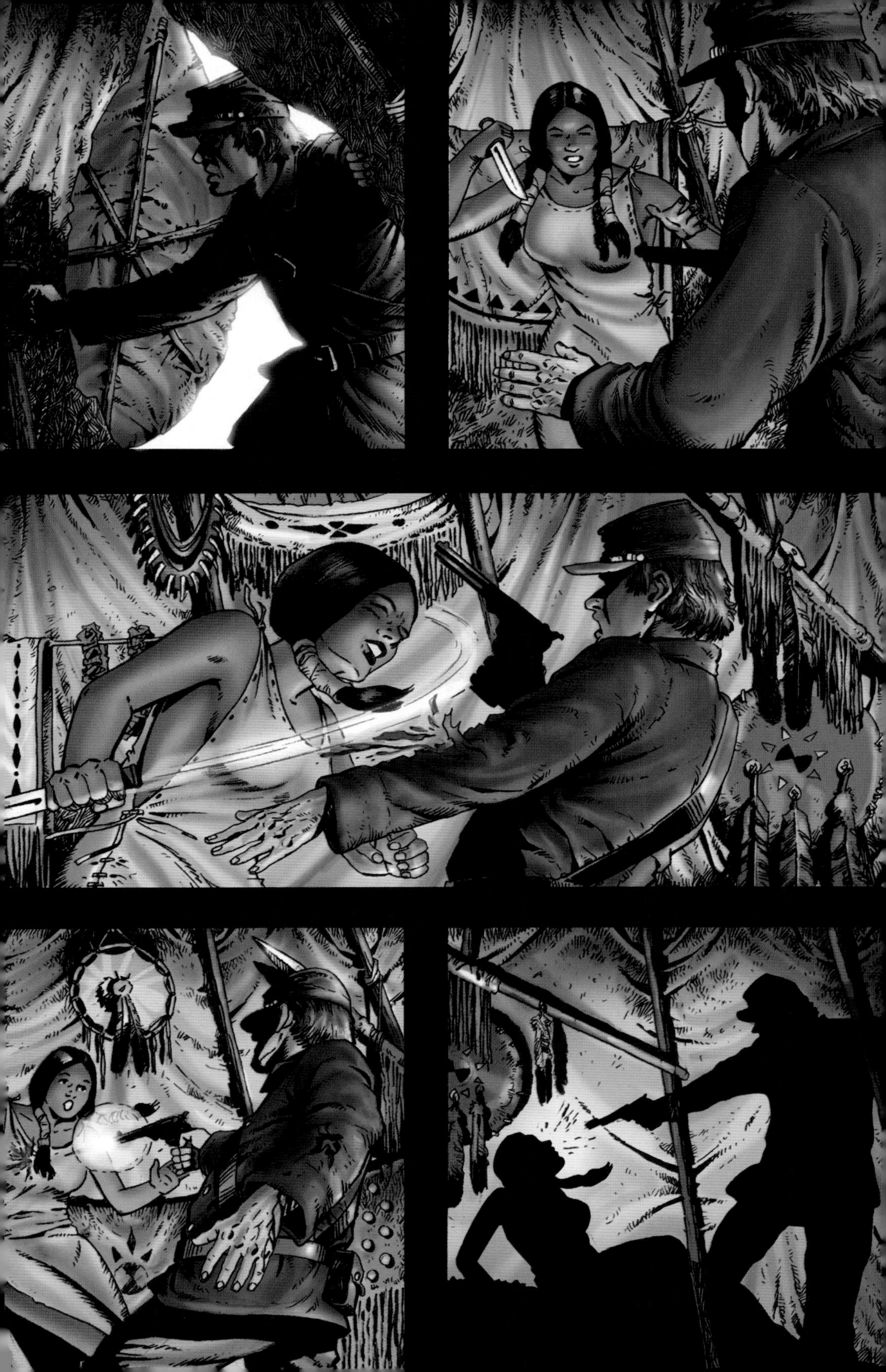

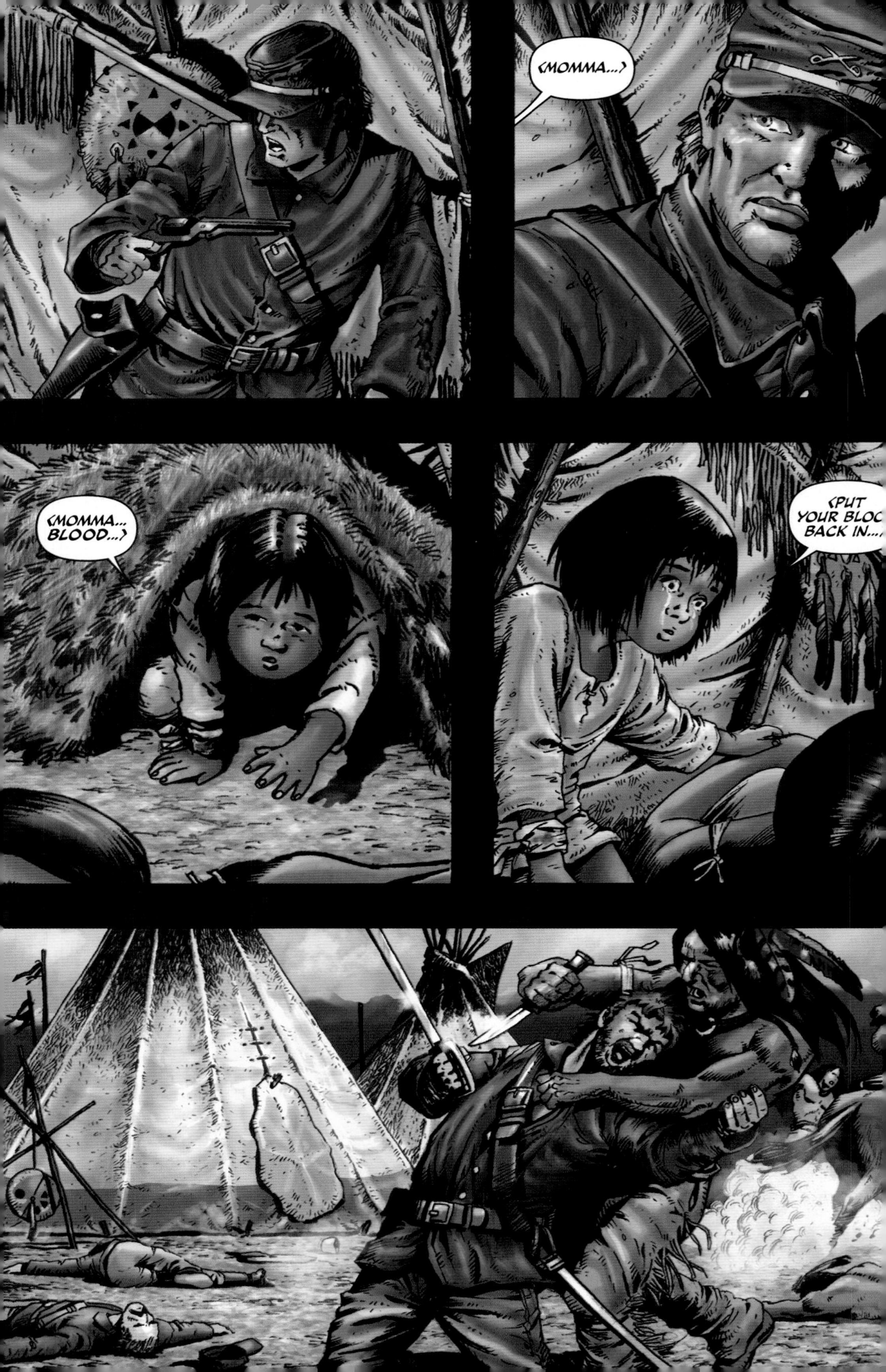

<MOMMA...>
<MOMMA... BLOOD...>
<PUT YOUR BLOC BACK IN...>

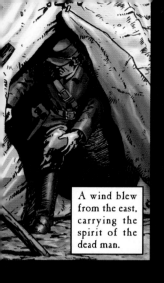

A wind blew from the east, carrying the spirit of the dead man.

As the wind neared the house a white coyote appeared, running ahead of the wind.

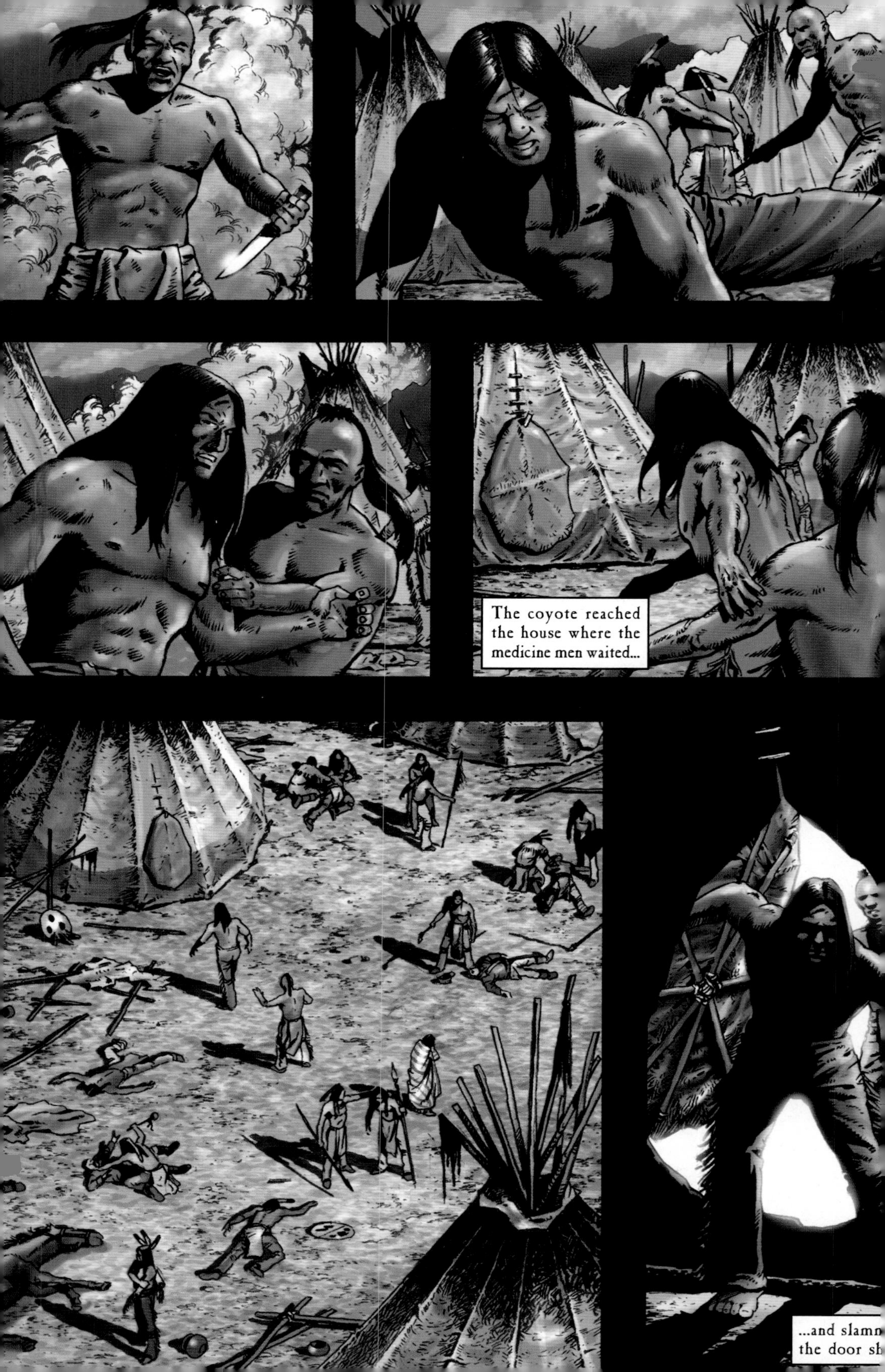
The coyote reached the house where the medicine men waited...
...and slamn
the door sh

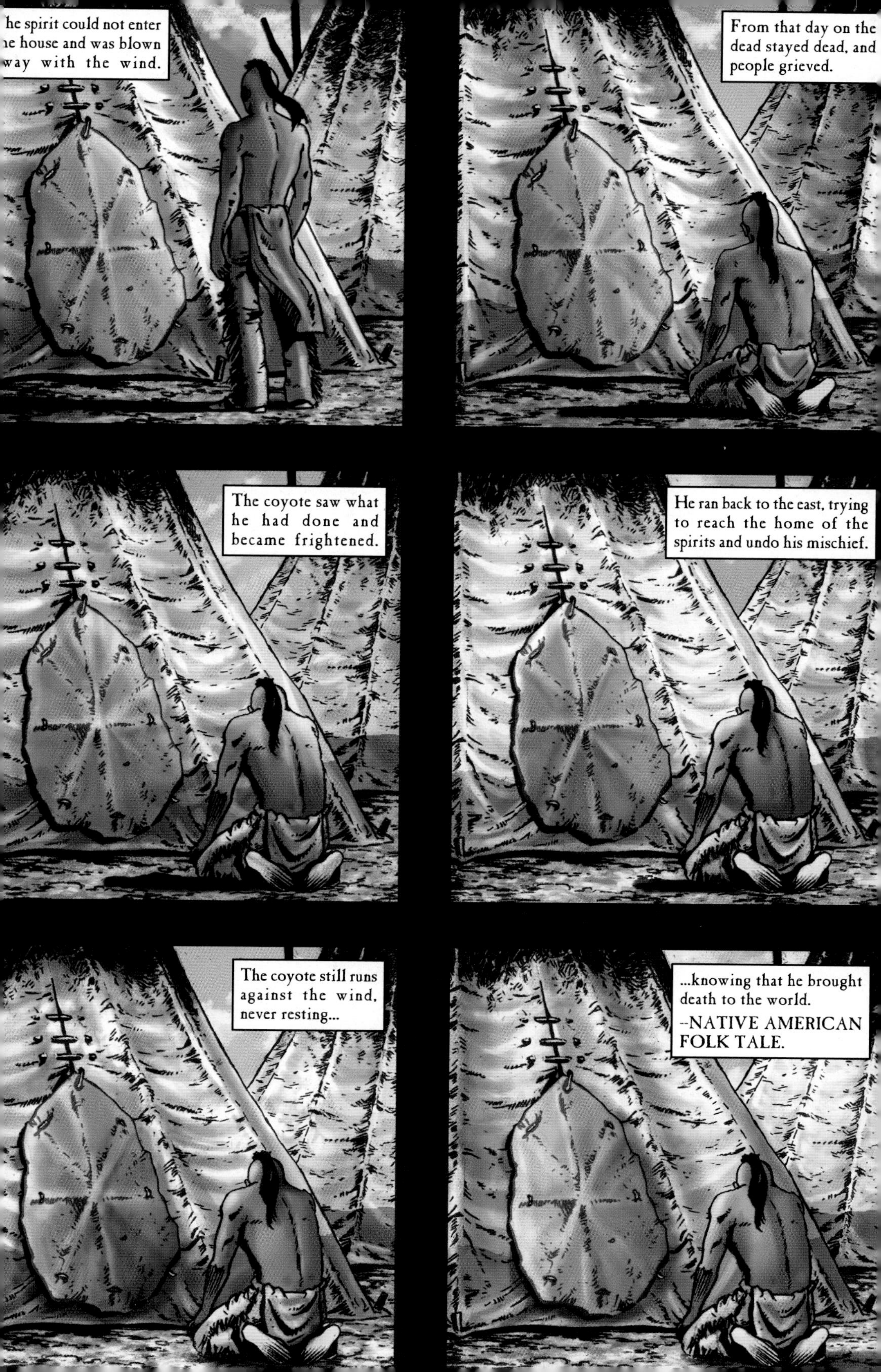
he spirit could not enter
ne house and was blown
way with the wind.
From that day on the dead stayed dead, and people grieved.
The coyote saw what he had done and became frightened.
He ran back to the east, trying to reach the home of the spirits and undo his mischief.
The coyote still runs against the wind, never resting...
...knowing that he brought death to the world.
--NATIVE AMERICAN FOLK TALE.

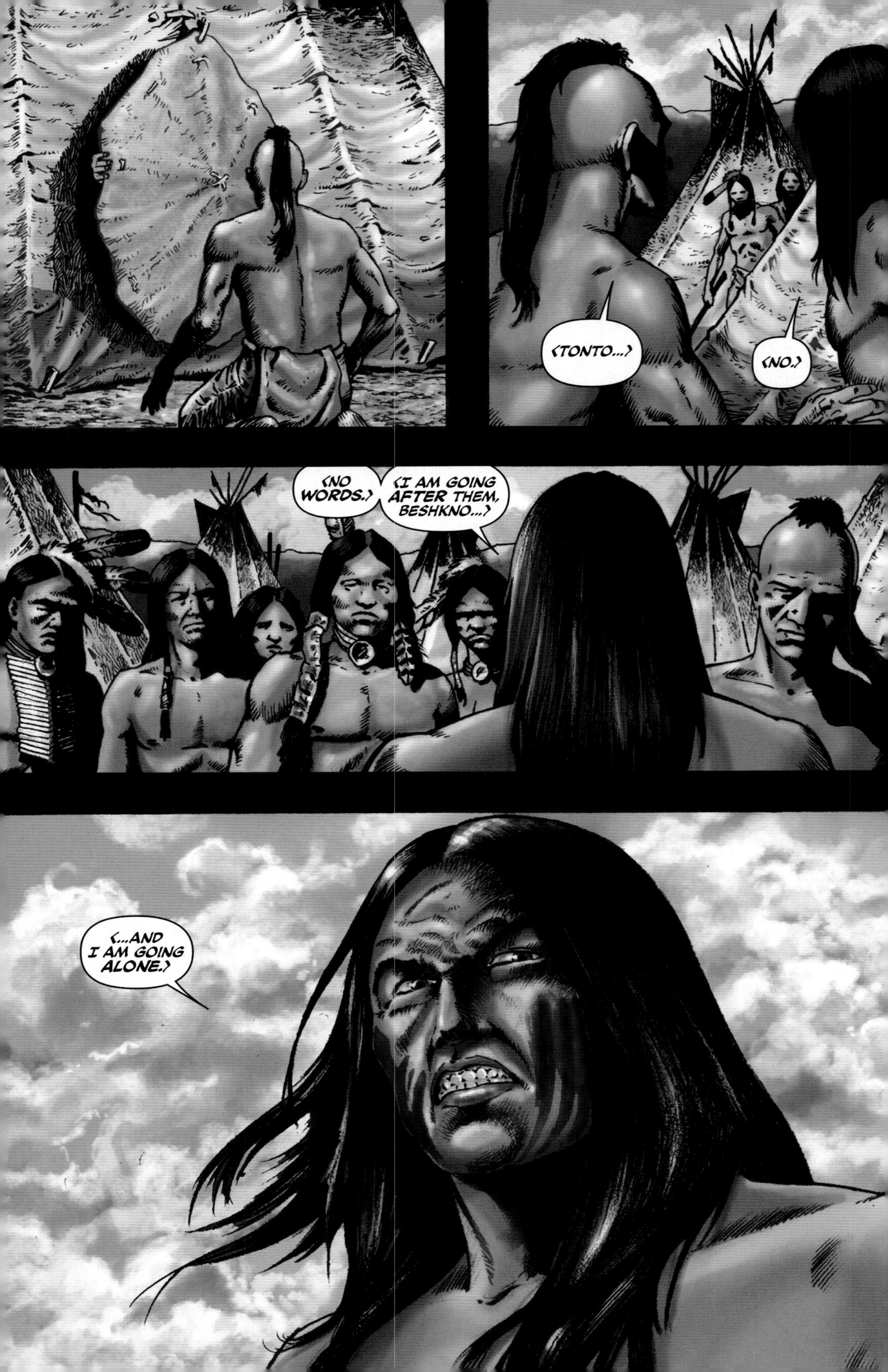
<TONTO...>
<NO.>
<NO WORDS.>
<I AM GOING AFTER THEM, BESHKNO...>
<...AND I AM GOING ALONE.>

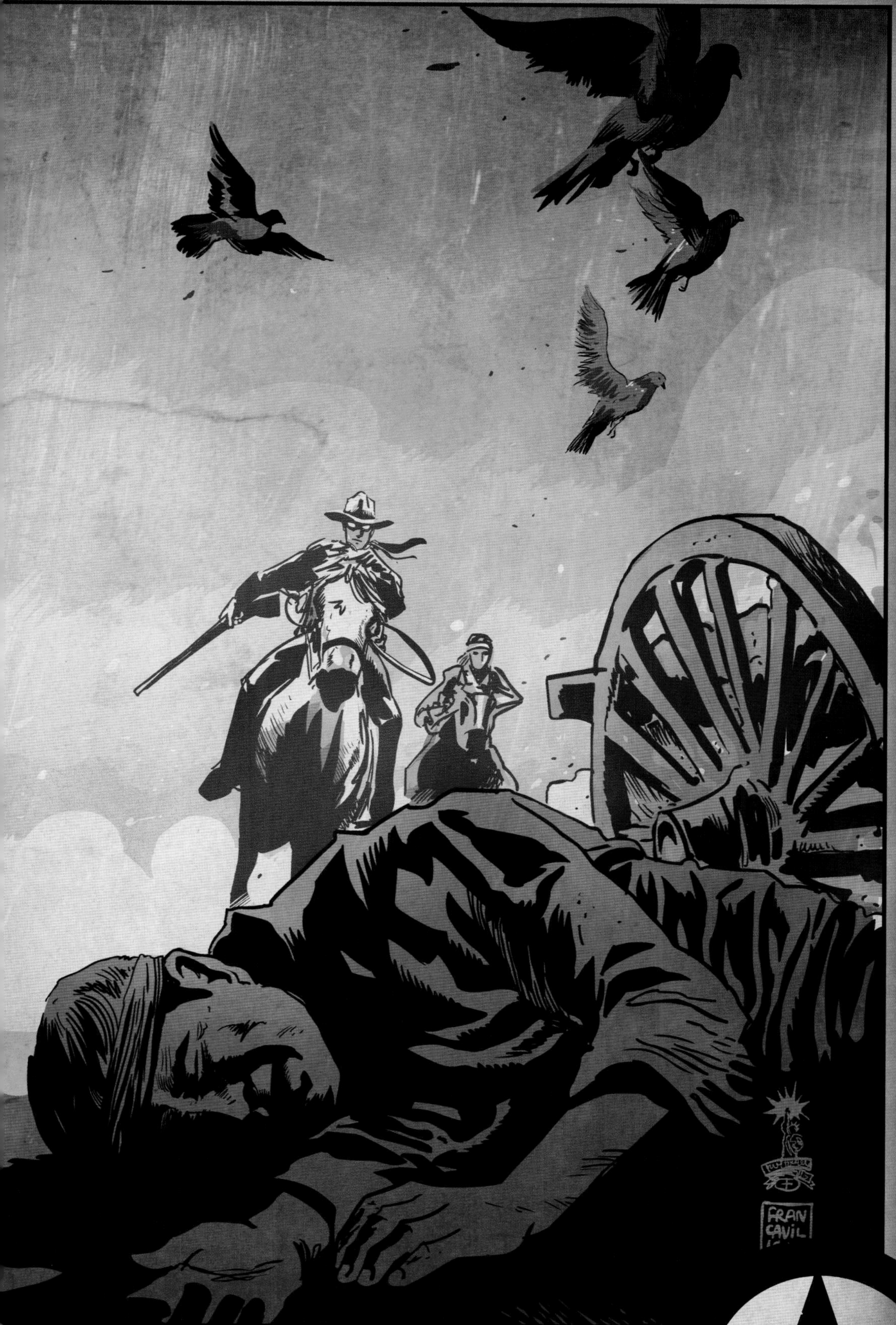

COVER BY FRANCESCO FRANCAVILLA

9

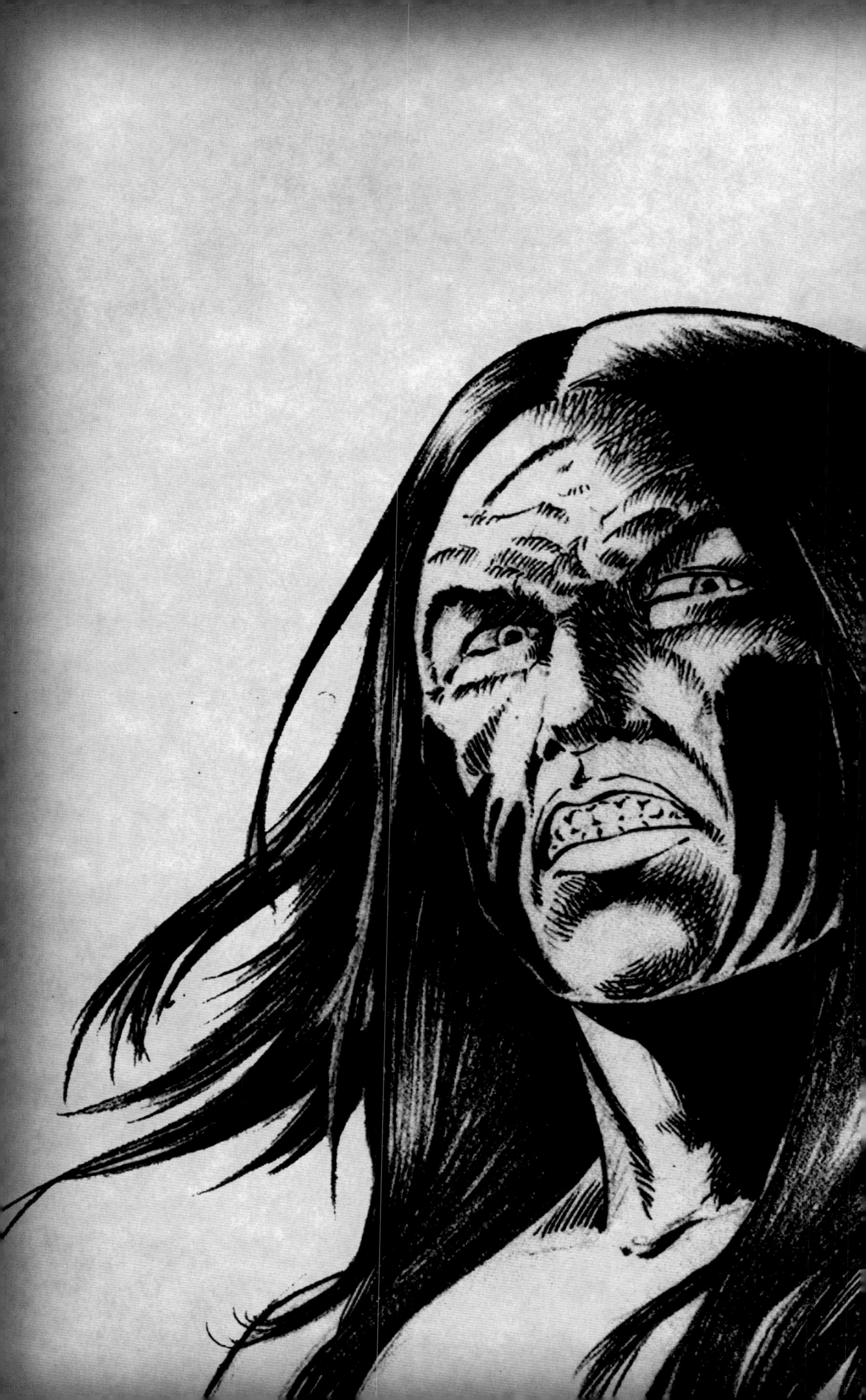

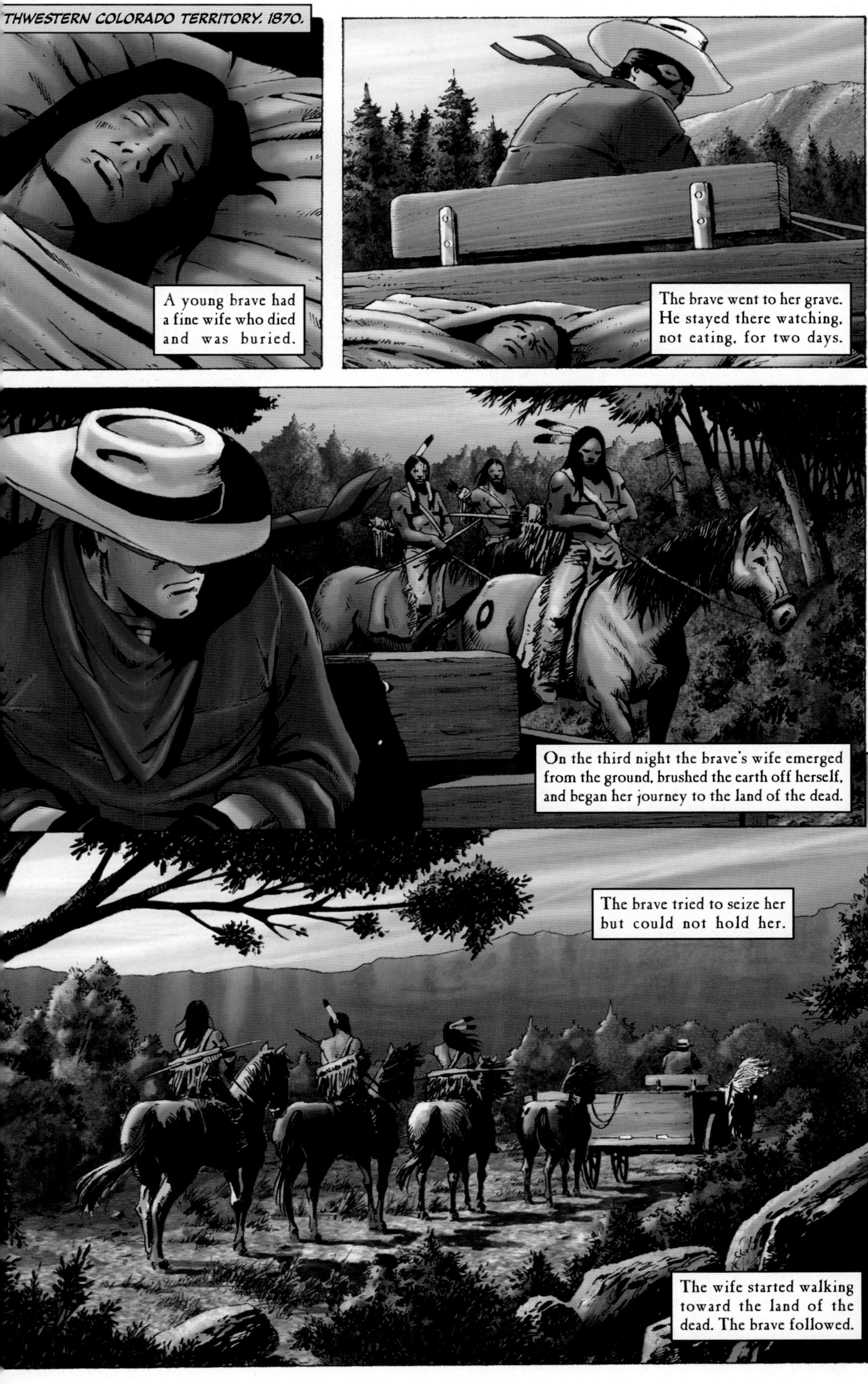
THWESTERN COLORADO TERRITORY. 1870.
A young brave had a fine wife who died and was buried.
The brave went to her grave. He stayed there watching, not eating, for two days.
On the third night the brave's wife emerged from the ground, brushed the earth off herself, and began her journey to the land of the dead.
The brave tried to seize her but could not hold her.
The wife started walking toward the land of the dead. The brave followed.

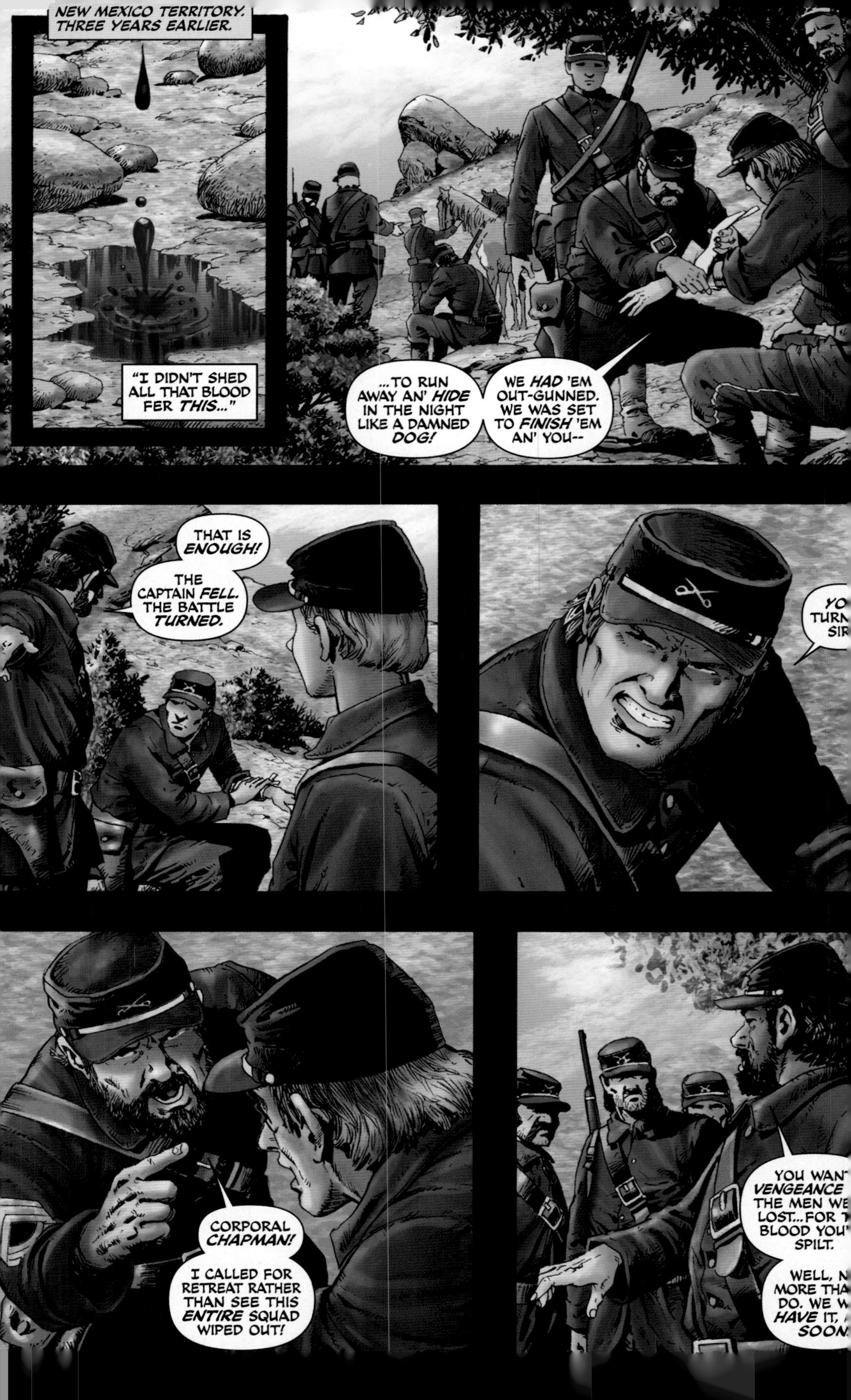
NEW MEXICO TERRITORY. THREE YEARS EARLIER.
"I DIDN'T SHED ALL THAT BLOOD FER THIS..."
...TO RUN AWAY AN' HIDE IN THE NIGHT LIKE A DAMNED DOG!
WE HAD 'EM OUT-GUNNED. WE WAS SET TO FINISH 'EM AN' YOU--
THAT IS ENOUGH!
THE CAPTAIN FELL. THE BATTLE TURNED.
YO TURN SIR
CORPORAL CHAPMAN!
I CALLED FOR RETREAT RATHER THAN SEE THIS ENTIRE SQUAD WIPED OUT!
YOU WAN VENGEANCE THE MEN WE LOST...FOR BLOOD YOU SPILT.
WELL, MORE THA DO. WE W HAVE IT, SOON

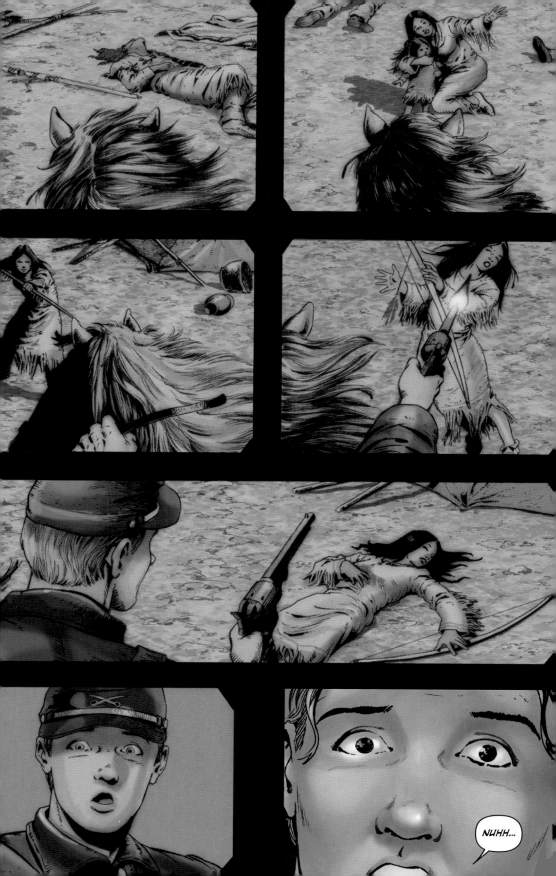

NUHH...

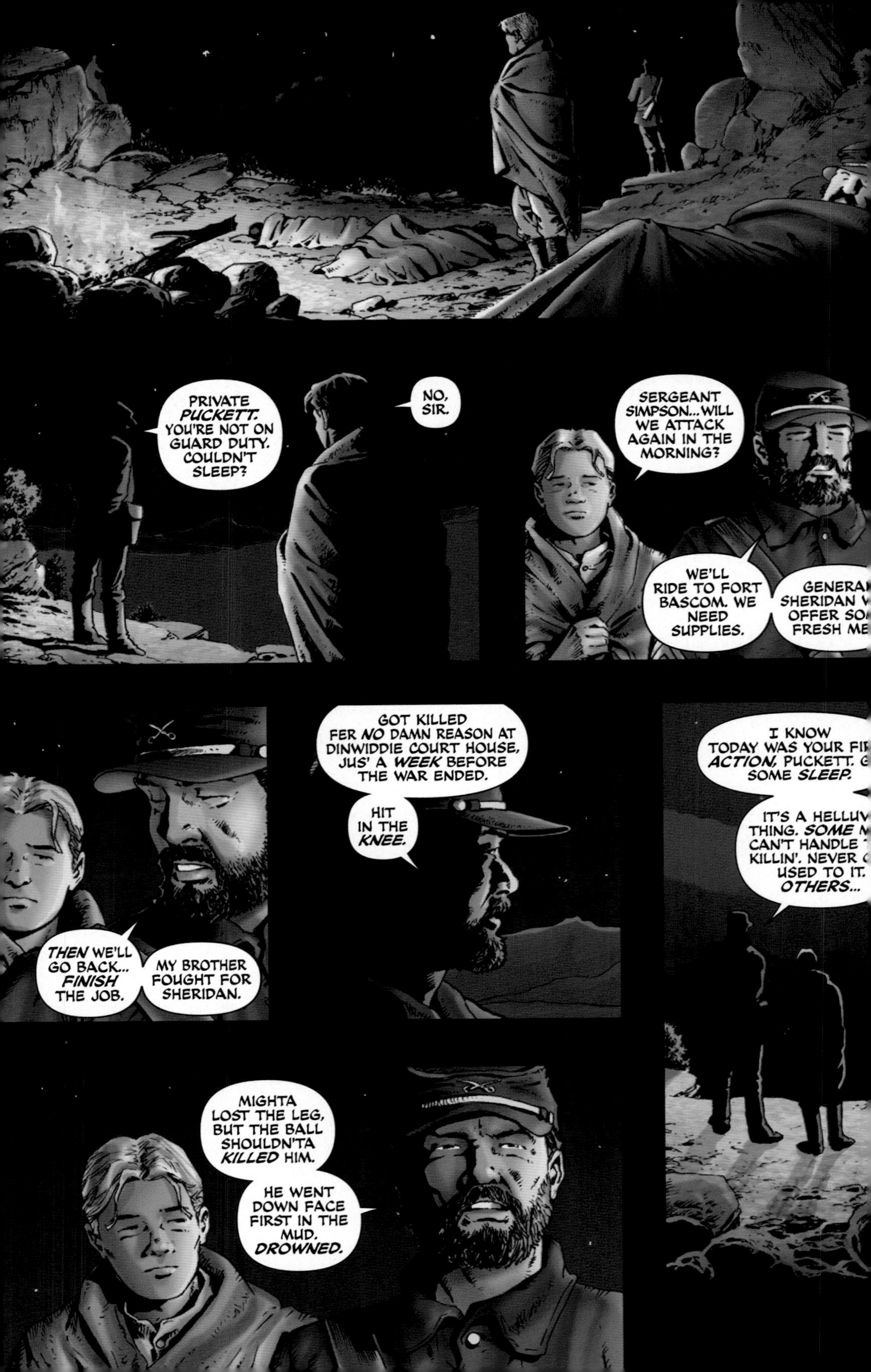
PRIVATE PUCKETT. YOU'RE NOT ON GUARD DUTY. COULDN'T SLEEP?
NO, SIR.
SERGEANT SIMPSON...WILL WE ATTACK AGAIN IN THE MORNING?
WE'LL RIDE TO FORT BASCOM. WE NEED SUPPLIES.
THEN WE'LL GO BACK... FINISH THE JOB.
MY BROTHER FOUGHT FOR SHERIDAN.
GOT KILLED FER NO DAMN REASON AT DINWIDDIE COURT HOUSE, JUS' A WEEK BEFORE THE WAR ENDED.
HIT IN THE KNEE.
MIGHTA LOST THE LEG, BUT THE BALL SHOULDN'TA KILLED HIM.
HE WENT DOWN FACE FIRST IN THE MUD. DROWNED.
USED TO IT.
OTHERS...

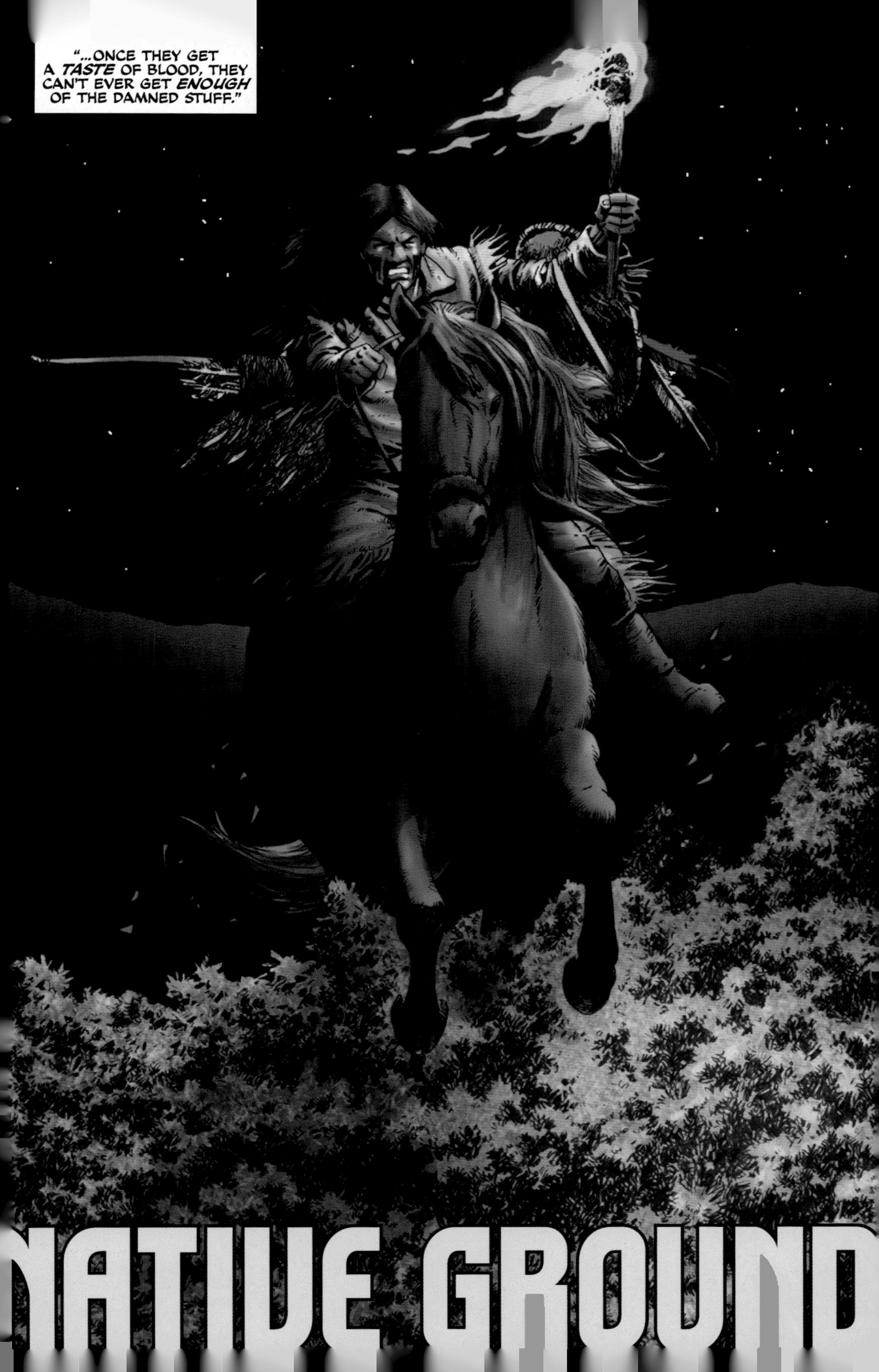
"...ONCE THEY GET A TASTE OF BLOOD, THEY CAN'T EVER GET ENOUGH OF THE DAMNED STUFF."
NATIVE GROUND

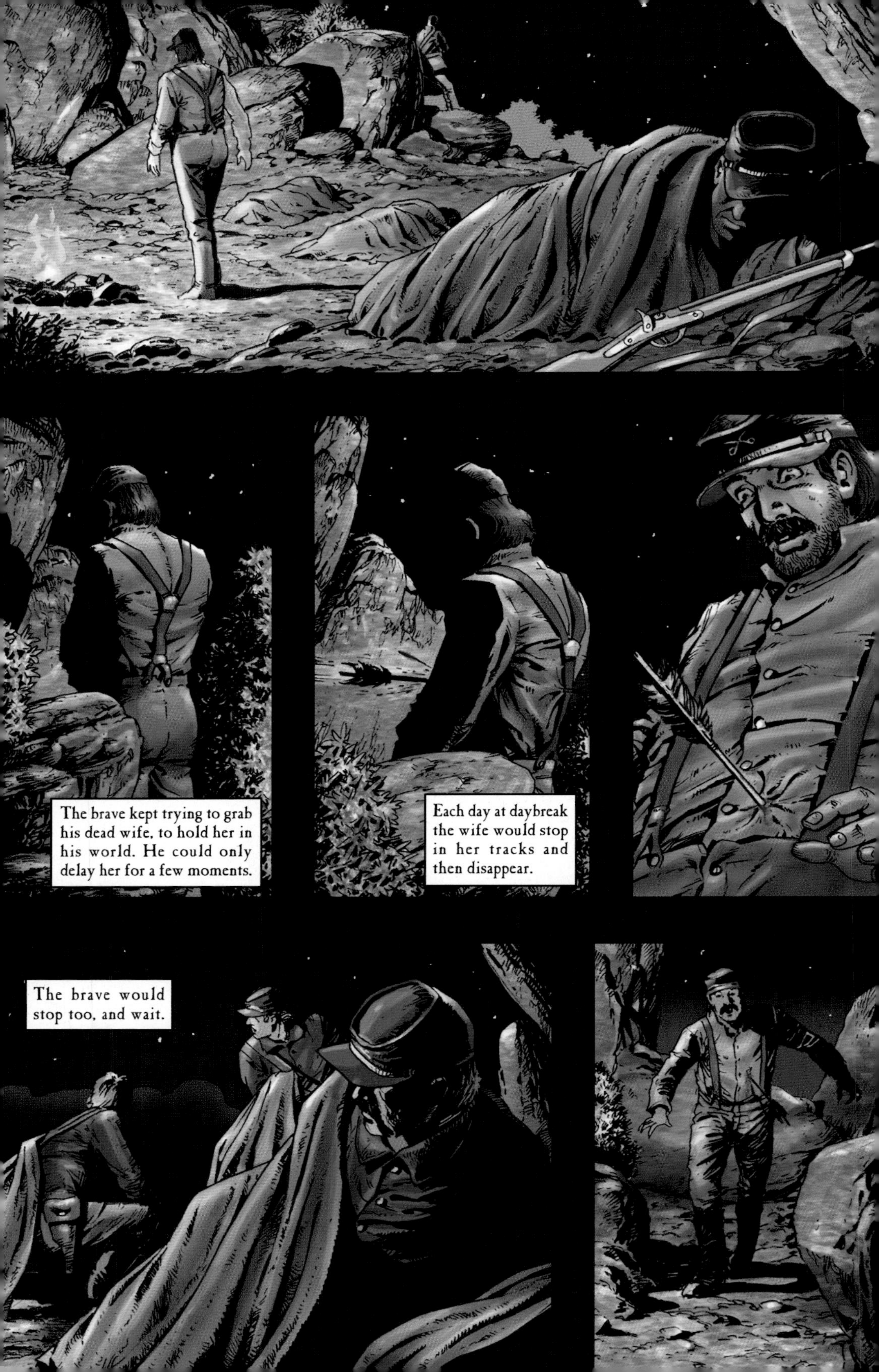
The brave kept trying to grab his dead wife, to hold her in his world. He could only delay her for a few moments.
Each day at daybreak the wife would stop in her tracks and then disappear.
The brave would stop too, and wait.

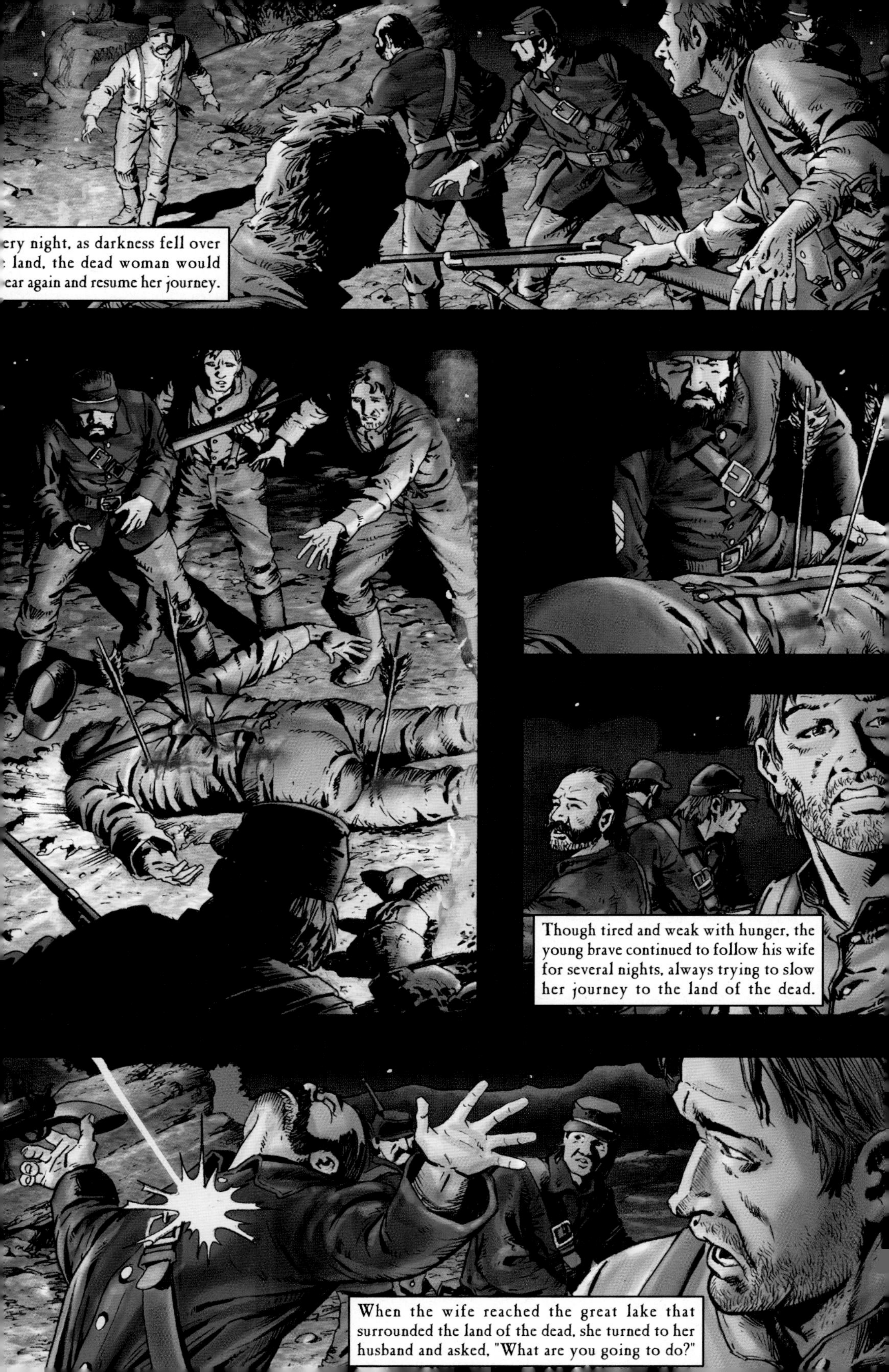
ery night, as darkness fell over
land, the dead woman would
ear again and resume her journey.
Though tired and weak with hunger, the young brave continued to follow his wife for several nights, always trying to slow her journey to the land of the dead.
When the wife reached the great lake that surrounded the land of the dead, she turned to her husband and asked, "What are you going to do?"

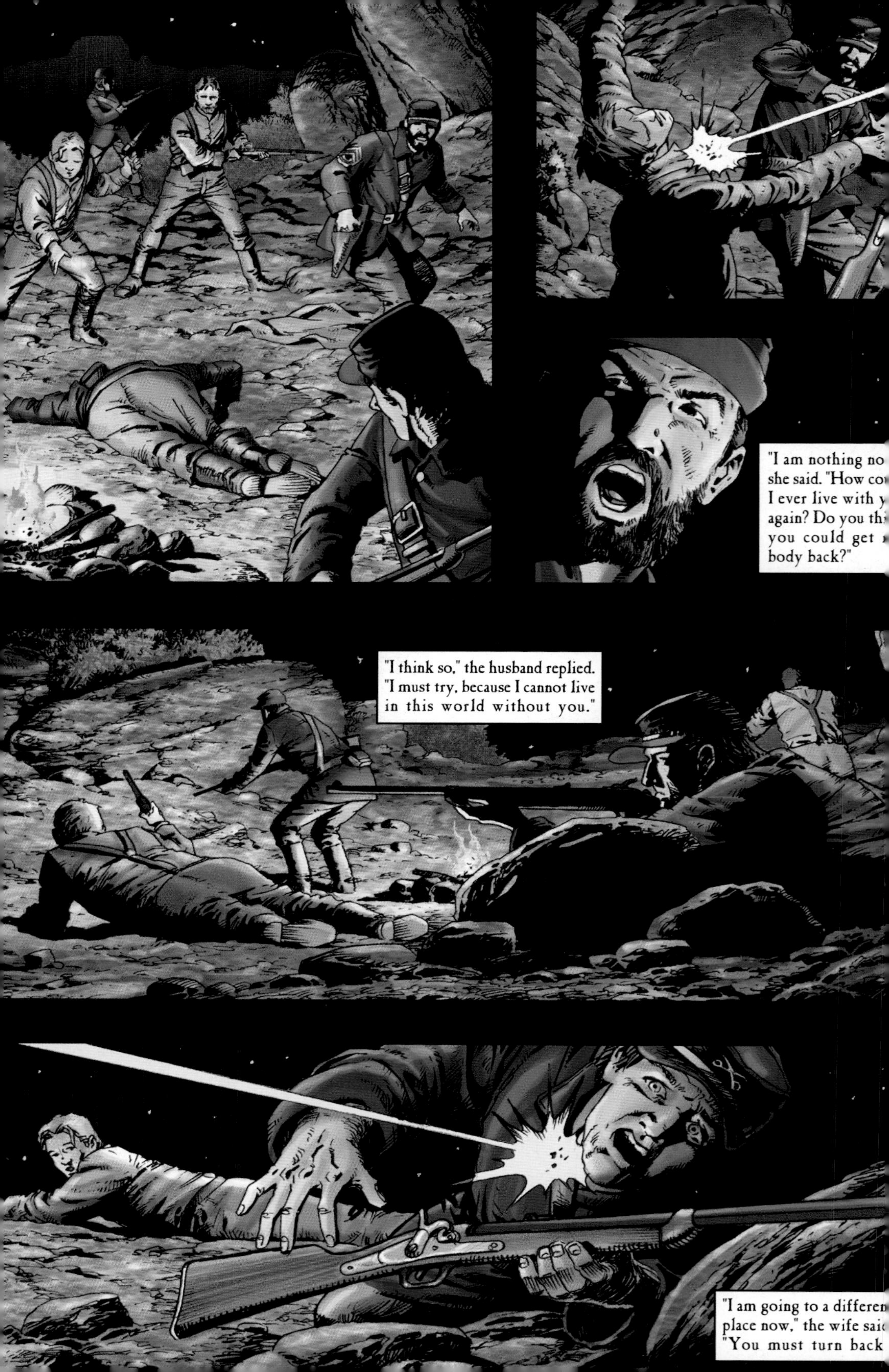
"I am nothing no she said. "How co I ever live with y again? Do you thi you could get body back?"
"I think so," the husband replied. "I must try, because I cannot live in this world without you."
"I am going to a differen place now," the wife sai "You must turn back

The wife walked across a vast bridge that led to the land of the dead. Her husband followed.

Black birds flew from the heavens, crashing into the black water.

They emerged as shimmering fish, leaping over the bridge, dripping black water onto the brave and his dead wife.

When the wife had crossed the bridge, she was met by the Chief of the dead.

The Chief's eyes were blank, sunken holes, but he sensed the presence of the wife and said, "Someone has come."

The fish cried out, "There are two. One of them is alive. He stinks."

"Do not let him enter the land of the dead," the fish pleaded.

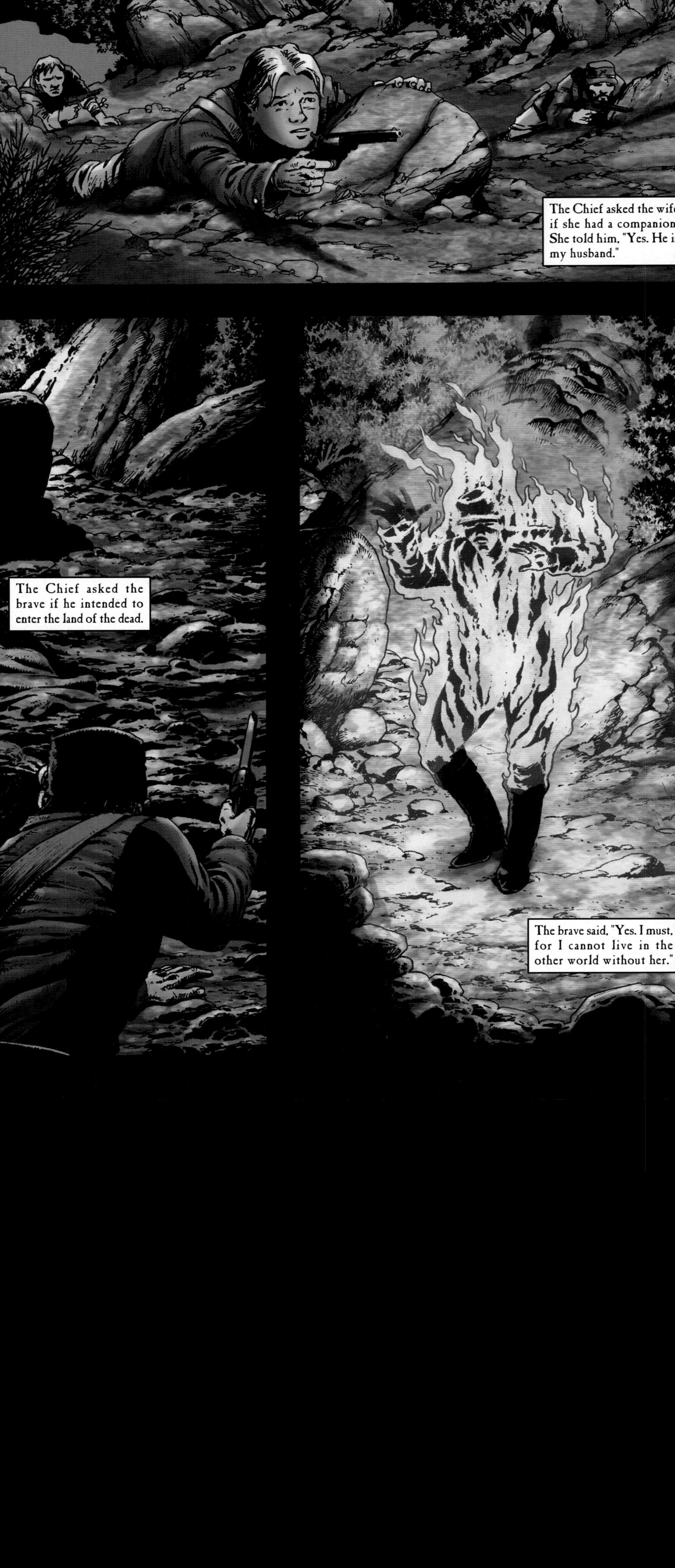
The Chief asked the wif
if she had a companion
She told him, "Yes. He i
my husband."
The Chief asked the brave if he intended to enter the land of the dead.
The brave said, "Yes. I must, for I cannot live in the other world without her."

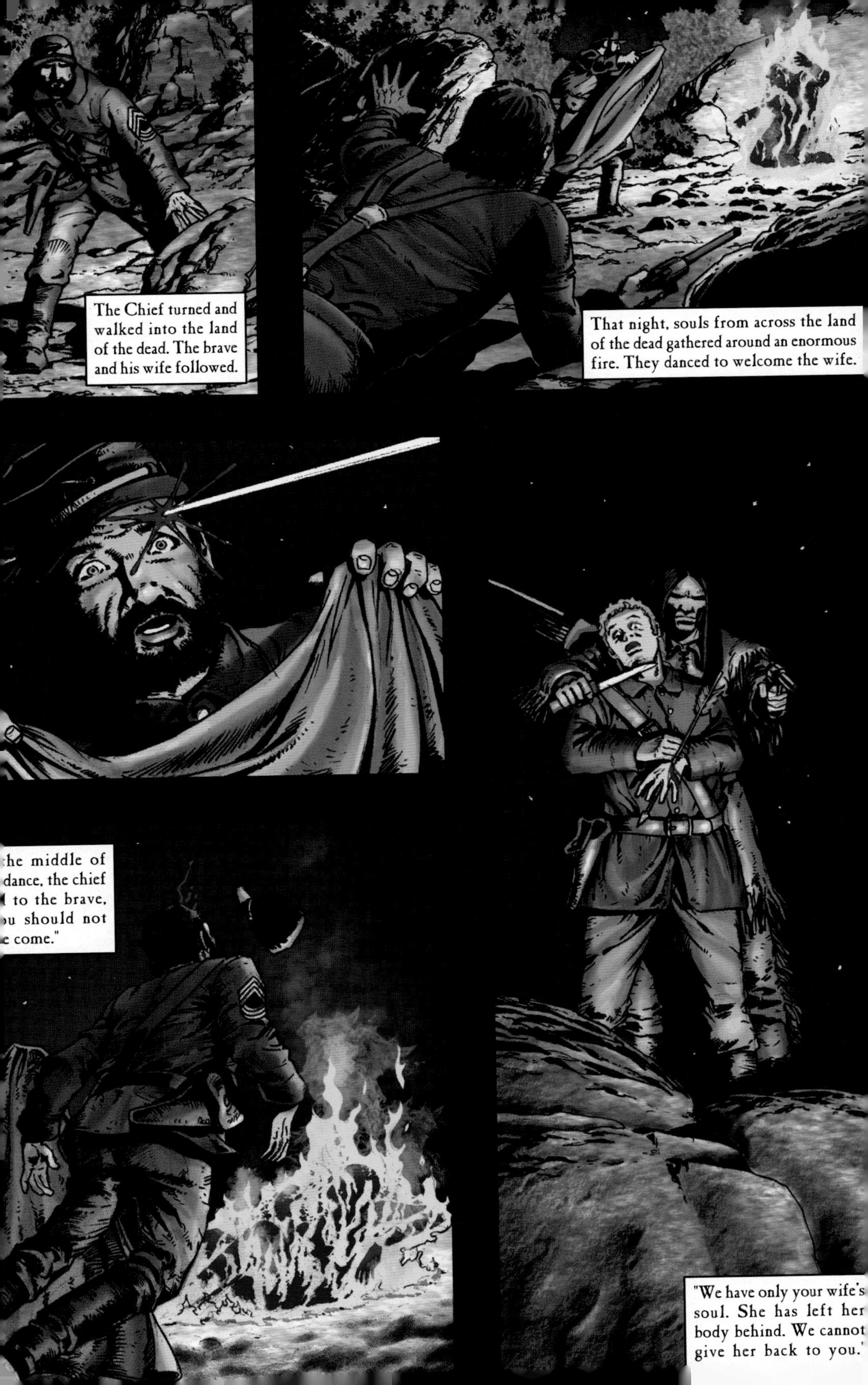
The Chief turned and walked into the land of the dead. The brave and his wife followed.
That night, souls from across the land of the dead gathered around an enormous fire. They danced to welcome the wife.
he middle of dance, the chief to the brave, u should not e come."
"We have only your wife's soul. She has left her body behind. We cannot give her back to you.'

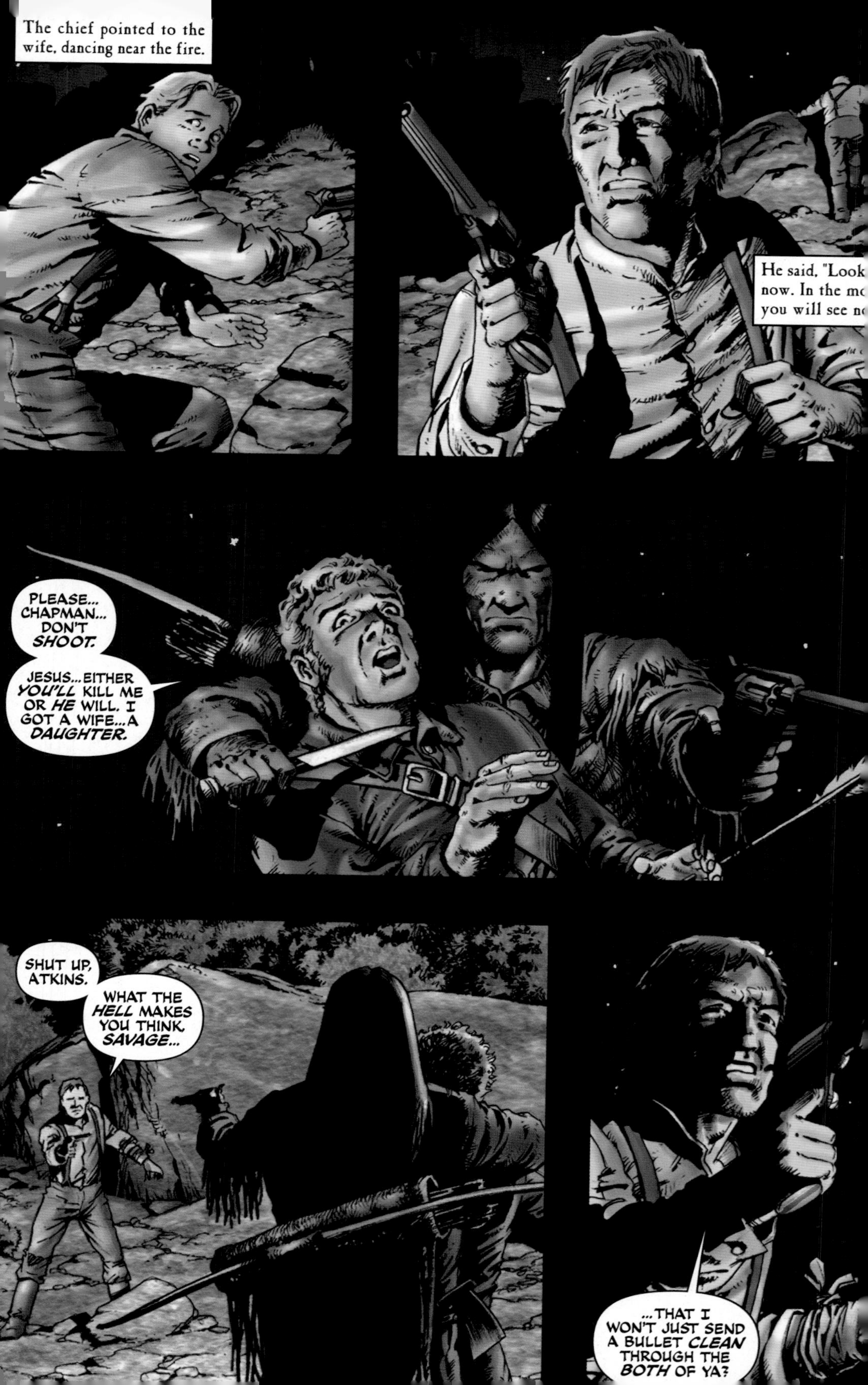
The chief pointed to the wife, dancing near the fire.
He said, "Look now. In the mo you will see n
PLEASE... CHAPMAN... DON'T SHOOT.
JESUS... EITHER YOU'LL KILL ME OR HE WILL. I GOT A WIFE... A DAUGHTER.
SHUT UP, ATKINS.
WHAT THE HELL MAKES YOU THINK, SAVAGE...
...THAT I WON'T JUST SEND A BULLET CLEAN THROUGH THE BOTH OF YA?

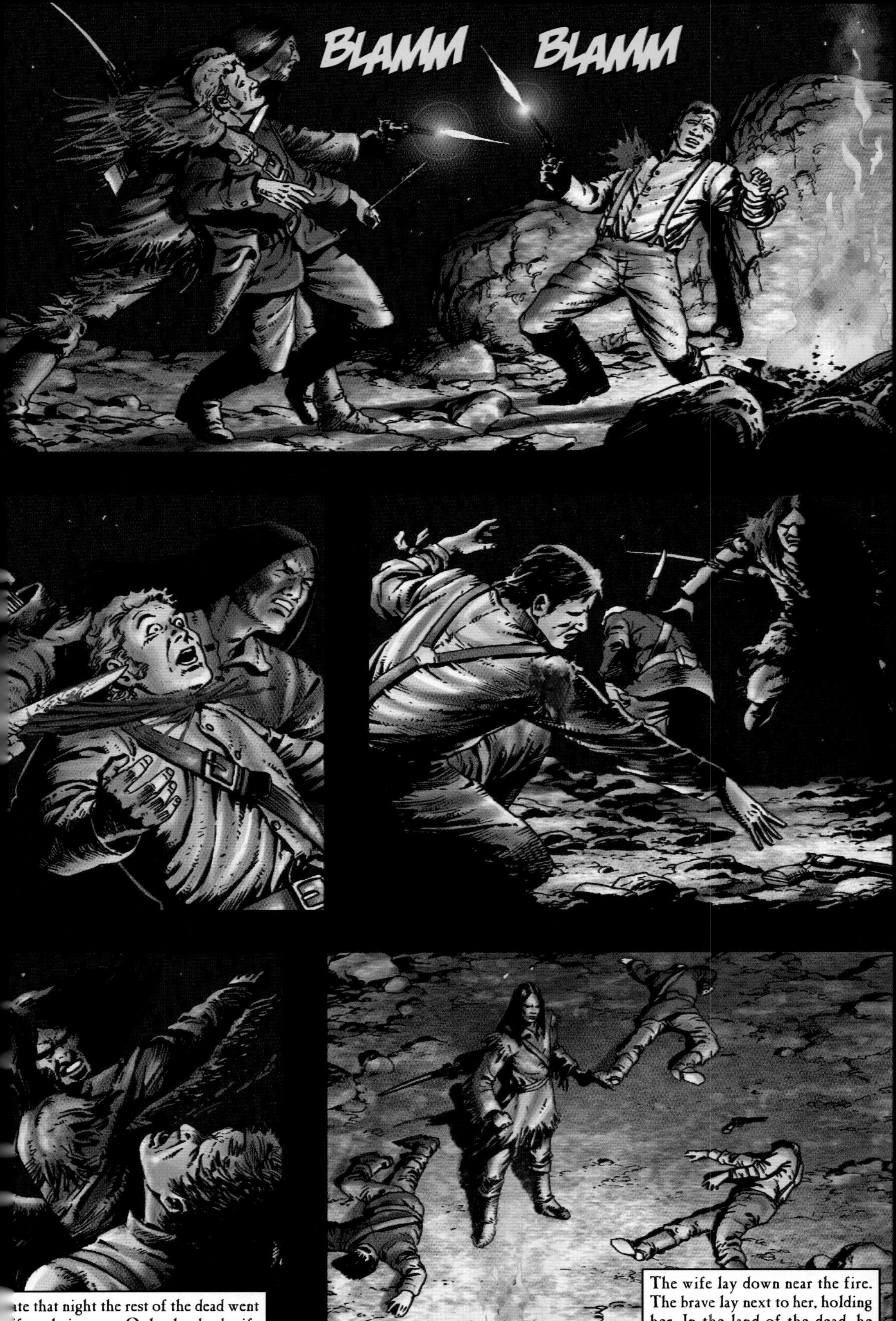
BLAMM
BLAMM
ate that night the rest of the dead went f to their tents. Only the dead wife d her husband remained by the fire.
The wife lay down near the fire. The brave lay next to her, holding her. In the land of the dead, he could touch her as if she still lived.

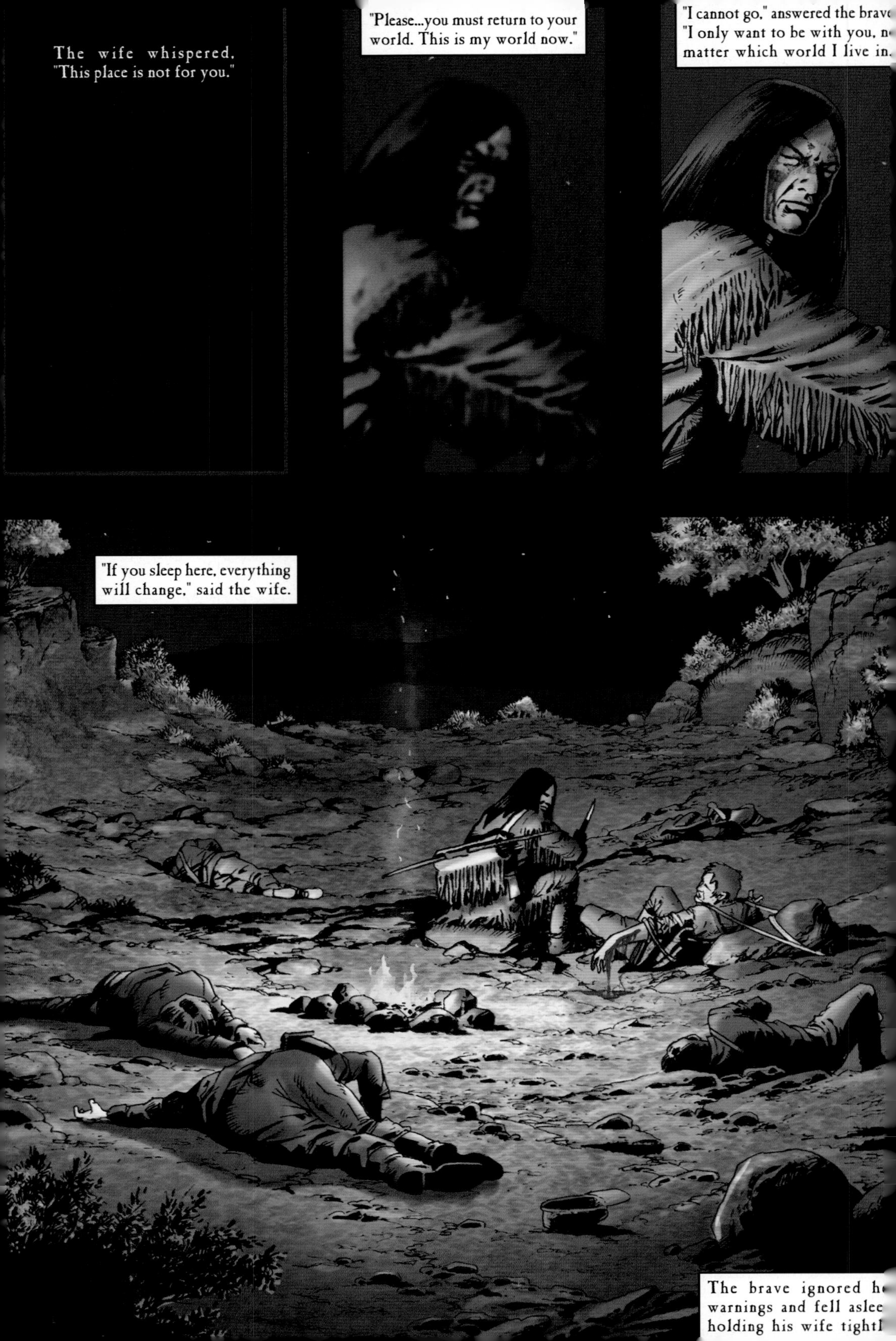
The wife whispered, "This place is not for you."
"Please...you must return to your world. This is my world now."
"I cannot go," answered the brav
"I only want to be with you, n
matter which world I live in.
"If you sleep here, everything will change," said the wife.
The brave ignored h
warnings and fell aslee
holding his wife tightl

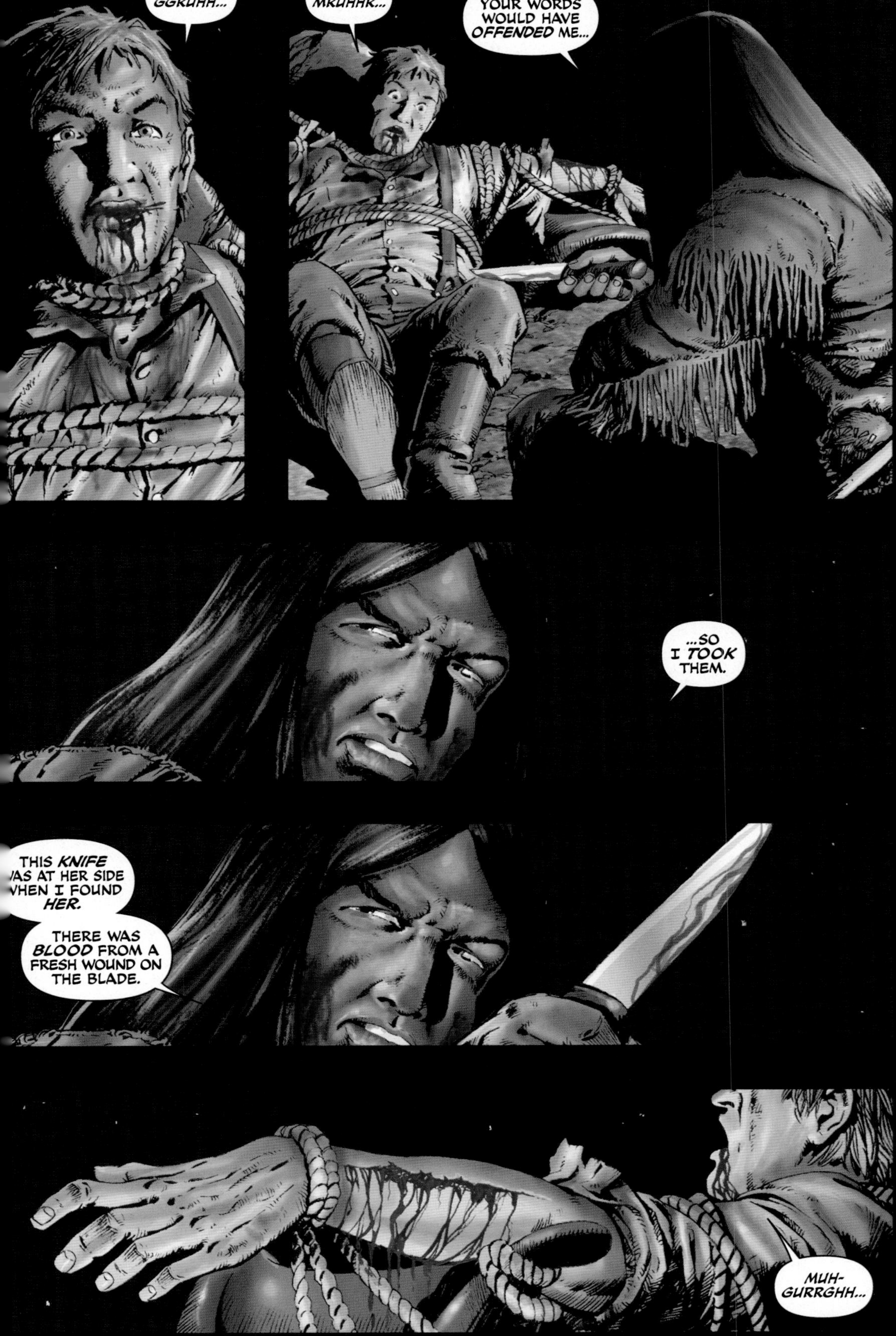
MMRURR-GGRUHH...
MMM-MRUHHR...
YOUR WORDS WOULD HAVE OFFENDED ME...
...SO I TOOK THEM.
THIS KNIFE WAS AT HER SIDE WHEN I FOUND HER.
THERE WAS BLOOD FROM A FRESH WOUND ON THE BLADE.
MUH-GURRGHH...

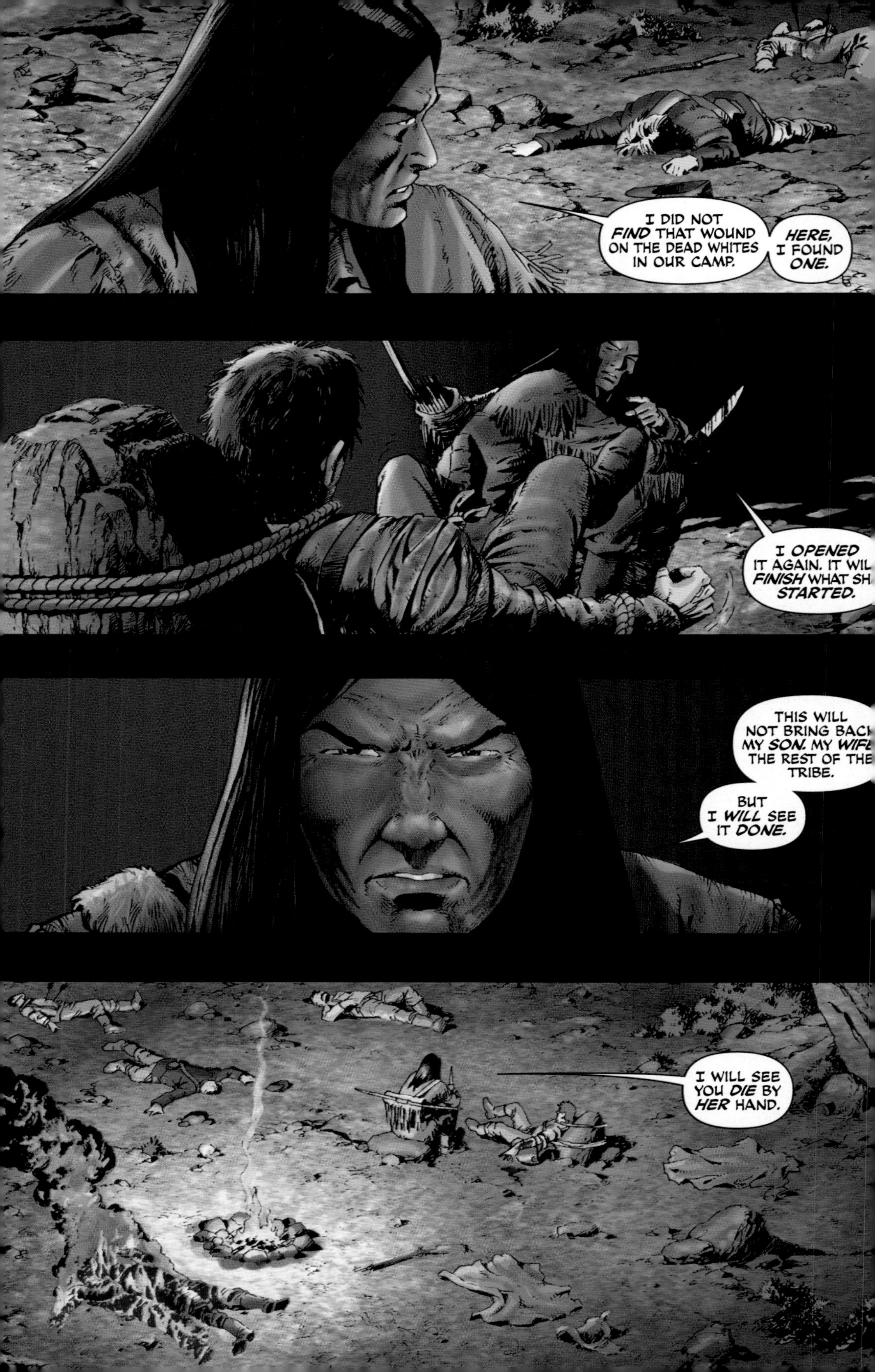
I DID NOT FIND THAT WOUND ON THE DEAD WHITES IN OUR CAMP.
HERE, I FOUND ONE.
I OPENED IT AGAIN. IT WIL FINISH WHAT SH STARTED.
THIS WILL NOT BRING BAC MY SON. MY WIF THE REST OF THE TRIBE.
BUT I WILL SEE IT DONE.
I WILL SEE YOU DIE BY HER HAND.

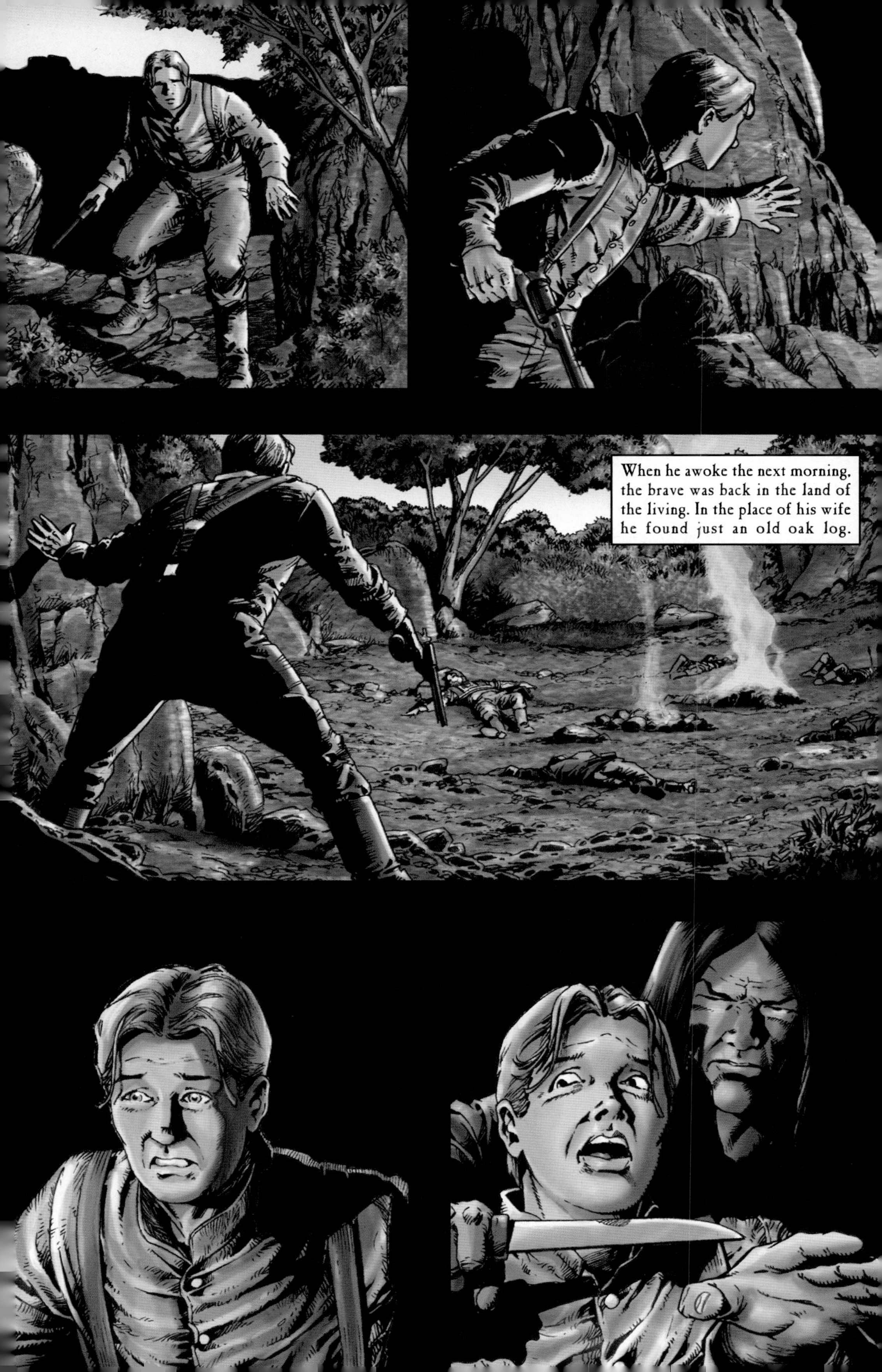
When he awoke the next morning, the brave was back in the land of the living. In the place of his wife he found just an old oak log.

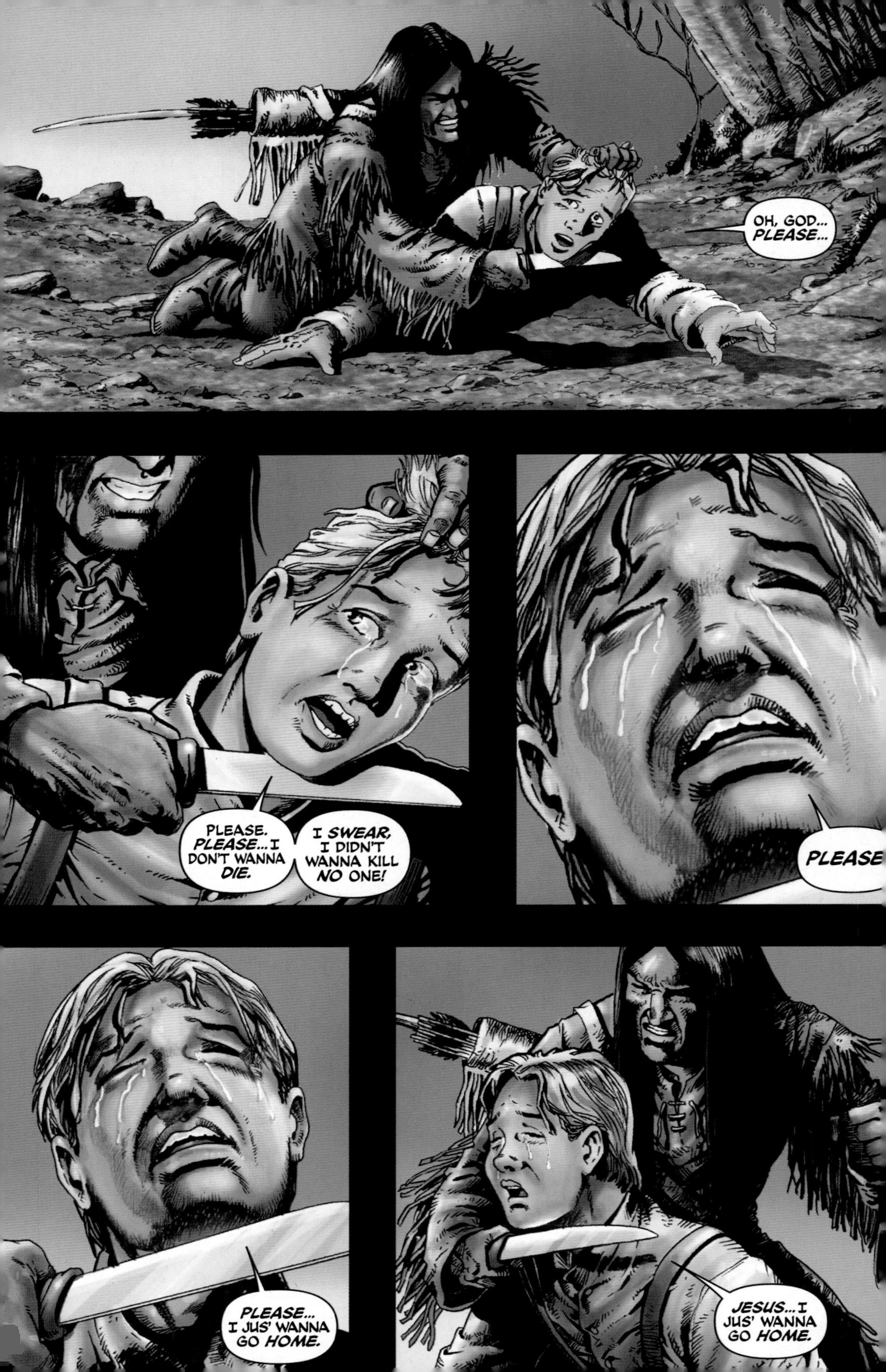
OH, GOD... PLEASE...
PLEASE. PLEASE... I DON'T WANNA DIE.
I SWEAR, I DIDN'T WANNA KILL NO ONE!
PLEASE
PLEASE... I JUS' WANNA GO HOME.
JESUS... I JUS' WANNA GO HOME.

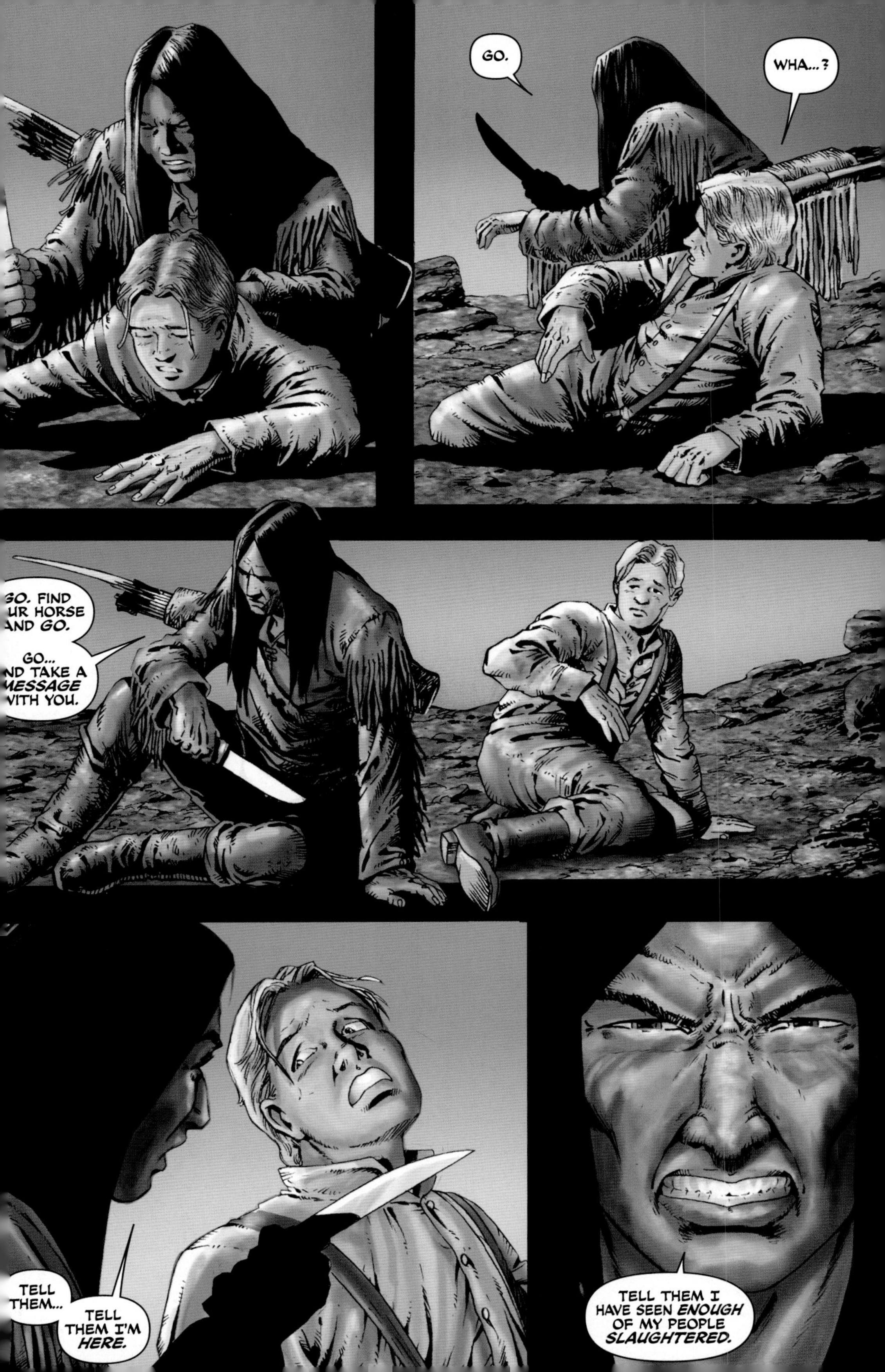
GO.
WHA...?
GO. FIND UR HORSE AND GO.
GO... ND TAKE A MESSAGE WITH YOU.
TELL THEM...
TELL THEM I'M HERE.
TELL THEM I HAVE SEEN ENOUGH OF MY PEOPLE SLAUGHTERED.

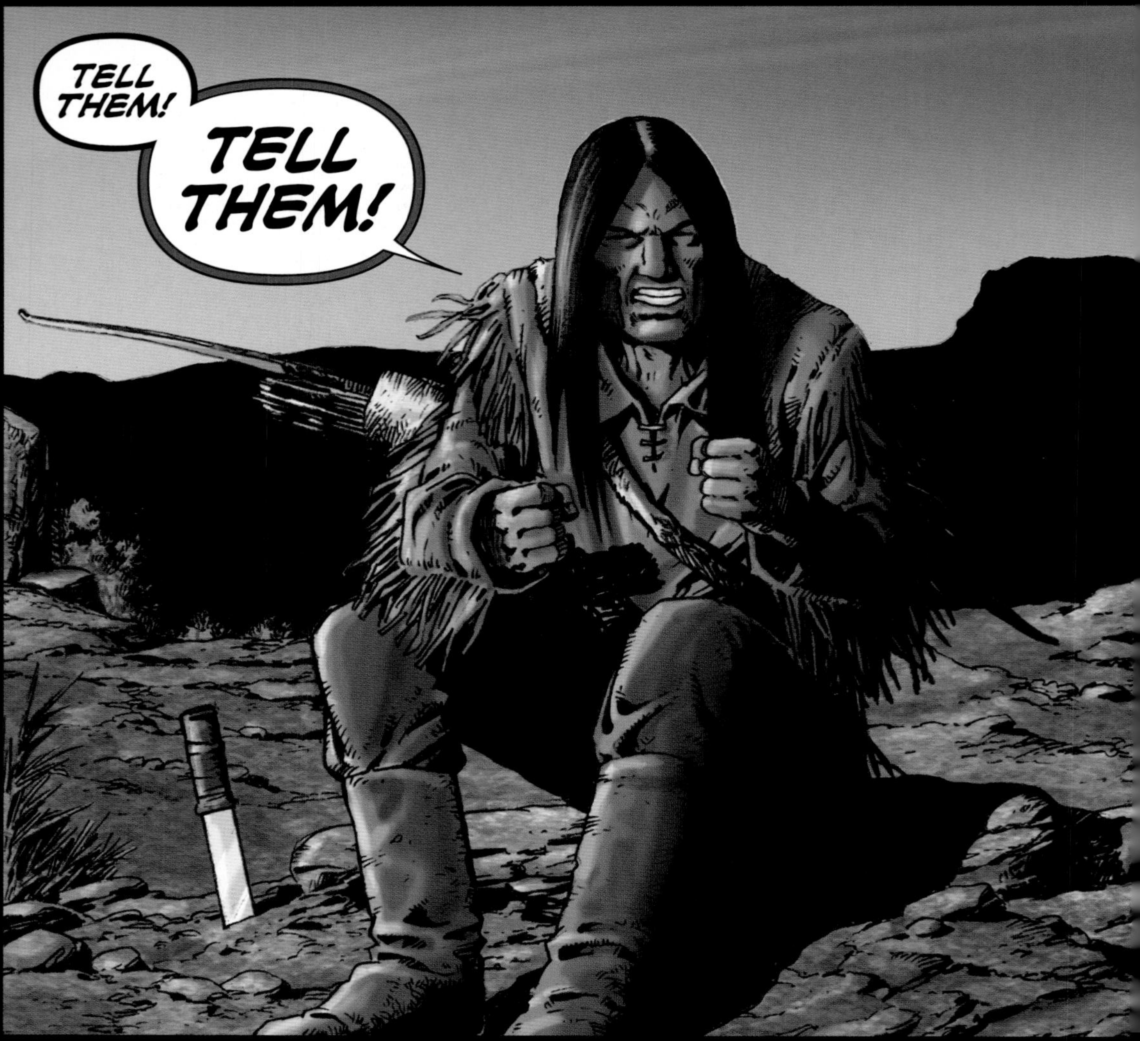
TELL THEM!
TELL THEM!

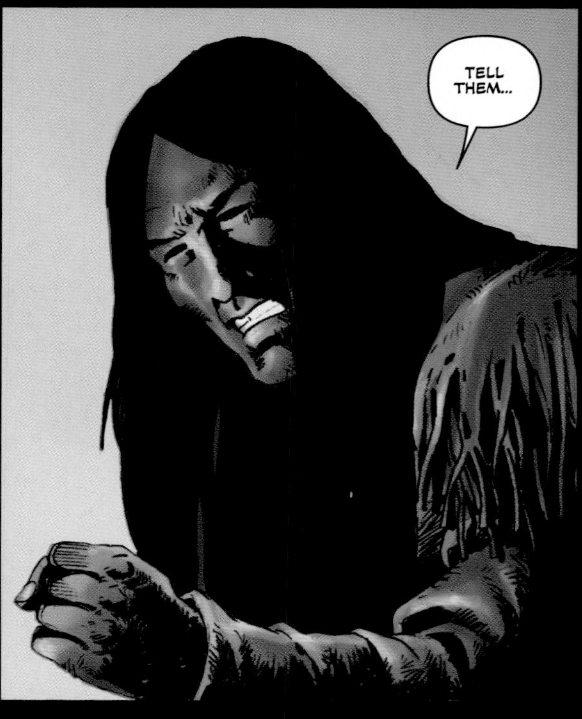
TELL THEM...

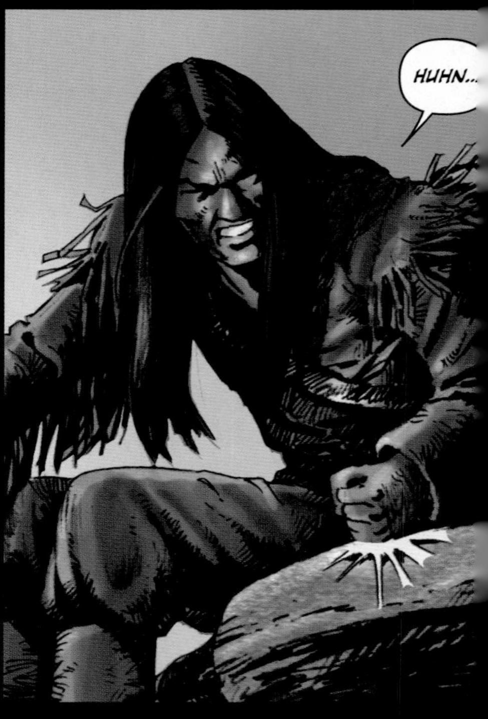
HUHN...

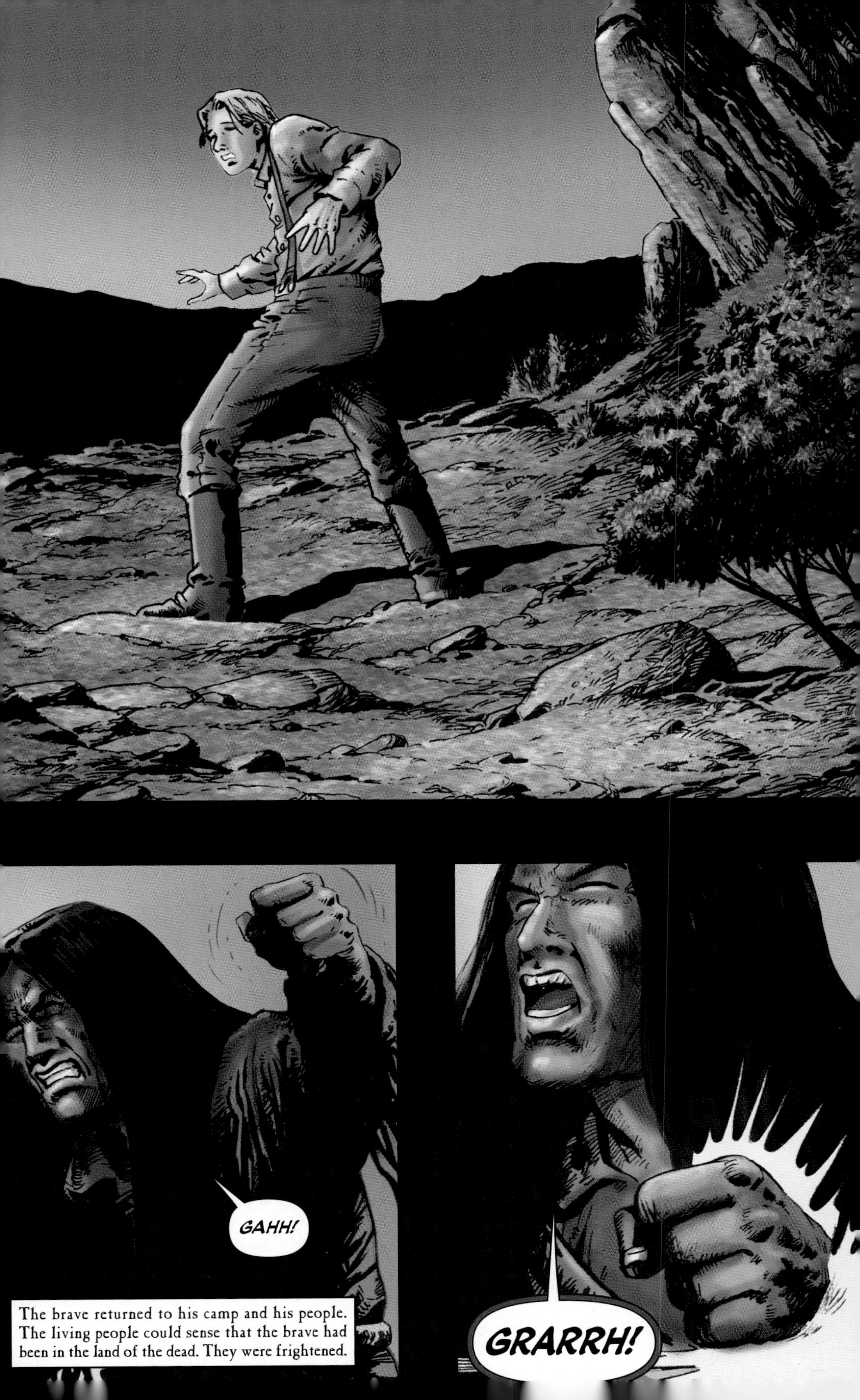
GAHH!
The brave returned to his camp and his people. The living people could sense that the brave had been in the land of the dead. They were frightened.
GRARRH!

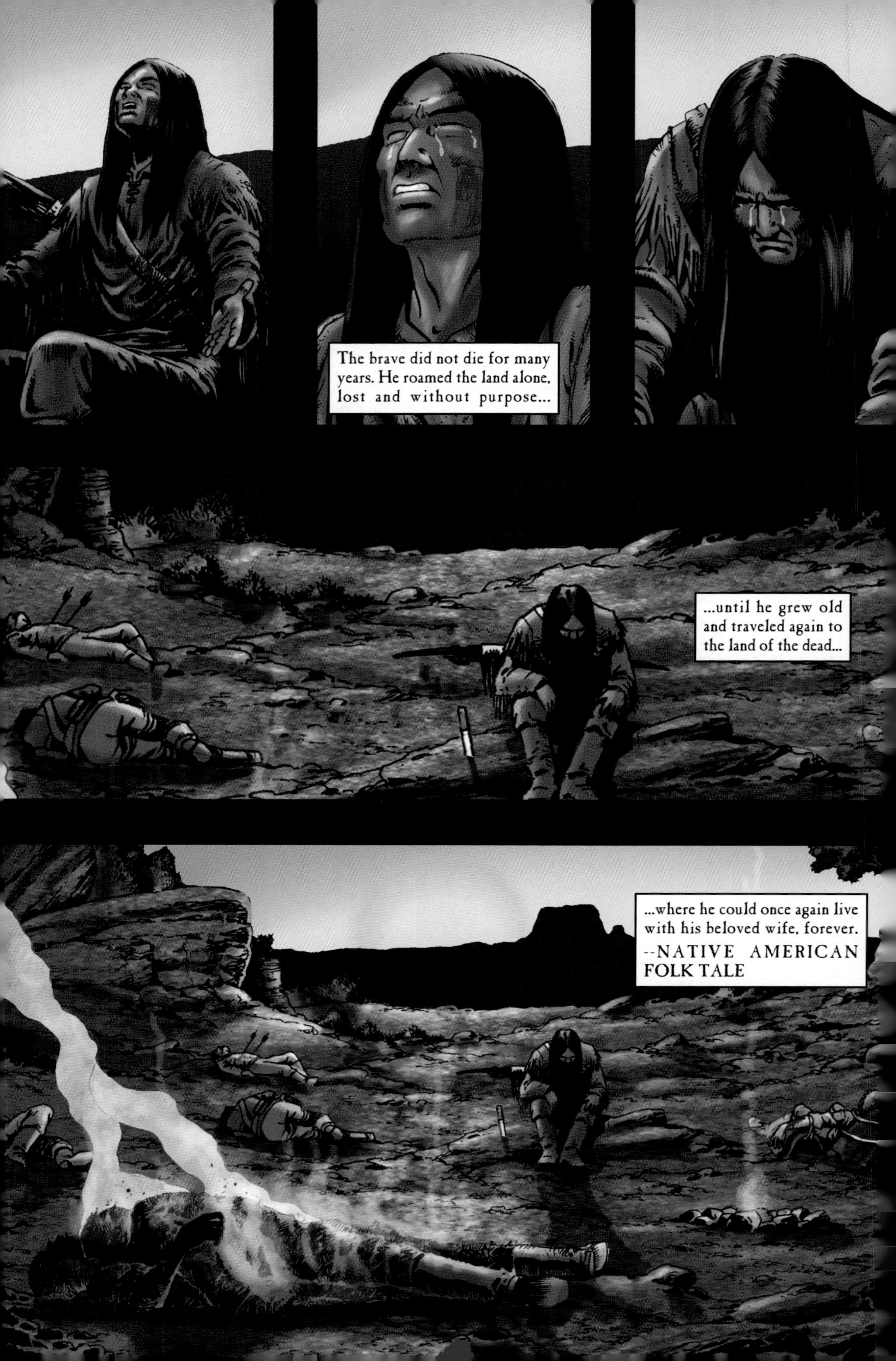
The brave did not die for many years. He roamed the land alone, lost and without purpose...
...until he grew old and traveled again to the land of the dead...
...where he could once again live with his beloved wife, forever.
--NATIVE AMERICAN FOLK TALE

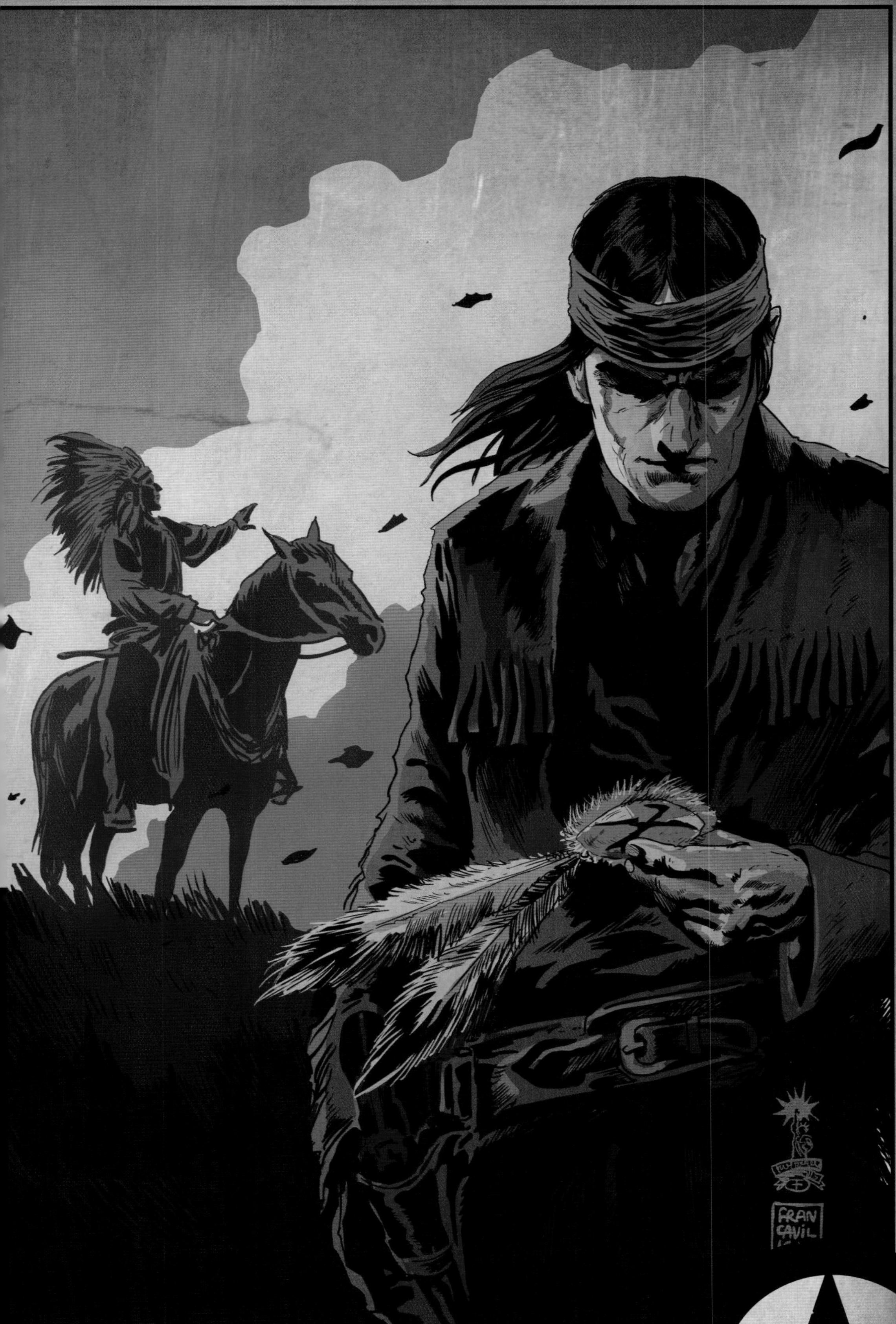
FRAN
CAVIL

COVER BY **FRANCESCO FRANCAVILLA**

10

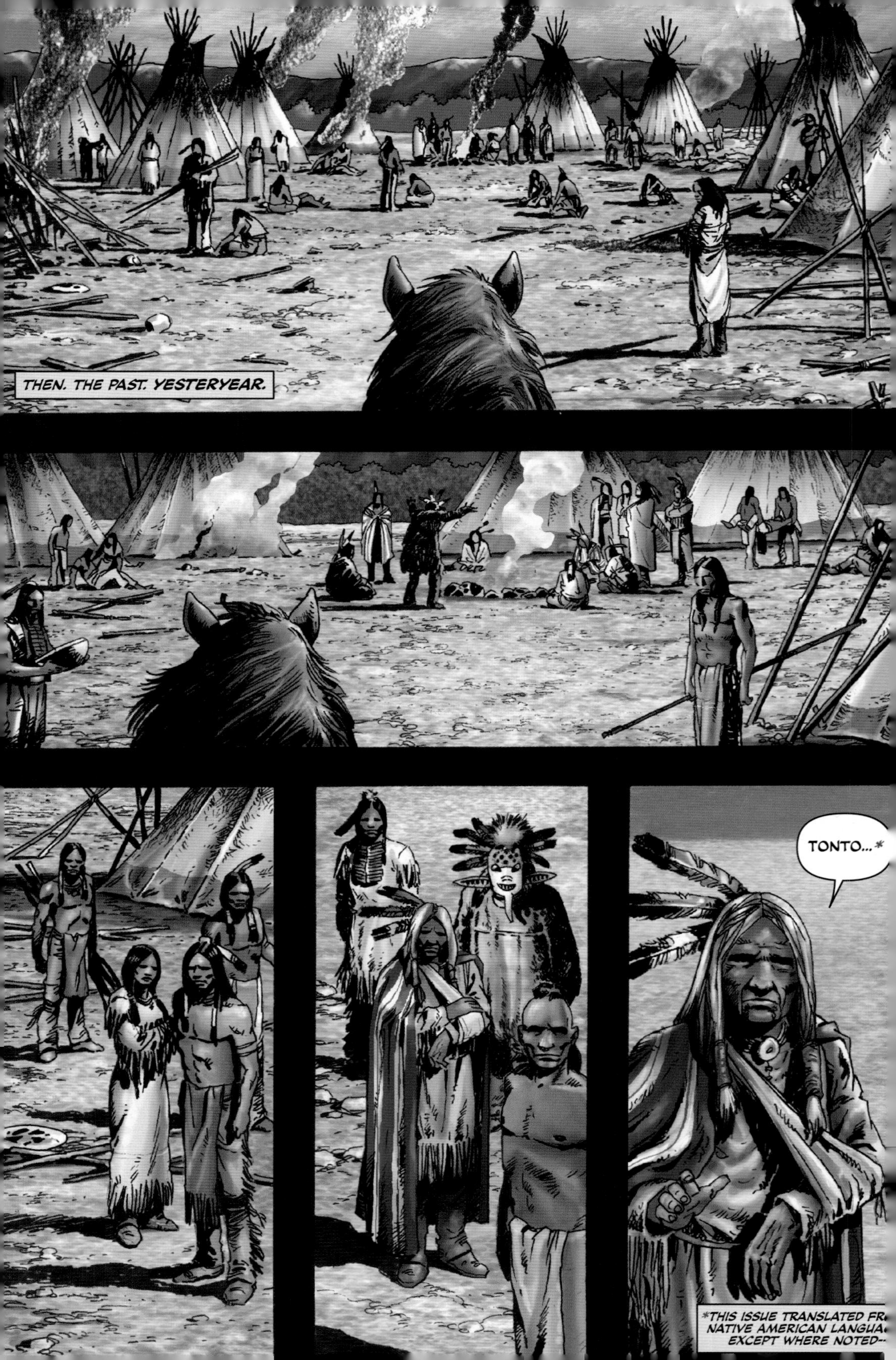
THEN. THE PAST. YESTERYEAR.
TONTO...*
*THIS ISSUE TRANSLATED FR
NATIVE AMERICAN LANGUA
EXCEPT WHERE NOTED--

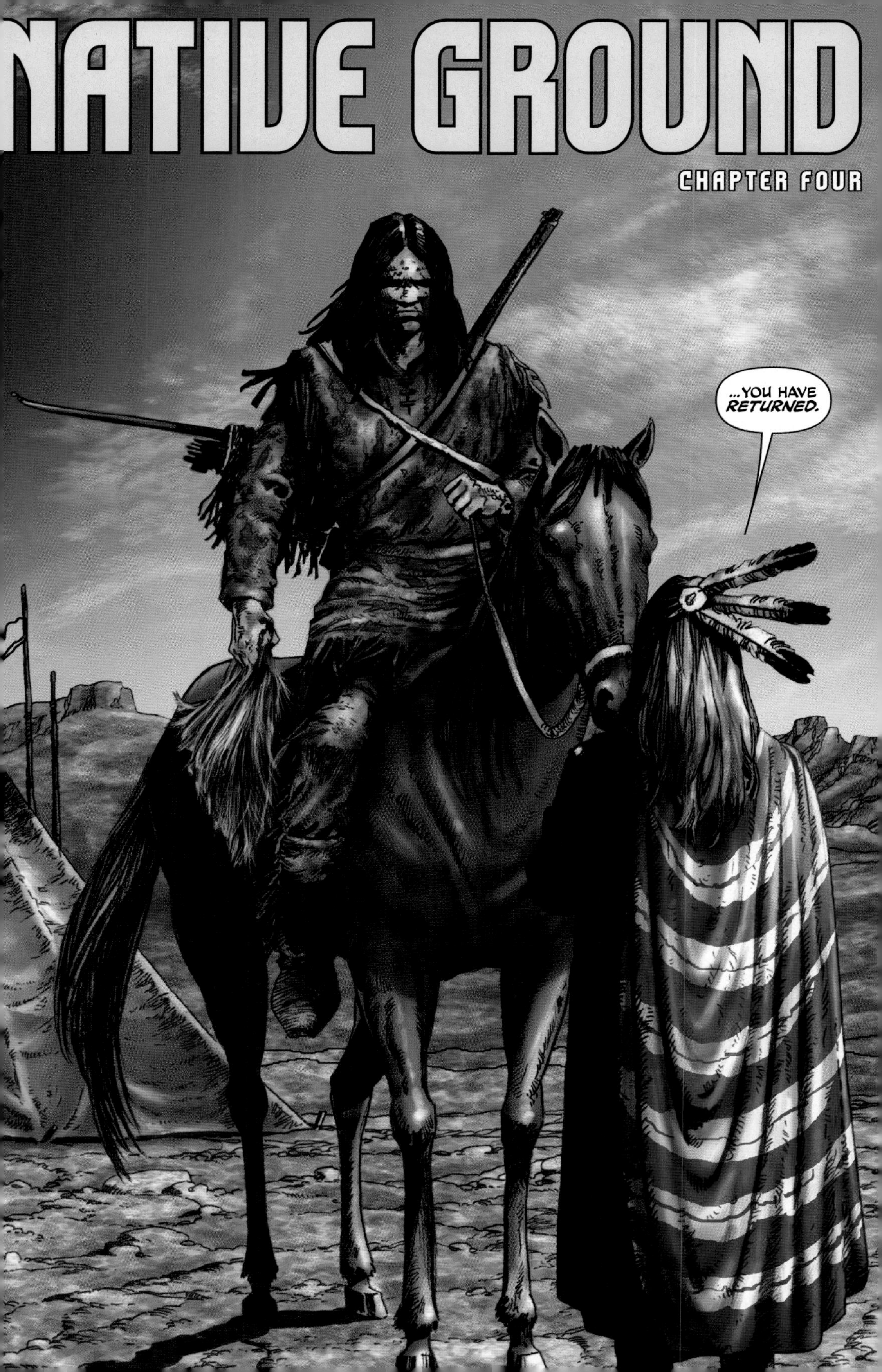
NATIVE GROUND
CHAPTER FOUR
...YOU HAVE RETURNED.

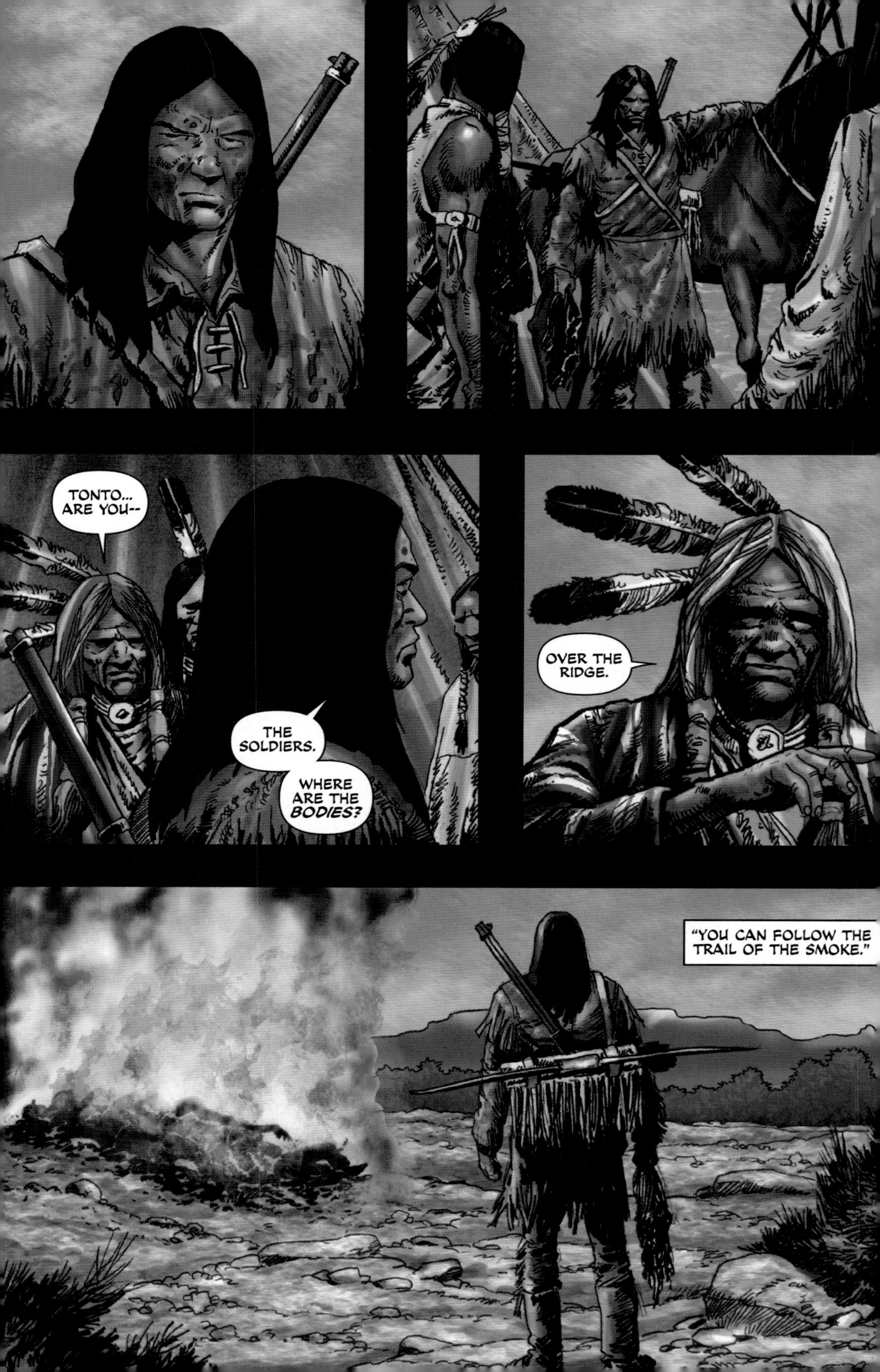
TONTO... ARE YOU--
THE SOLDIERS.
WHERE ARE THE *BODIES?*
OVER THE RIDGE.
"YOU CAN FOLLOW THE TRAIL OF THE SMOKE."

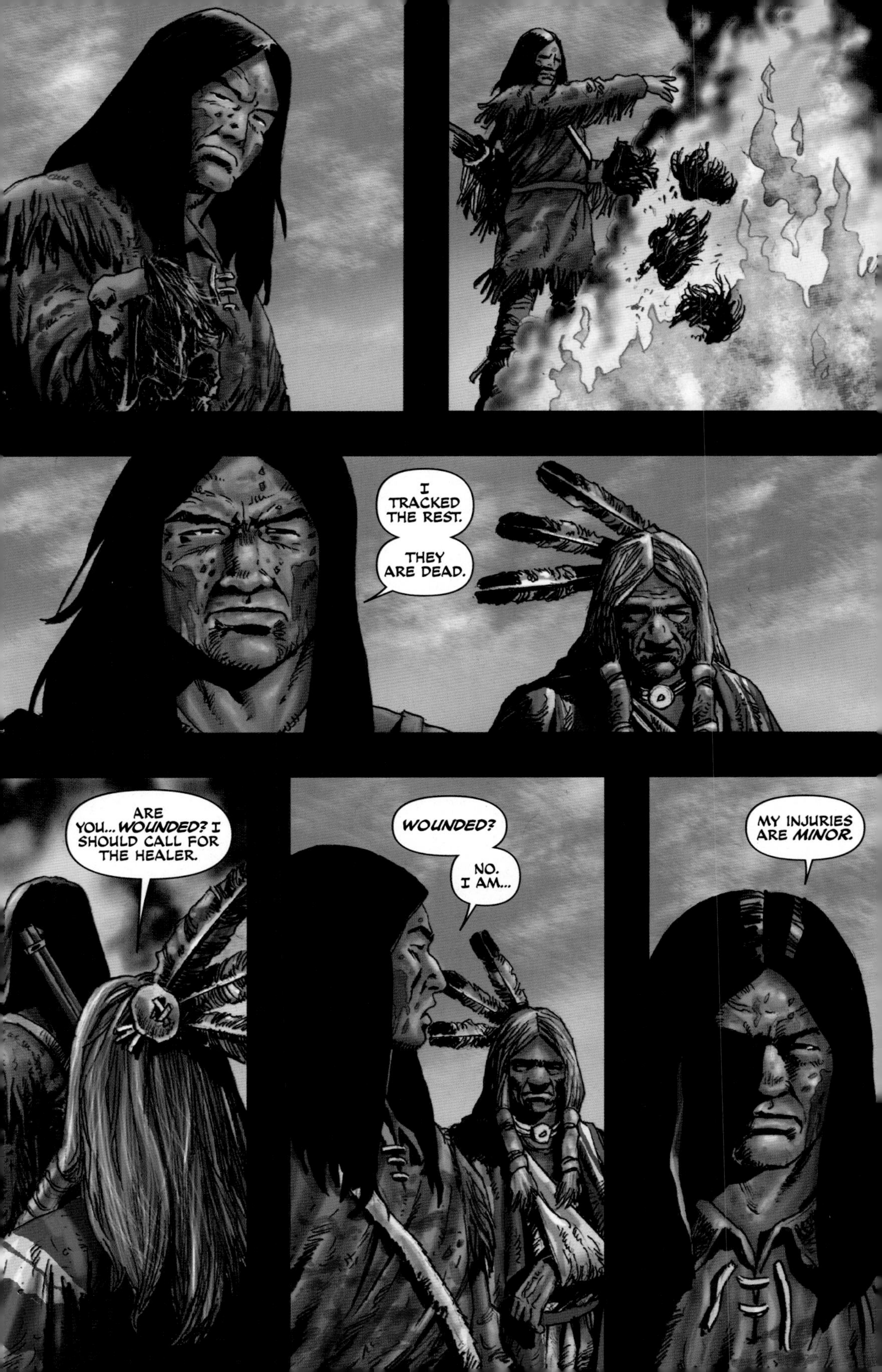
I TRACKED THE REST.
THEY ARE DEAD.
ARE YOU...*WOUNDED?* I SHOULD CALL FOR THE HEALER.
WOUNDED?
NO. I AM...
MY INJURIES ARE *MINOR.*

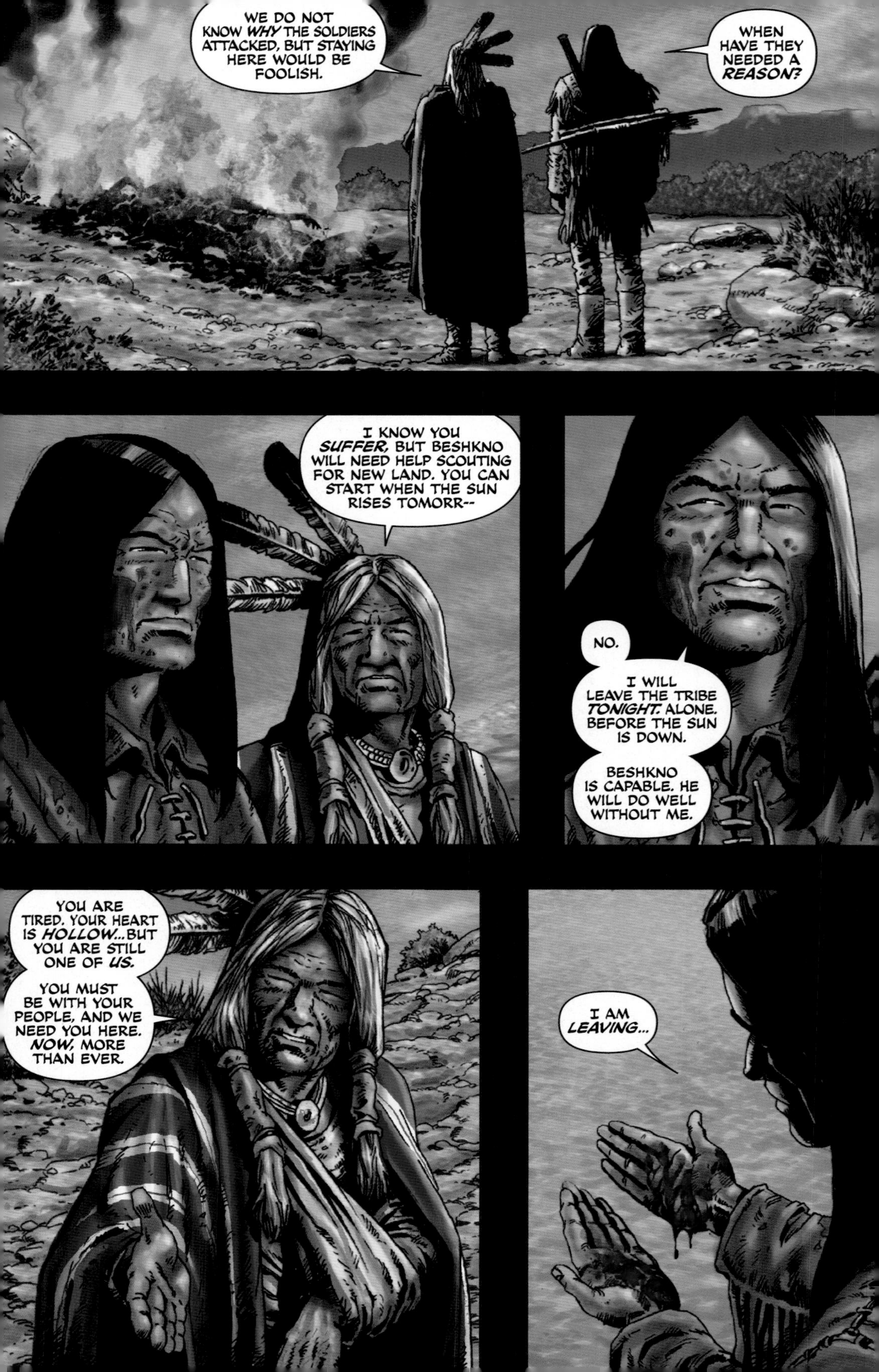
WE DO NOT KNOW WHY THE SOLDIERS ATTACKED, BUT STAYING HERE WOULD BE FOOLISH.
WHEN HAVE THEY NEEDED A REASON?
I KNOW YOU SUFFER, BUT BESHKNO WILL NEED HELP SCOUTING FOR NEW LAND. YOU CAN START WHEN THE SUN RISES TOMORR--
NO.
I WILL LEAVE THE TRIBE TONIGHT. ALONE. BEFORE THE SUN IS DOWN.
BESHKNO IS CAPABLE. HE WILL DO WELL WITHOUT ME.
YOU ARE TIRED. YOUR HEART IS HOLLOW...BUT YOU ARE STILL ONE OF US.
YOU MUST BE WITH YOUR PEOPLE, AND WE NEED YOU HERE. NOW, MORE THAN EVER.
I AM LEAVING...

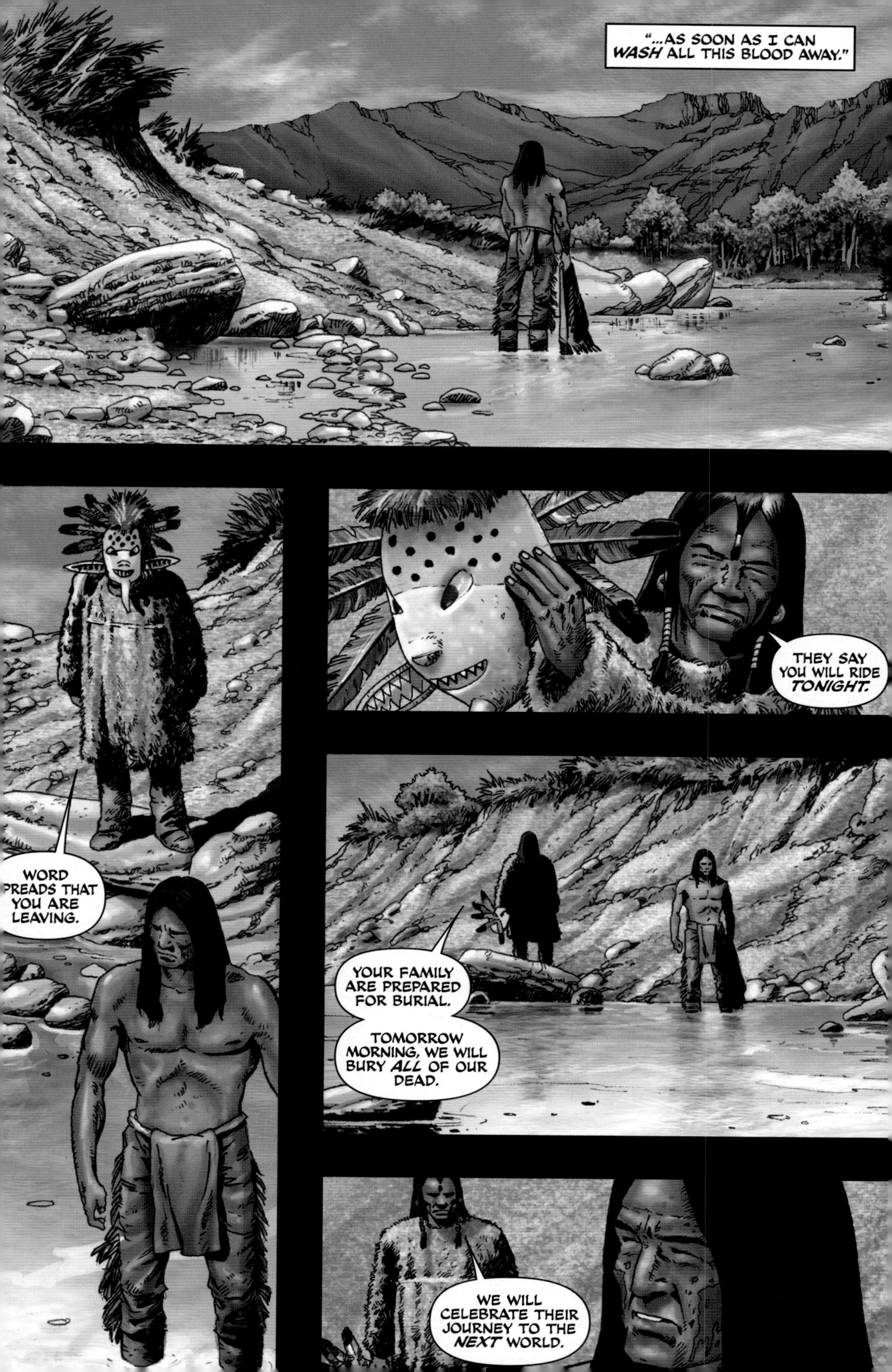
"...AS SOON AS I CAN *WASH* ALL THIS BLOOD AWAY."
THEY SAY YOU WILL RIDE *TONIGHT.*
WORD PREADS THAT YOU ARE LEAVING.
YOUR FAMILY ARE PREPARED FOR BURIAL.
TOMORROW MORNING, WE WILL BURY *ALL* OF OUR DEAD.
WE WILL CELEBRATE THEIR JOURNEY TO THE *NEXT* WORLD.

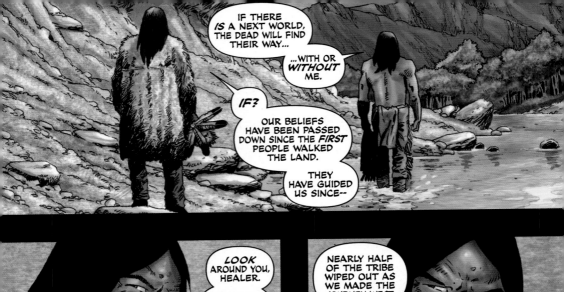

IF THERE *IS* A NEXT WORLD, THE DEAD WILL FIND THEIR WAY...

...WITH OR *WITHOUT* ME.

IF?

OUR BELIEFS HAVE BEEN PASSED DOWN SINCE THE *FIRST* PEOPLE WALKED THE LAND.

THEY HAVE GUIDED US SINCE--

LOOK AROUND YOU, HEALER.

OUR HOMELANDS *LOST* TO US FOREVER.

NEARLY HALF OF THE TRIBE WIPED OUT AS WE MADE THE JOURNEY WEST.

AND *STILL,* IT'S NOT ENOUGH.

STILL WE LIVE AND DI AT THE *WHI* OF THE WHITES.

THIS IS WHERE YOUR *BELIEFS...* YOUR *GODS...* HAVE GUIDED US.

THIS IS THE *FRUIT* YOUR FAITH HAS BORNE.

YOUR *PAIN* SPEAKS FOR YOU.

I UNDERSTAND.

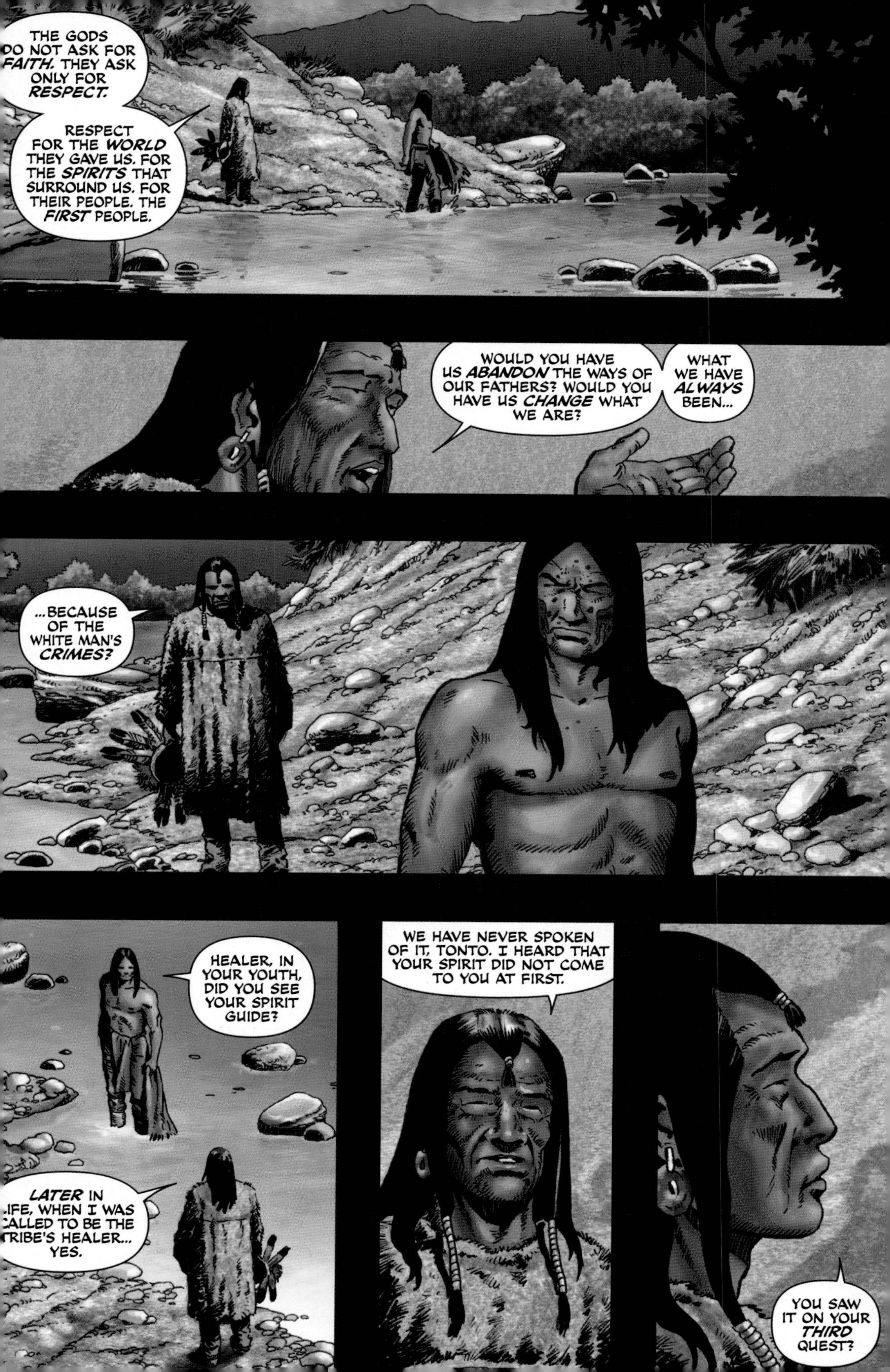
THE GODS DO NOT ASK FOR FAITH. THEY ASK ONLY FOR RESPECT.
RESPECT FOR THE WORLD THEY GAVE US. FOR THE SPIRITS THAT SURROUND US. FOR THEIR PEOPLE. THE FIRST PEOPLE.
WOULD YOU HAVE US ABANDON THE WAYS OF OUR FATHERS? WOULD YOU HAVE US CHANGE WHAT WE ARE?
WHAT WE HAVE ALWAYS BEEN...
...BECAUSE OF THE WHITE MAN'S CRIMES?
HEALER, IN YOUR YOUTH, DID YOU SEE YOUR SPIRIT GUIDE?
LATER IN LIFE, WHEN I WAS CALLED TO BE THE TRIBE'S HEALER... YES.
WE HAVE NEVER SPOKEN OF IT, TONTO. I HEARD THAT YOUR SPIRIT DID NOT COME TO YOU AT FIRST.
YOU SAW IT ON YOUR THIRD QUEST?

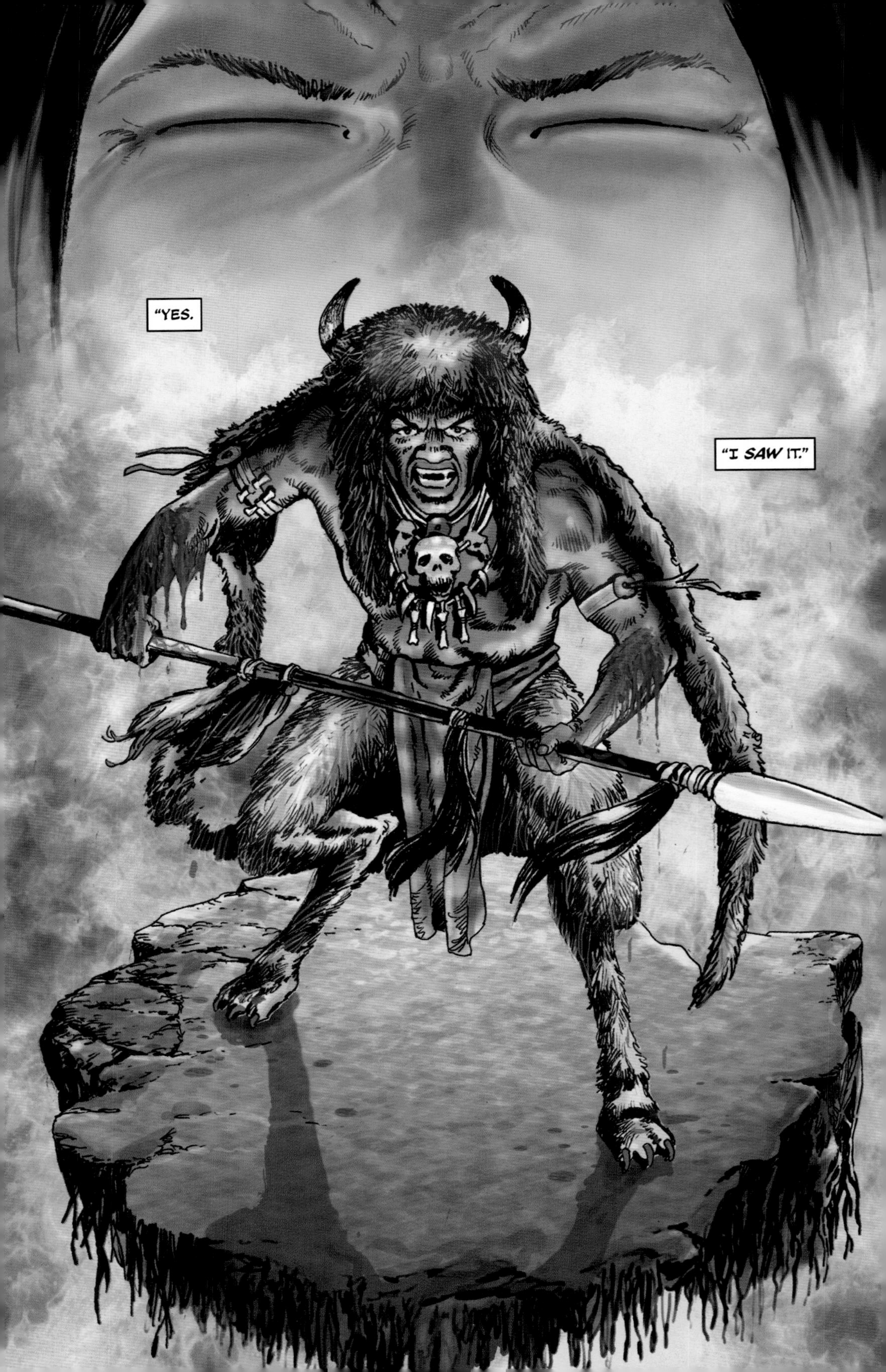
"YES.
"I SAW IT."

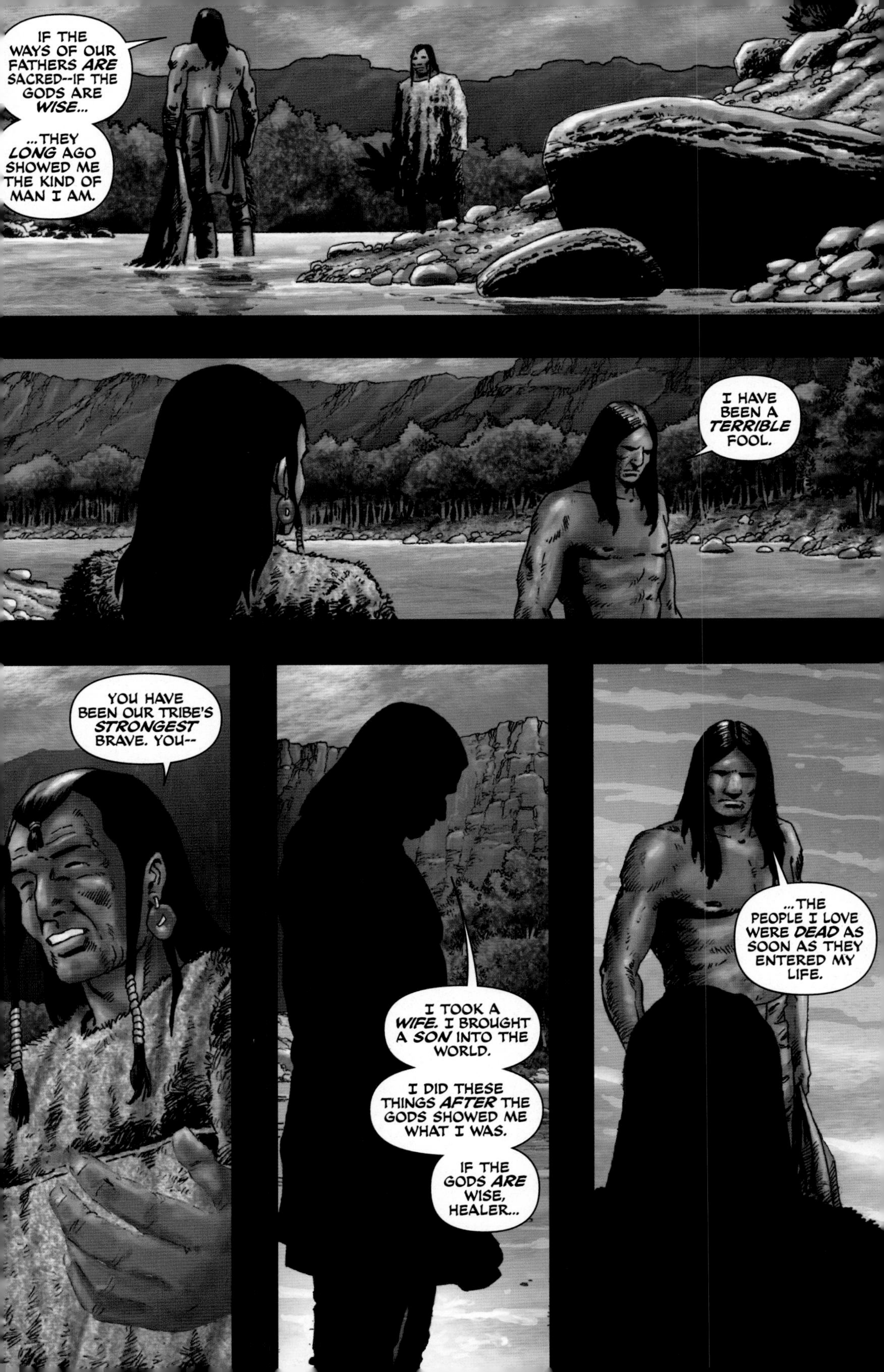
IF THE WAYS OF OUR FATHERS ARE SACRED--IF THE GODS ARE WISE...
...THEY LONG AGO SHOWED ME THE KIND OF MAN I AM.
I HAVE BEEN A TERRIBLE FOOL.
YOU HAVE BEEN OUR TRIBE'S STRONGEST BRAVE. YOU--
I TOOK A WIFE. I BROUGHT A SON INTO THE WORLD.
I DID THESE THINGS AFTER THE GODS SHOWED ME WHAT I WAS.
IF THE GODS ARE WISE, HEALER...
...THE PEOPLE I LOVE WERE DEAD AS SOON AS THEY ENTERED MY LIFE.

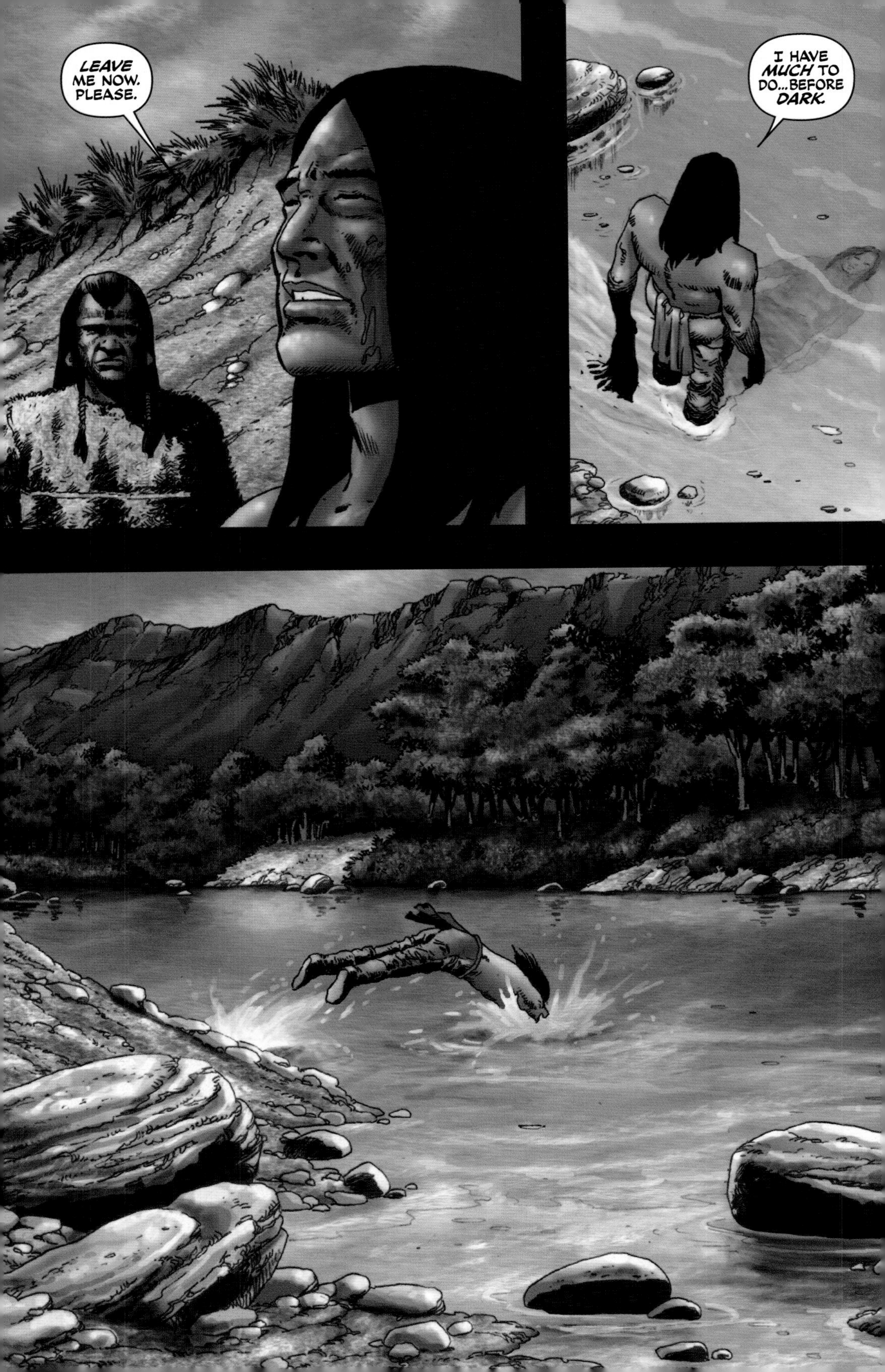

LEAVE ME NOW. PLEASE.
I HAVE MUCH TO DO...BEFORE DARK.

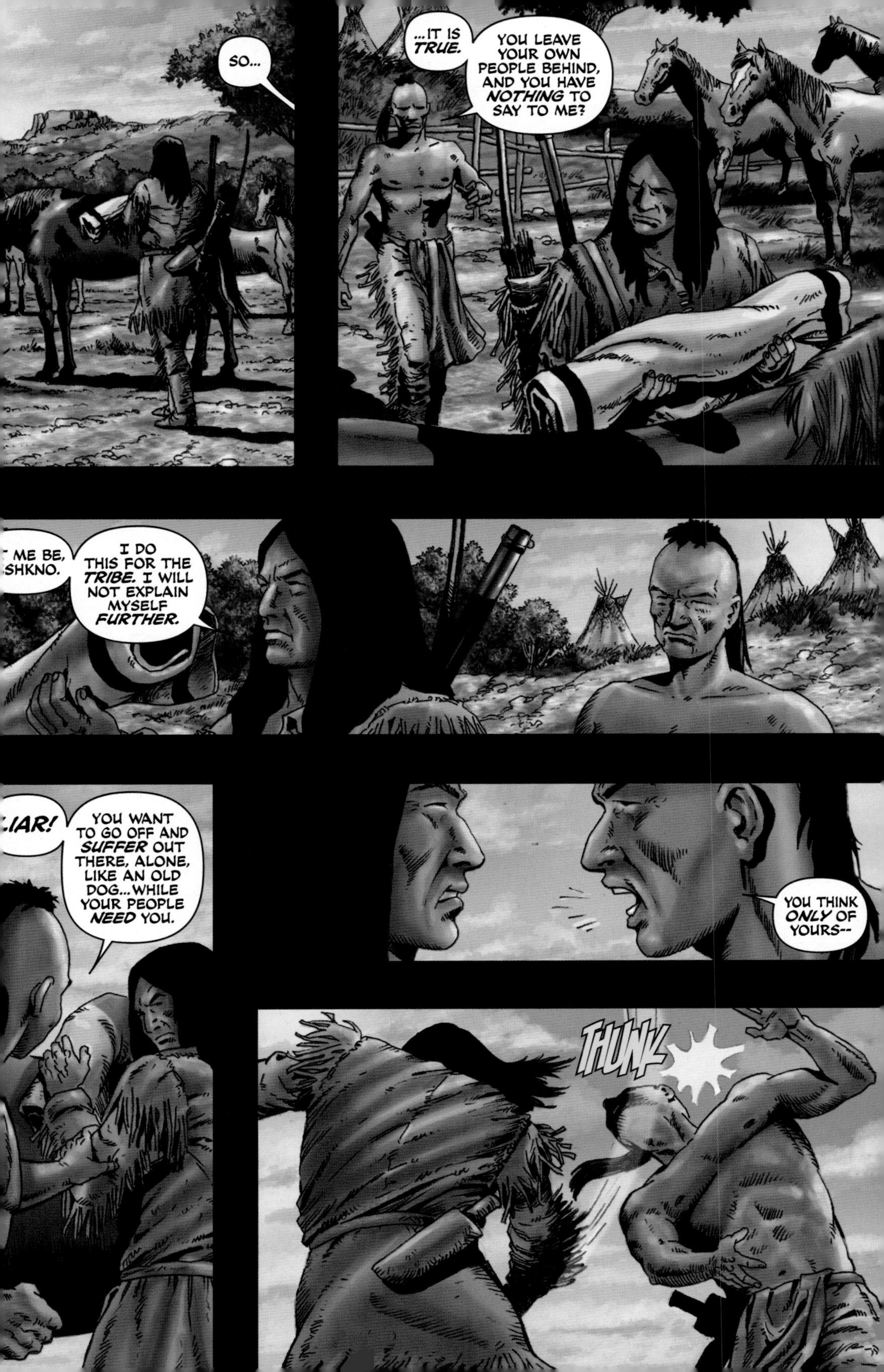

SO...
...IT IS TRUE.
YOU LEAVE YOUR OWN PEOPLE BEHIND, AND YOU HAVE NOTHING TO SAY TO ME?
ME BE, SHKNO.
I DO THIS FOR THE TRIBE. I WILL NOT EXPLAIN MYSELF FURTHER.
IAR!
YOU WANT TO GO OFF AND SUFFER OUT THERE, ALONE, LIKE AN OLD DOG...WHILE YOUR PEOPLE NEED YOU.
YOU THINK ONLY OF YOURS--
THUNK

WHUD

KRUKK

SPLGT

SPK

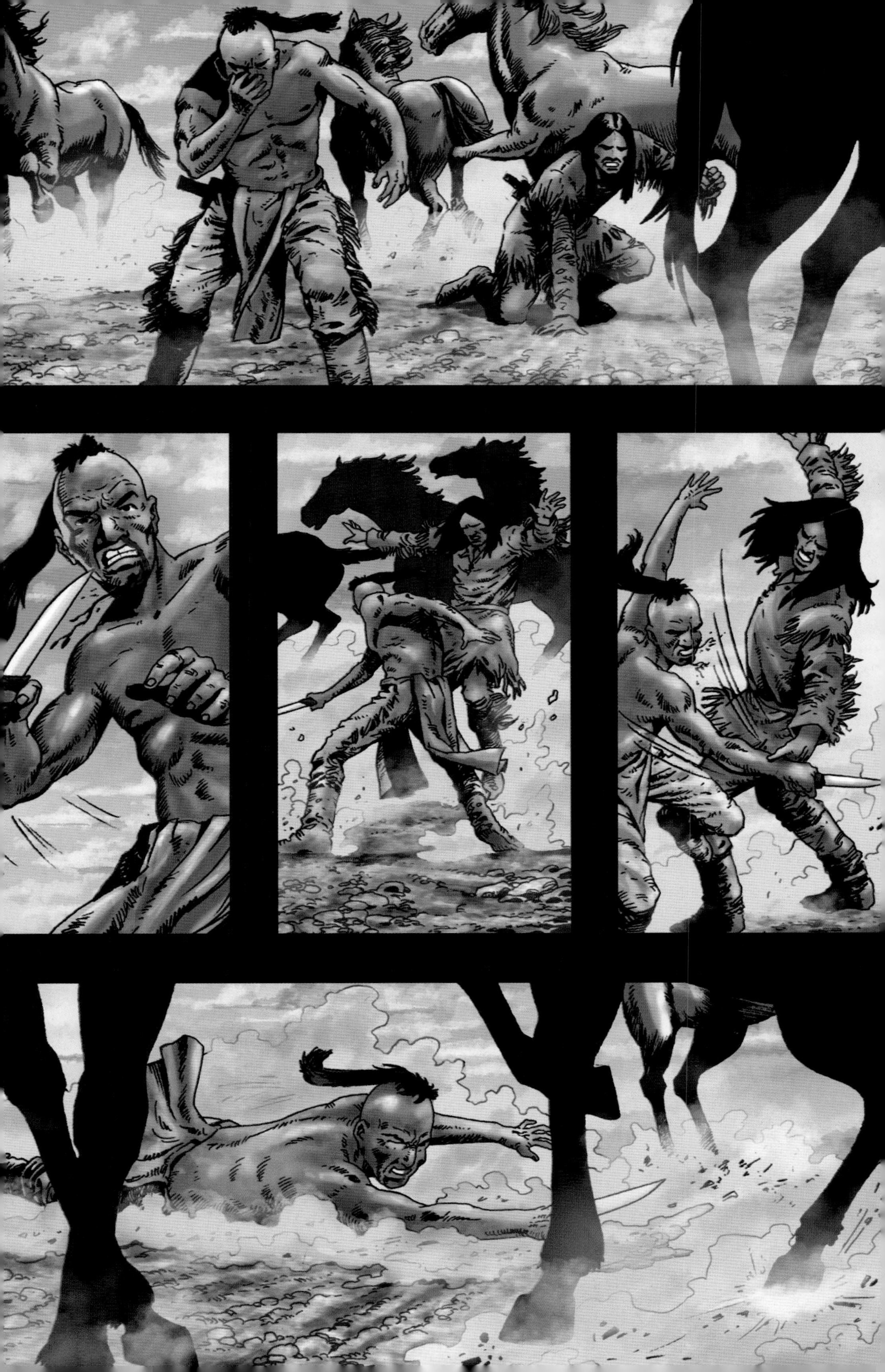

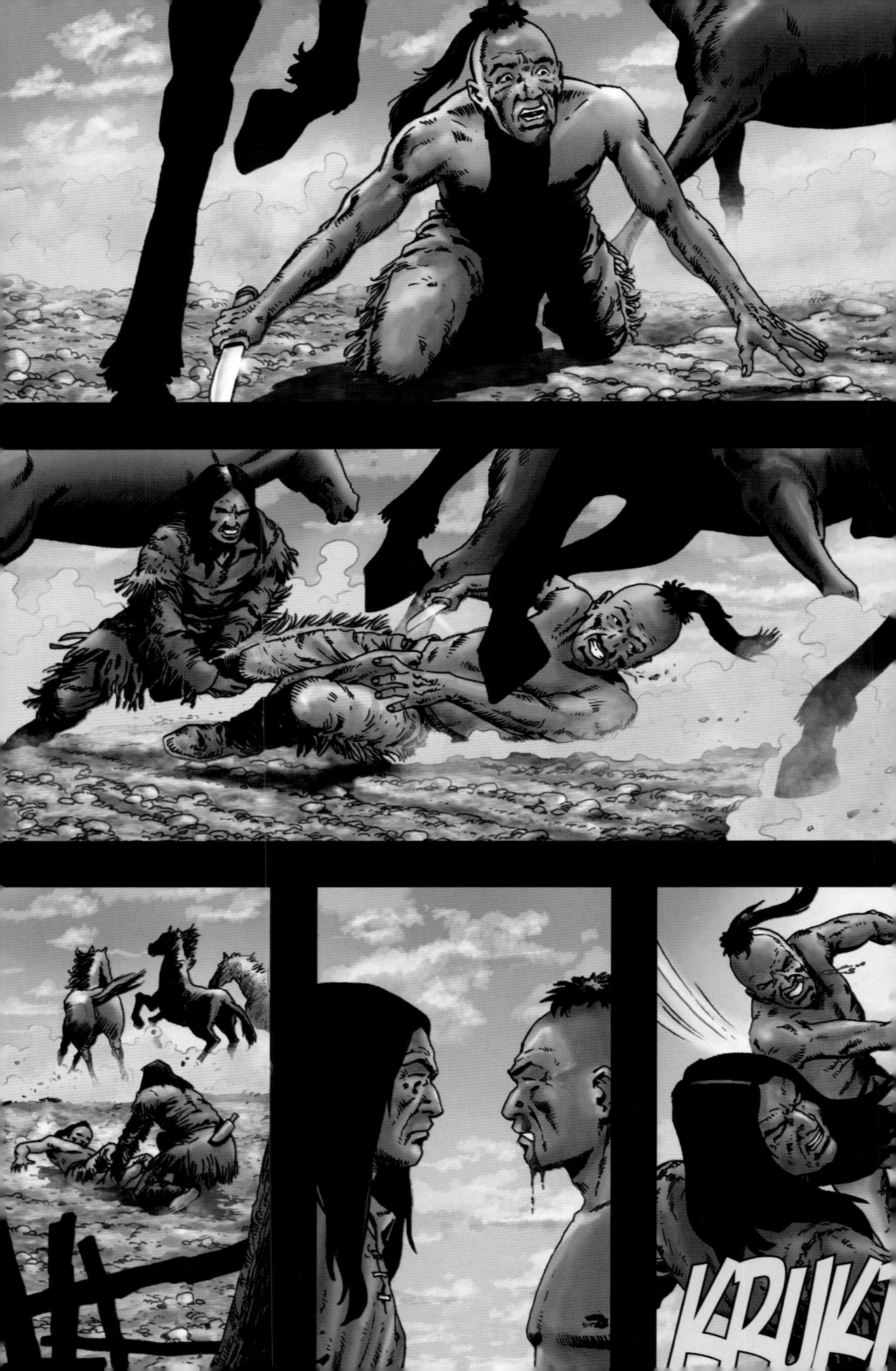
KRUK!

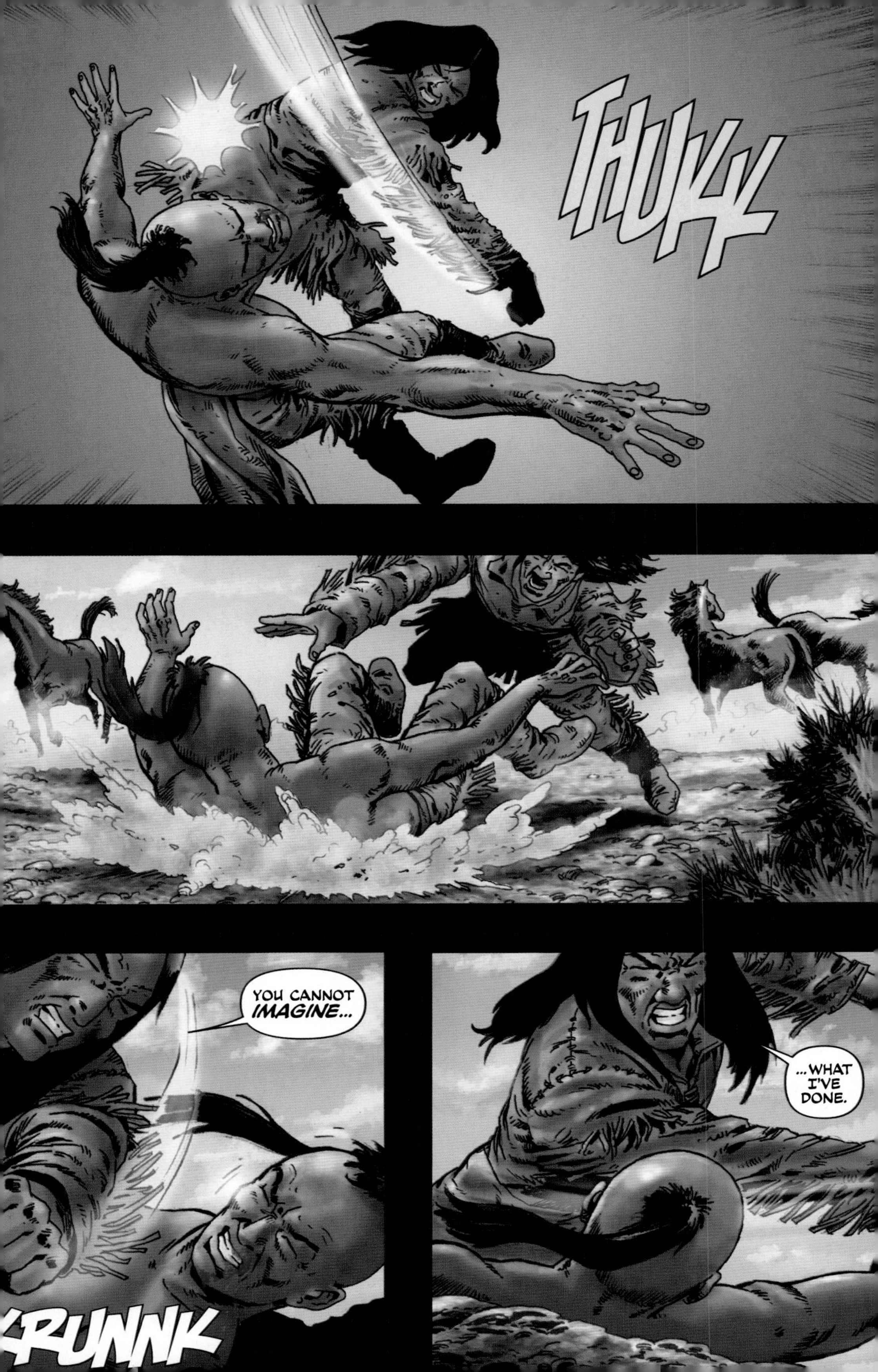
THUKK
YOU CANNOT IMAGINE...
KRUNNK
...WHAT I'VE DONE.

‡HUHHK‡ WHAT I'VE *DONE*...

YOU SPILLED THE BLOOD OF *DEMONS*.

OUR DEAD *CRIED* FOR JUSTICE. *YOUR* DEAD CRIED FOR IT.

YOU GAVE IT.

I DIDN'T HEAR *THEM*. I HEARD NOTHING BUT MY *OWN* RAGE.

I DIDN'[T] DO IT FO[R] *THEM*. I [DID] IT FOR M[E] AND I LE[FT] IT UNDON[E.]

BESHKNO... I LEFT ONE *ALIVE*.

THE TRIBE WILL *NEVER* BE SAFE WHILE HE IS ALIVE TO TELL WHAT I'VE DONE.

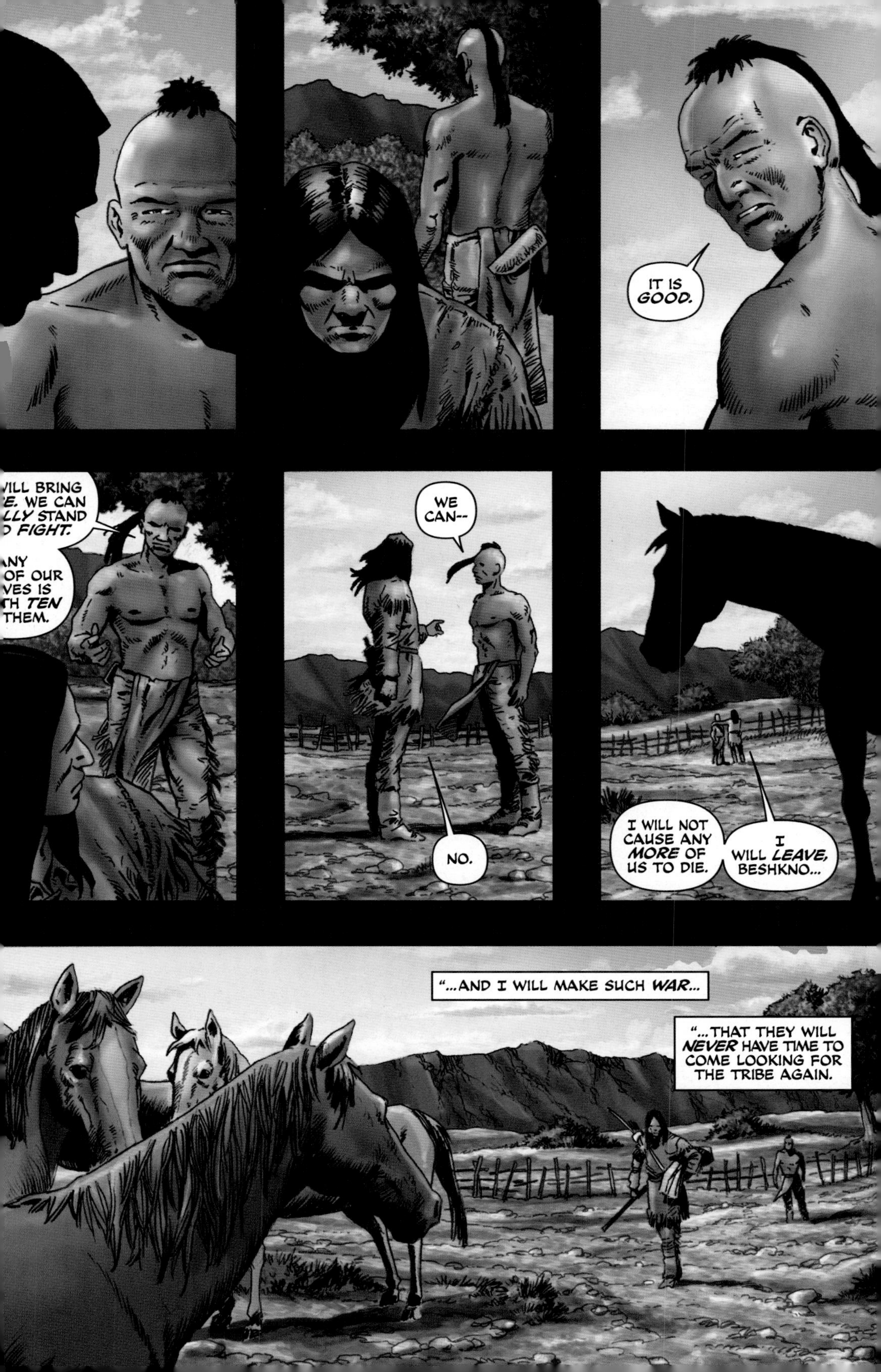

IT IS GOOD.
...ILL BRING ...E. WE CAN ...LLY STAND ...D FIGHT.
...ANY ...OF OUR ...VES IS ...TH TEN ...THEM.
WE CAN--
NO.
I WILL NOT CAUSE ANY MORE OF US TO DIE.
I WILL LEAVE, BESHKNO...
"...AND I WILL MAKE SUCH WAR...
"...THAT THEY WILL NEVER HAVE TIME TO COME LOOKING FOR THE TRIBE AGAIN.

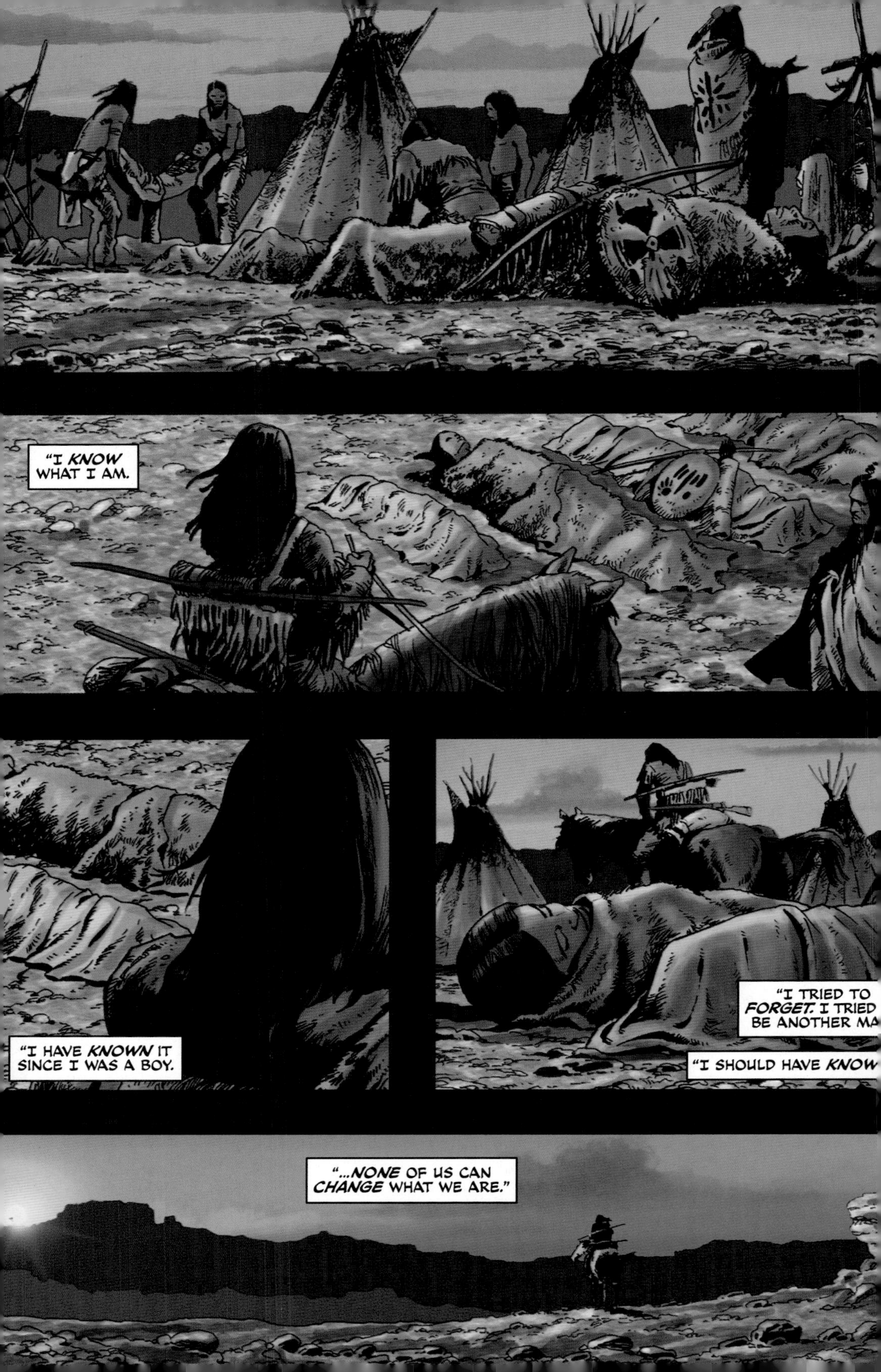
"I KNOW WHAT I AM.
"I HAVE KNOWN IT SINCE I WAS A BOY.
"I TRIED TO FORGET. I TRIED BE ANOTHER MA
"I SHOULD HAVE KNOW
"...NONE OF US CAN CHANGE WHAT WE ARE."

THREE YEARS LATER. SOUTHERN COLORADO TERRITORY. UTE COUNTRY.

SO... YOU ARE HIM.*

*THIS SCENE SPOKEN IN ENGLISH--JR.

THE *WHITE* MAN WITH THE *BLACK* FACE.

I SUPPOSE I AM. YOU *LEAD* THIS TRIBE?

I HAVE BEEN *CHIEF* OF THE UTE TRIBE SINCE BEFORE YOU STOOD ON TWO LEGS.

UTE HAVE *MUCH* TROUBLE WITH WHITES.

MUCH *FIGHTING.* MUCH *KILLING.*

I *KNOW.*

YOU *KNOW,* BUT YOU *CAME.*

YES. I CAME...

...FOR *HIM.*

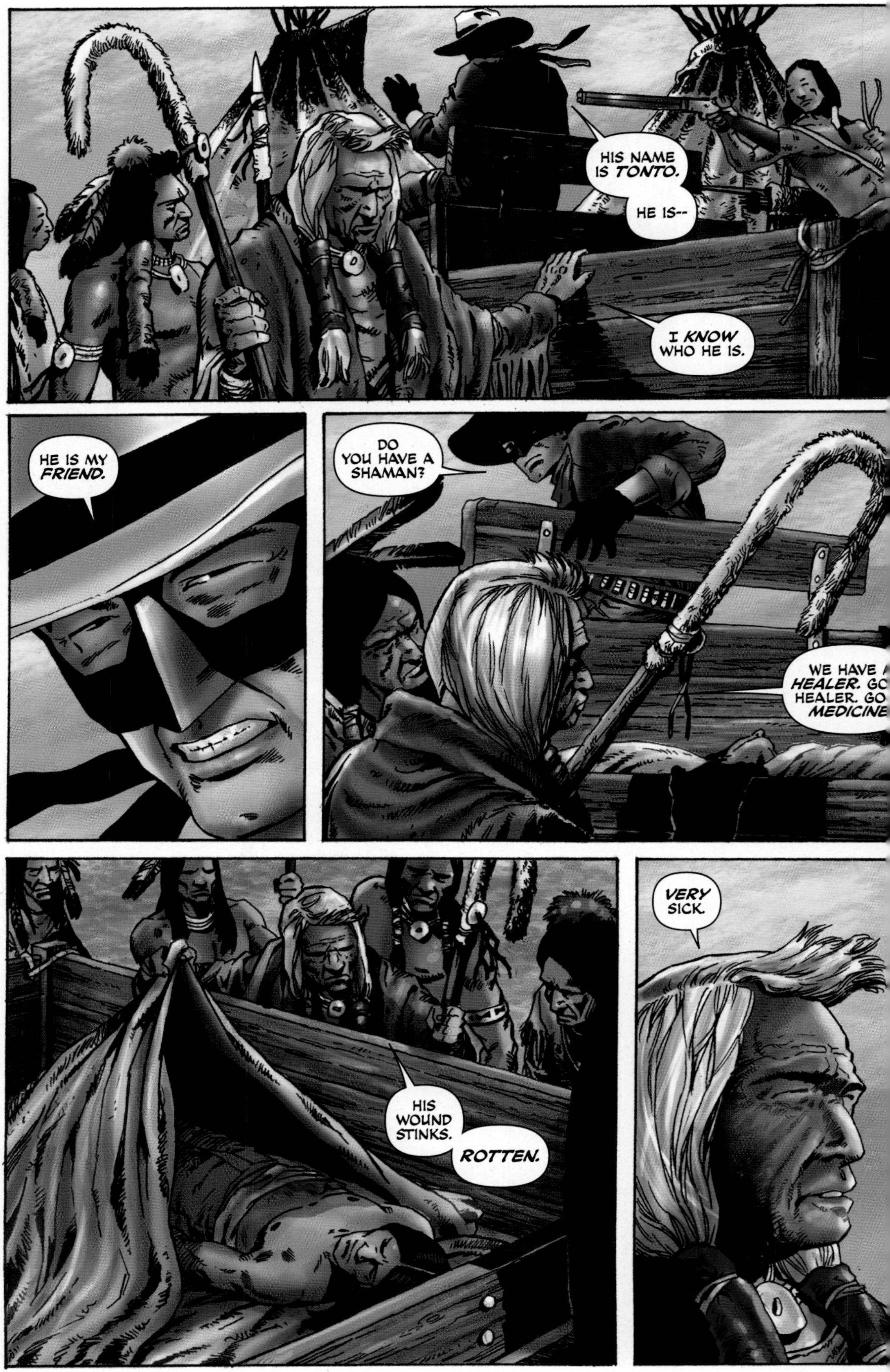
HIS NAME IS TONTO.
HE IS--
I KNOW WHO HE IS.
HE IS MY FRIEND.
DO YOU HAVE A SHAMAN?
WE HAVE A HEALER. GO HEALER. GO MEDICINE
HIS WOUND STINKS.
ROTTEN.
VERY SICK.

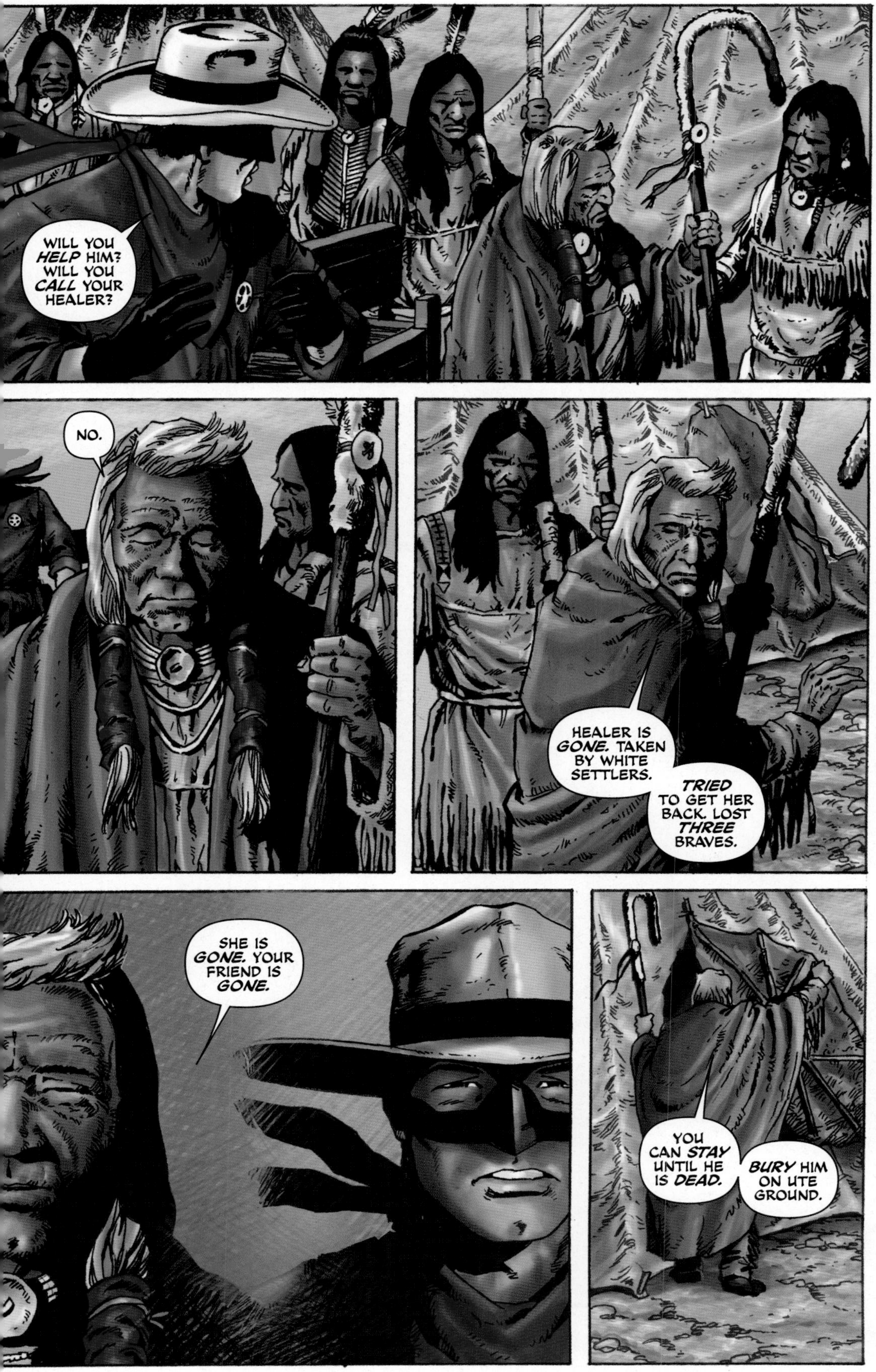
WILL YOU HELP HIM? WILL YOU CALL YOUR HEALER?
NO.
HEALER IS GONE. TAKEN BY WHITE SETTLERS.
TRIED TO GET HER BACK. LOST THREE BRAVES.
SHE IS GONE. YOUR FRIEND IS GONE.
YOU CAN STAY UNTIL HE IS DEAD.
BURY HIM ON UTE GROUND.

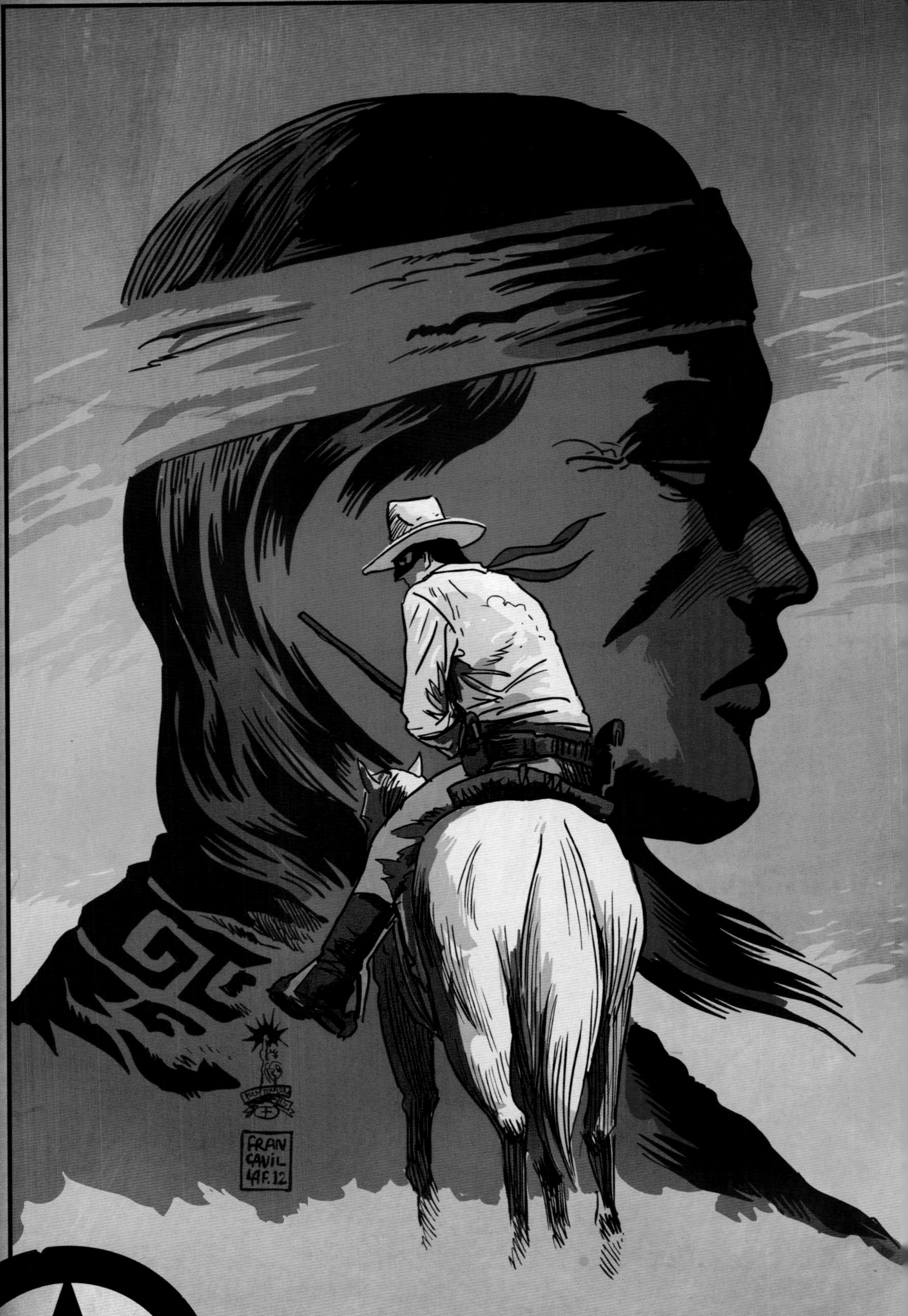
FRAN
CAVIL
14F.12

11

COVER BY **FRANCESCO FRANCAVILLA**

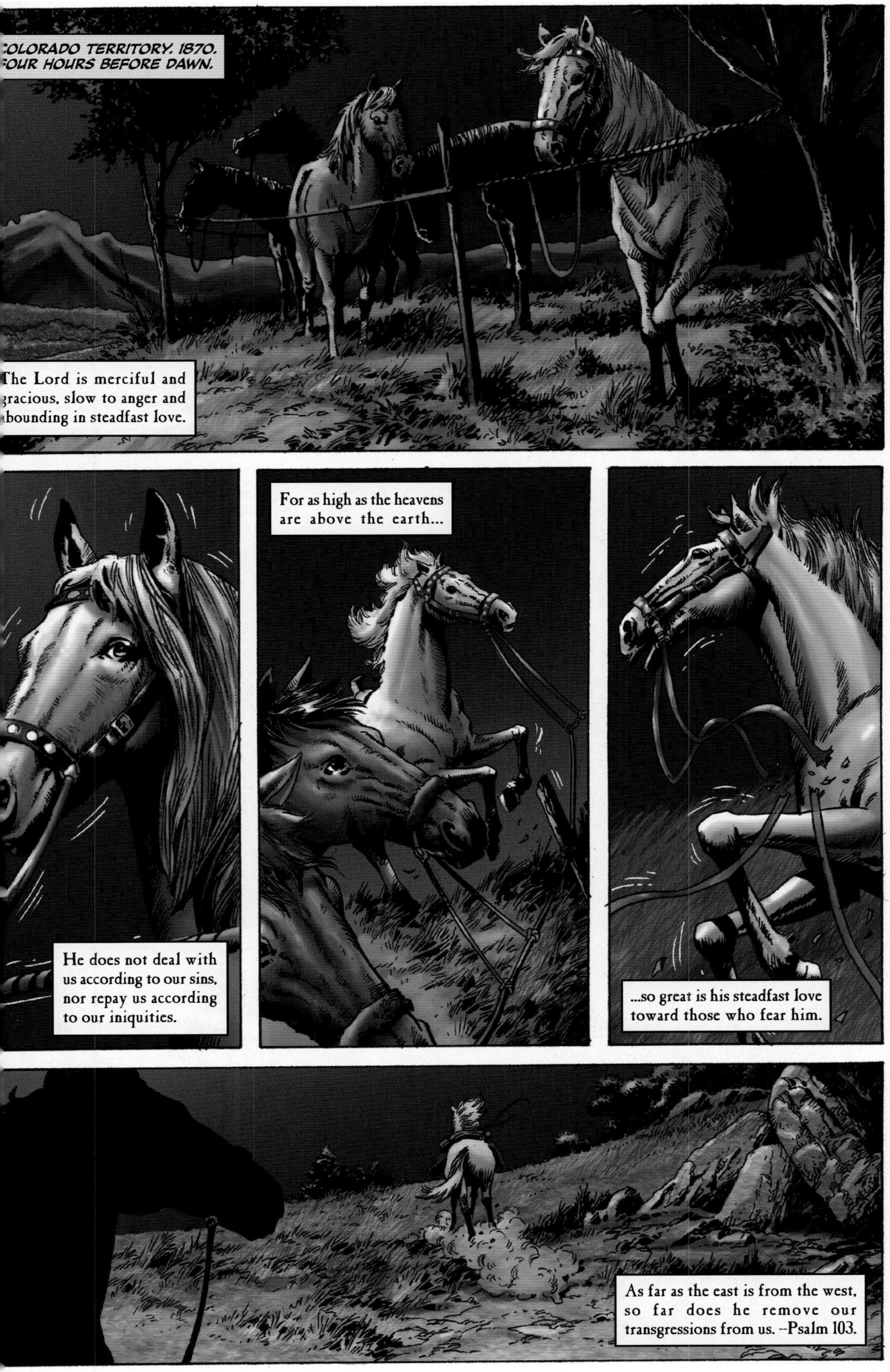
COLORADO TERRITORY. 1870. FOUR HOURS BEFORE DAWN.
The Lord is merciful and gracious, slow to anger and abounding in steadfast love.
He does not deal with us according to our sins, nor repay us according to our iniquities.
For as high as the heavens are above the earth...
...so great is his steadfast love toward those who fear him.
As far as the east is from the west, so far does he remove our transgressions from us. --Psalm 103.

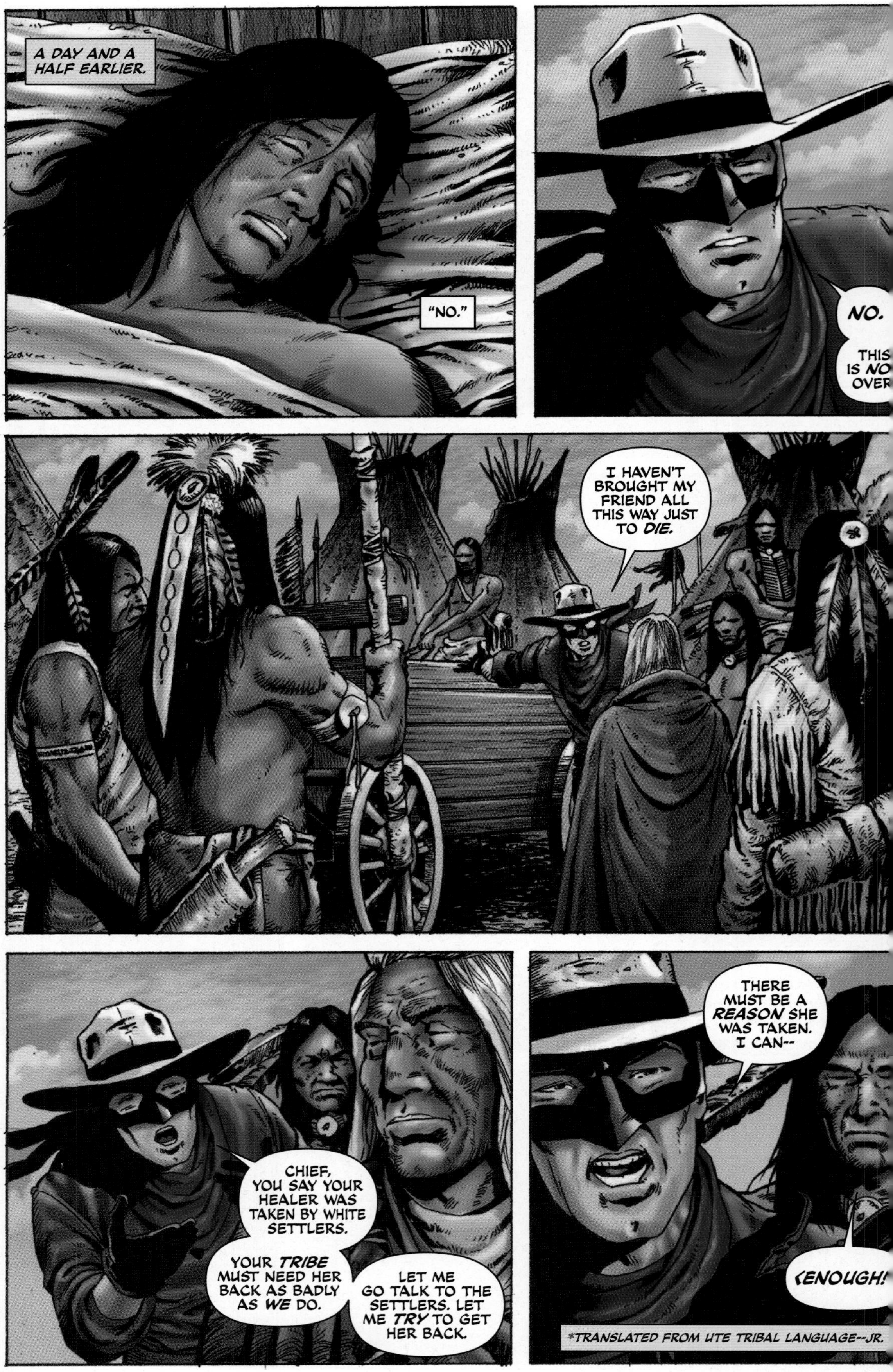

A DAY AND A HALF EARLIER.
"NO."
NO.
THIS IS NO OVER
I HAVEN'T BROUGHT MY FRIEND ALL THIS WAY JUST TO *DIE.*
CHIEF, YOU SAY YOUR HEALER WAS TAKEN BY WHITE SETTLERS.
YOUR *TRIBE* MUST NEED HER BACK AS BADLY AS *WE* DO.
LET ME GO TALK TO THE SETTLERS. LET ME *TRY* TO GET HER BACK.
THERE MUST BE A *REASON* SHE WAS TAKEN. I CAN--
‹ENOUGH!
*TRANSLATED FROM UTE TRIBAL LANGUAGE--JR.

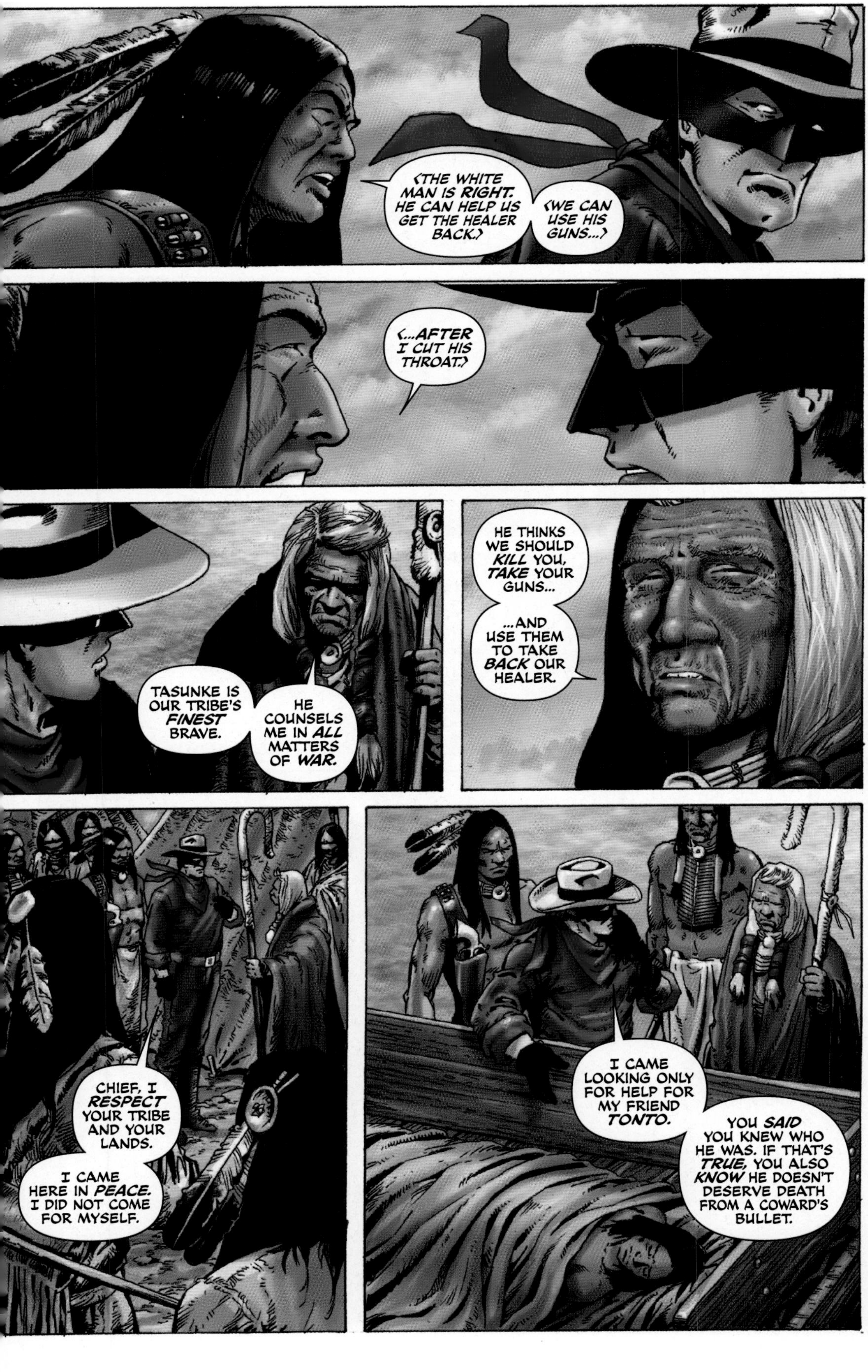
‹THE WHITE MAN IS RIGHT. HE CAN HELP US GET THE HEALER BACK.›
‹WE CAN USE HIS GUNS...›
‹...AFTER I CUT HIS THROAT.›
TASUNKE IS OUR TRIBE'S FINEST BRAVE.
HE COUNSELS ME IN ALL MATTERS OF WAR.
HE THINKS WE SHOULD KILL YOU, TAKE YOUR GUNS...
...AND USE THEM TO TAKE BACK OUR HEALER.
CHIEF, I RESPECT YOUR TRIBE AND YOUR LANDS.
I CAME HERE IN PEACE. I DID NOT COME FOR MYSELF.
I CAME LOOKING ONLY FOR HELP FOR MY FRIEND TONTO.
YOU SAID YOU KNEW WHO HE WAS. IF THAT'S TRUE, YOU ALSO KNOW HE DOESN'T DESERVE DEATH FROM A COWARD'S BULLET.

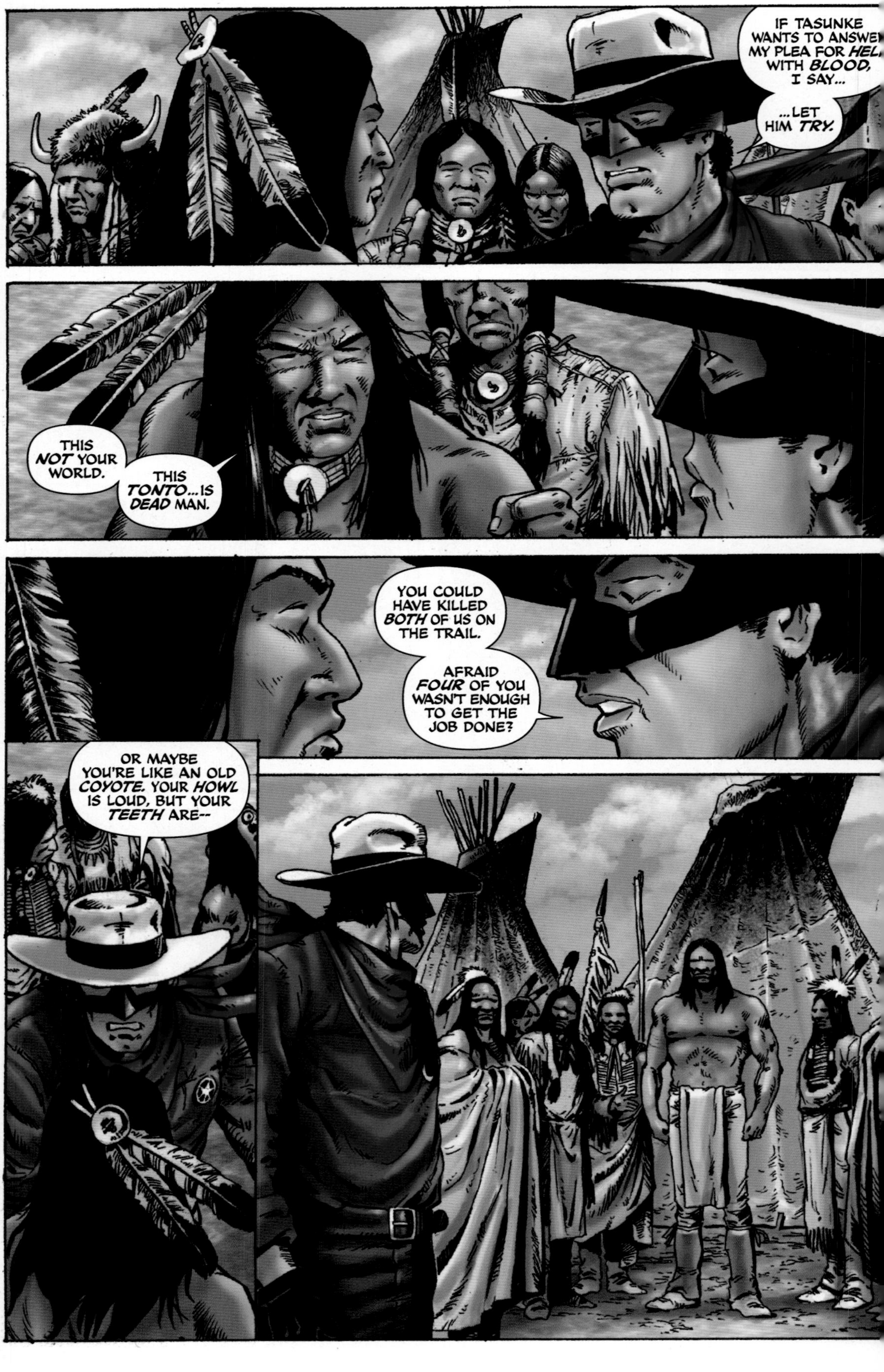

IF TASUNKE WANTS TO ANSWE MY PLEA FOR HEL WITH BLOOD, I SAY...
...LET HIM TRY.
THIS NOT YOUR WORLD.
THIS TONTO...IS DEAD MAN.
YOU COULD HAVE KILLED BOTH OF US ON THE TRAIL.
AFRAID FOUR OF YOU WASN'T ENOUGH TO GET THE JOB DONE?
OR MAYBE YOU'RE LIKE AN OLD COYOTE. YOUR HOWL IS LOUD, BUT YOUR TEETH ARE--

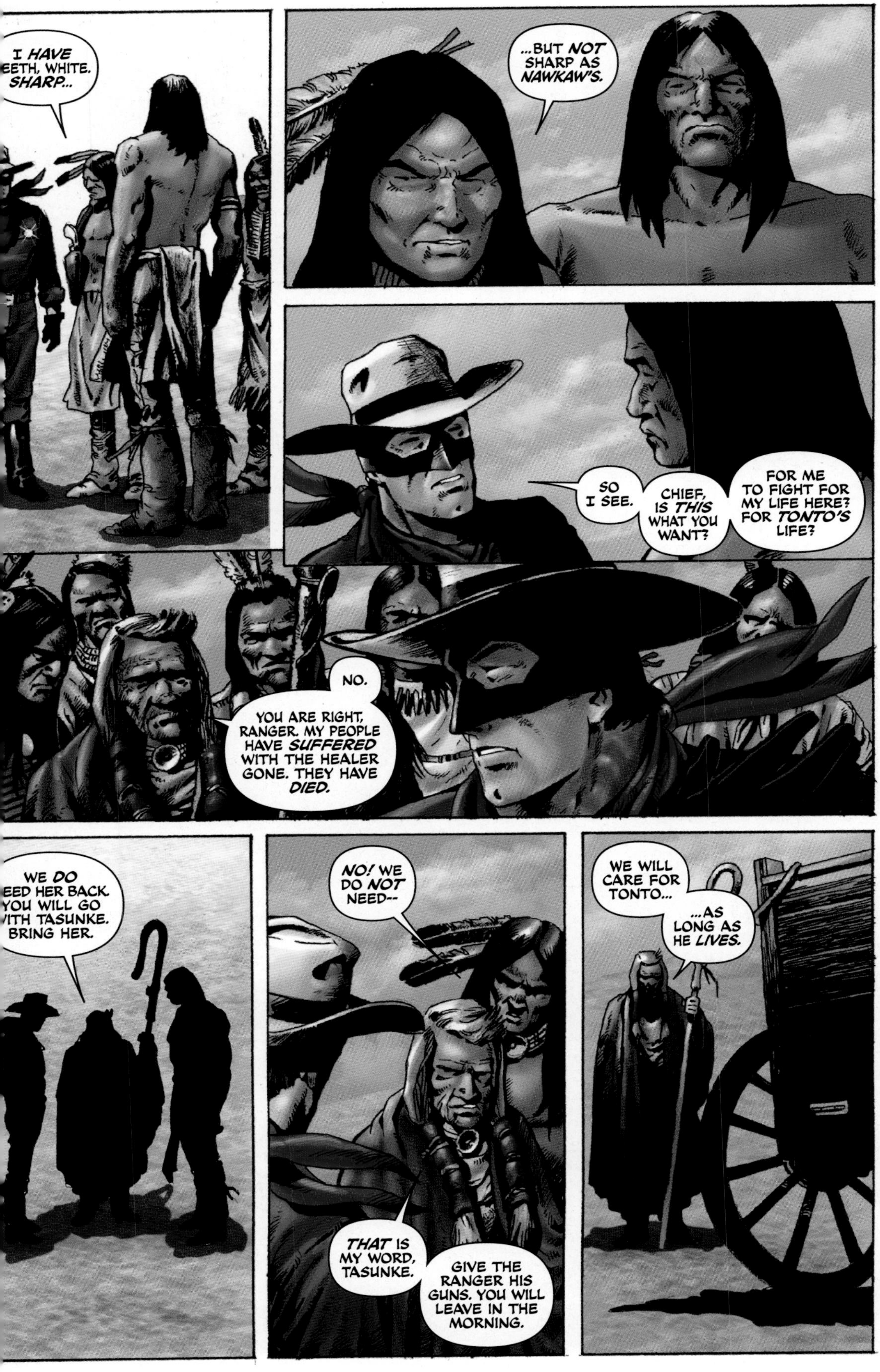
I HAVE
EETH, WHITE. SHARP...
...BUT NOT SHARP AS NAWKAW'S.
SO I SEE.
CHIEF, IS THIS WHAT YOU WANT?
FOR ME TO FIGHT FOR MY LIFE HERE? FOR TONTO'S LIFE?
NO.
YOU ARE RIGHT, RANGER. MY PEOPLE HAVE SUFFERED WITH THE HEALER GONE. THEY HAVE DIED.
WE DO
EED HER BACK. YOU WILL GO
VITH TASUNKE. BRING HER.
NO! WE DO NOT NEED--
THAT IS MY WORD, TASUNKE.
GIVE THE RANGER HIS GUNS. YOU WILL LEAVE IN THE MORNING.
WE WILL CARE FOR TONTO...
...AS LONG AS HE LIVES.

RANGER...

...THIS *RIFLE*. IT IS TONTO'S?

IT IS.

TASUNKE WILL CARRY IT WHEN YOU RIDE.

WE'RE GOING TO *TALK.* NOT *SHOOT.*

THESE SETTLERS HAVE KILLED OUR PEOPLE BEFORE.

NOT WITH *WORDS.* WITH *BULLETS.*

WE ONCE *HAD* GUNS. THEY WERE TAKEN, *ALONG* WITH OUR HEALER...AND THE *LIVES* OF OUR BRAVES.

IF *YOU* WERE CHIEF...

...WOULD *YO* HAVE YOUR BRAV RIDE UNARMED W A MASKED MAN A HIS GUNS?

TASUNKE CAN *BORROW* THE RIFLE.

I DON'T EXPECT HIM TO *USE* IT.

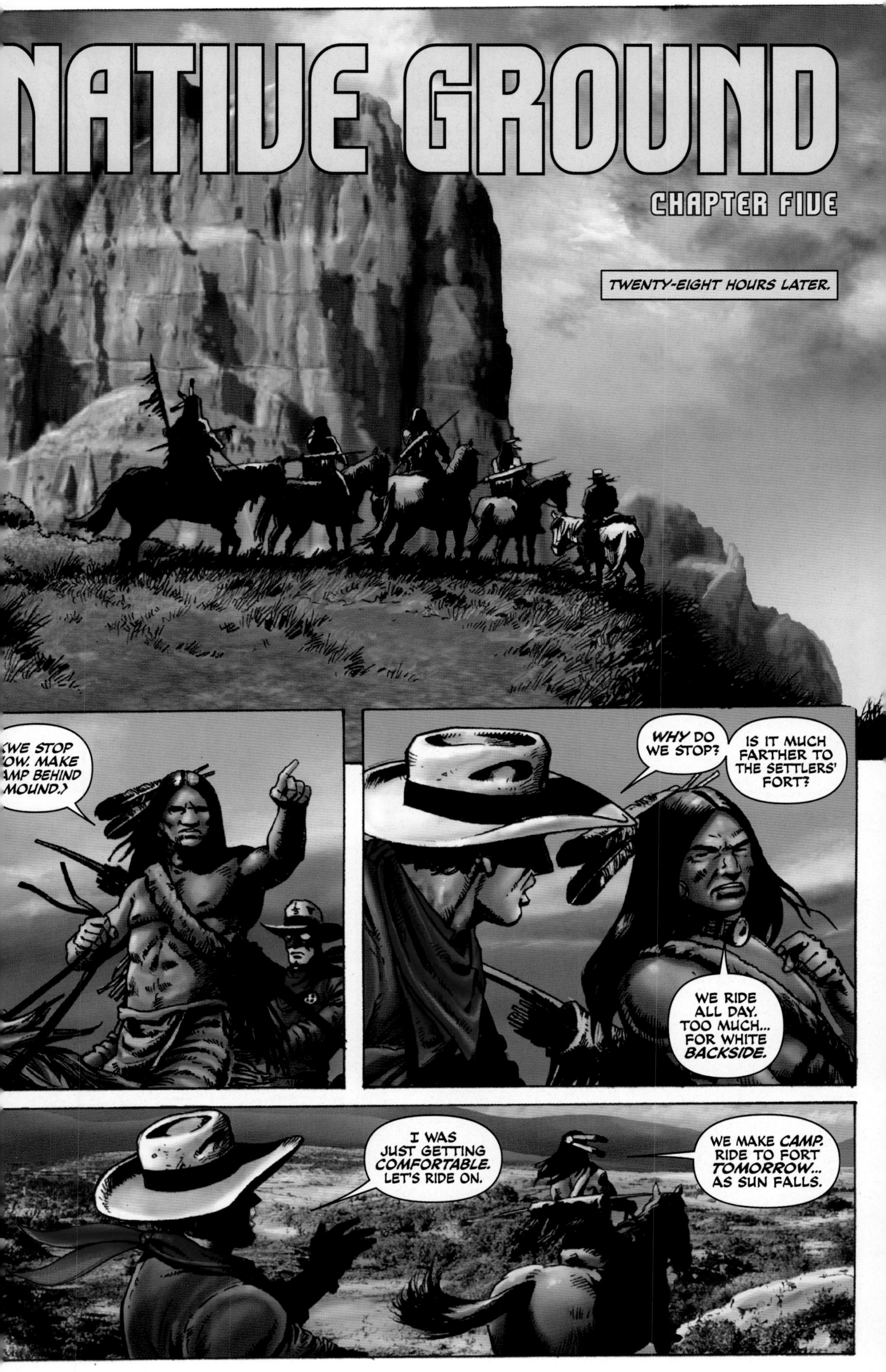
NATIVE GROUND
CHAPTER FIVE
TWENTY-EIGHT HOURS LATER.
<WE STOP
OW. MAKE
AMP BEHIND
MOUND.>
WHY DO WE STOP?
IS IT MUCH FARTHER TO THE SETTLERS' FORT?
WE RIDE ALL DAY. TOO MUCH... FOR WHITE BACKSIDE.
I WAS JUST GETTING COMFORTABLE. LET'S RIDE ON.
WE MAKE CAMP. RIDE TO FORT TOMORROW... AS SUN FALLS.

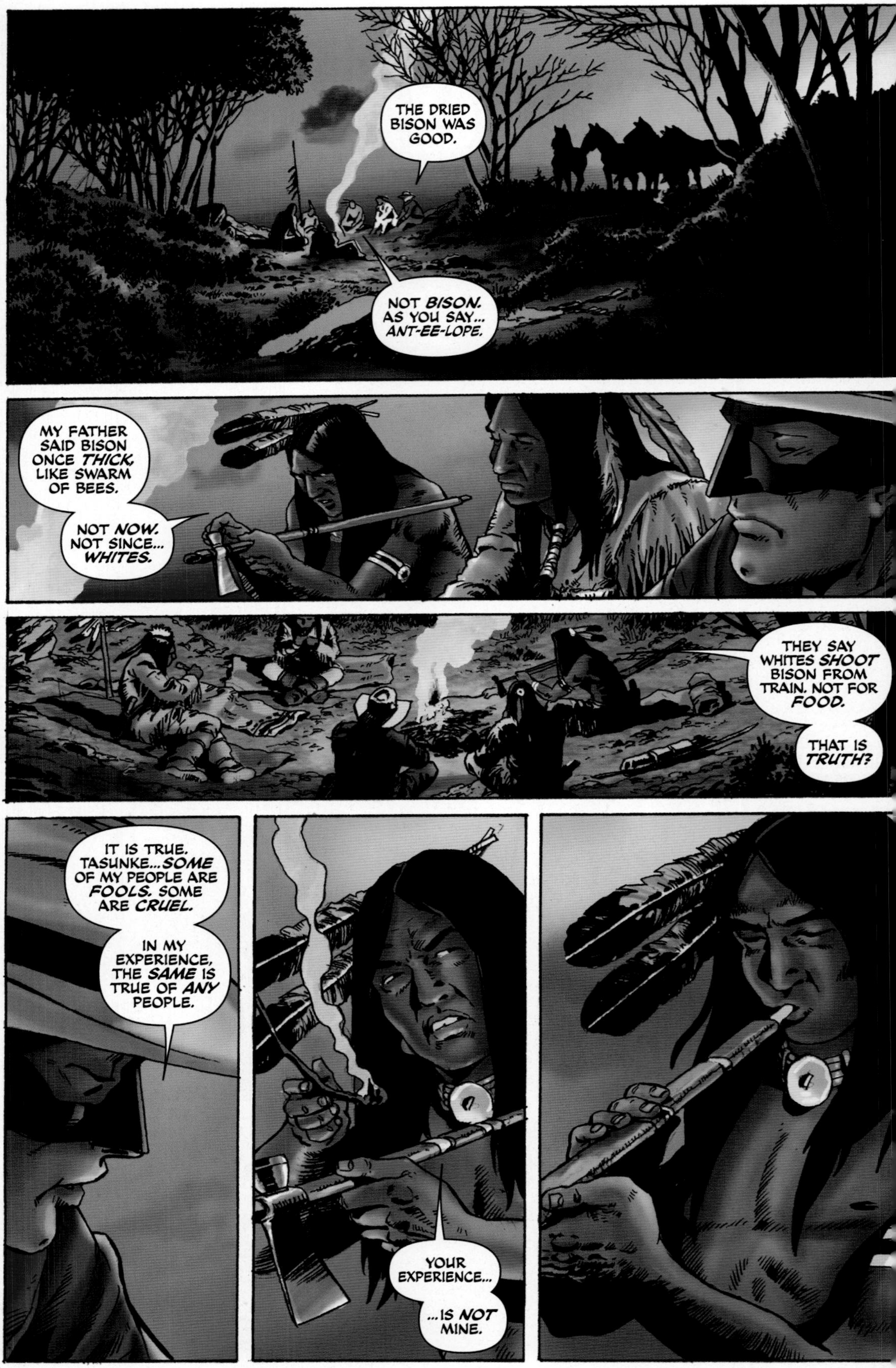
THE DRIED BISON WAS GOOD.
NOT *BISON.* AS YOU SAY... *ANT-EE-LOPE.*
MY FATHER SAID BISON ONCE *THICK,* LIKE SWARM OF BEES.
NOT *NOW.* NOT SINCE... *WHITES.*
THEY SAY WHITES *SHOOT* BISON FROM TRAIN. NOT FOR *FOOD.*
THAT IS *TRUTH?*
IT IS TRUE. TASUNKE... *SOME* OF MY PEOPLE ARE *FOOLS.* SOME ARE *CRUEL.*
IN MY EXPERIENCE, THE *SAME* IS TRUE OF *ANY* PEOPLE.
YOUR EXPERIENCE...
...IS *NOT* MINE.

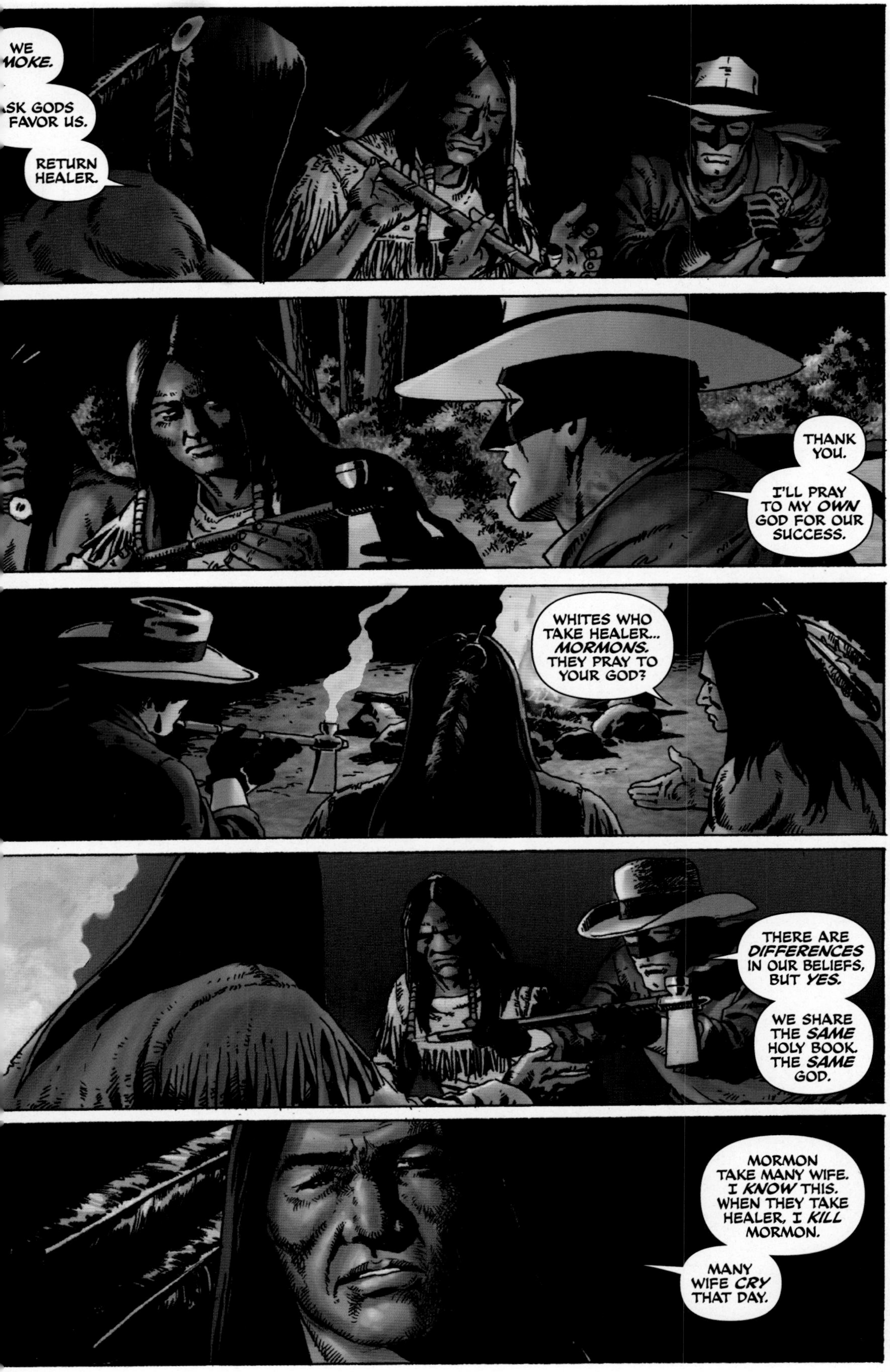
WE
MOKE.
SK GODS FAVOR US.
RETURN HEALER.
THANK YOU.
I'LL PRAY TO MY *OWN* GOD FOR OUR SUCCESS.
WHITES WHO TAKE HEALER... *MORMONS.* THEY PRAY TO YOUR GOD?
THERE ARE *DIFFERENCES* IN OUR BELIEFS, BUT *YES.*
WE SHARE THE *SAME* HOLY BOOK. THE *SAME* GOD.
MORMON TAKE MANY WIFE. I *KNOW* THIS. WHEN THEY TAKE HEALER, I *KILL* MORMON.
MANY WIFE *CRY* THAT DAY.

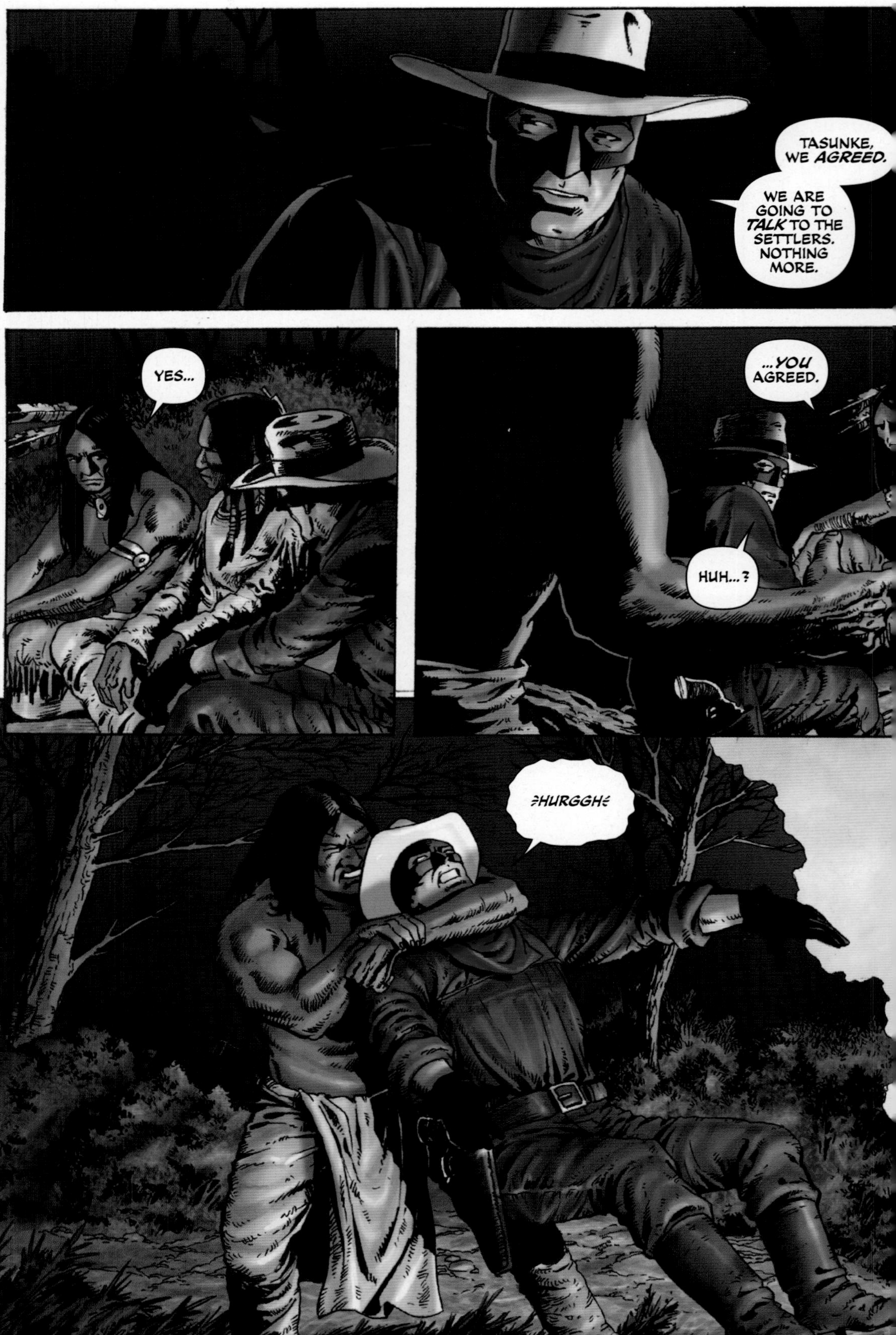
TASUNKE, WE *AGREED.*
WE ARE GOING TO *TALK* TO THE SETTLERS. NOTHING MORE.
YES...
...*YOU* AGREED.
HUH...?
HURGGH

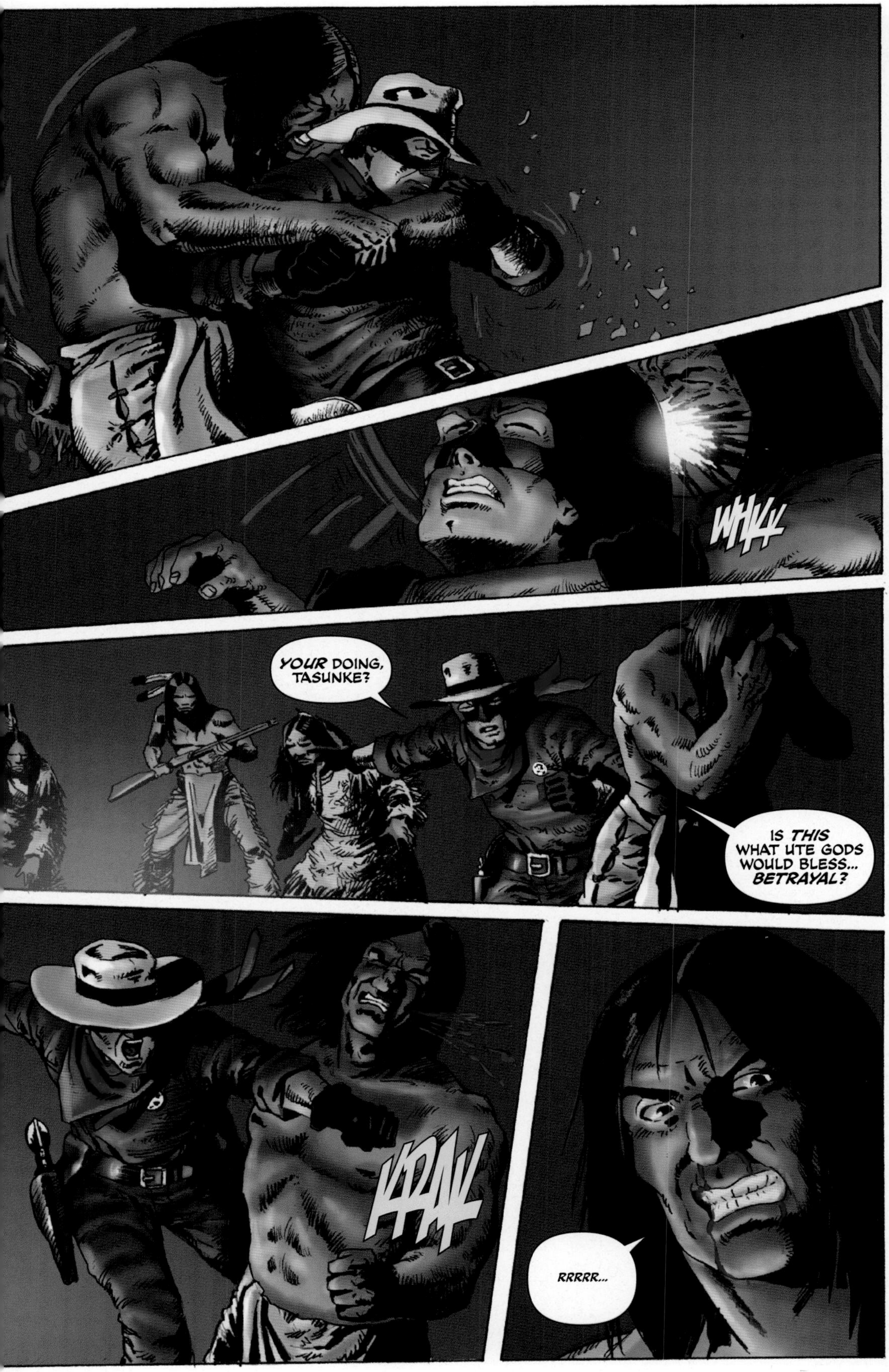
WHUK
YOUR DOING, TASUNKE?
IS THIS WHAT UTE GODS WOULD BLESS... BETRAYAL?
KRAK
RRRRR...

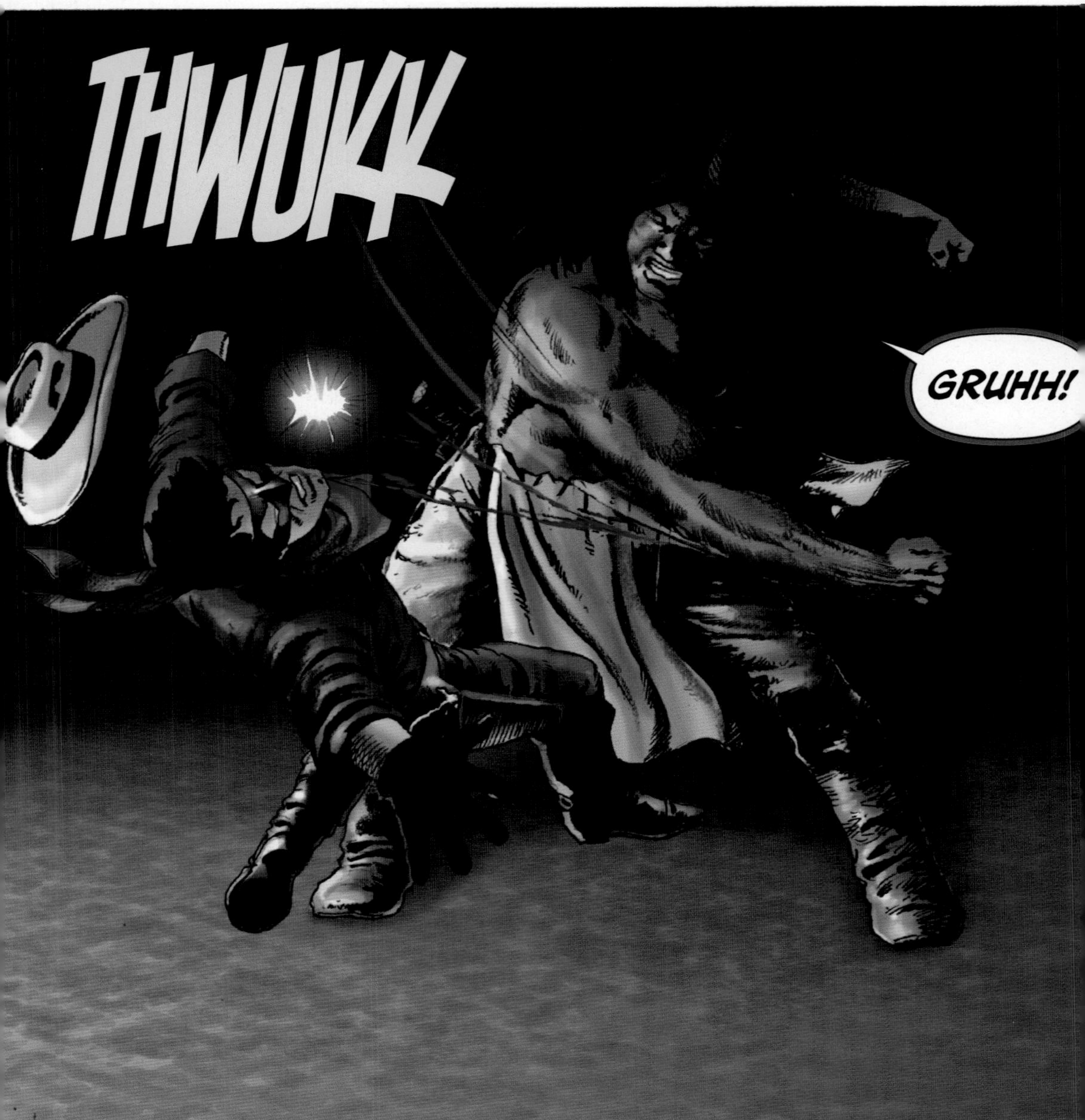
THWUKK
GRUHH!

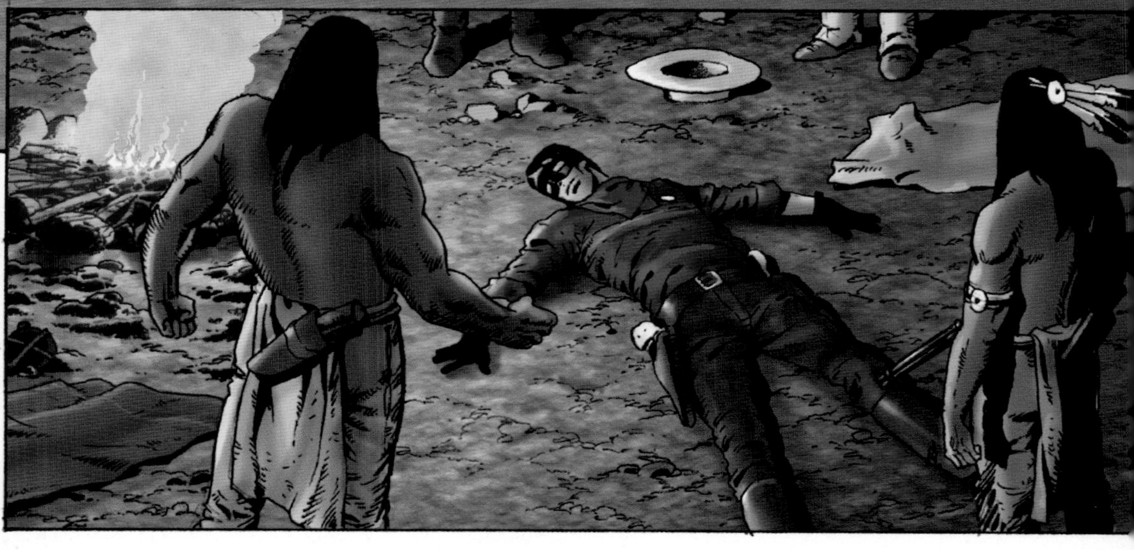

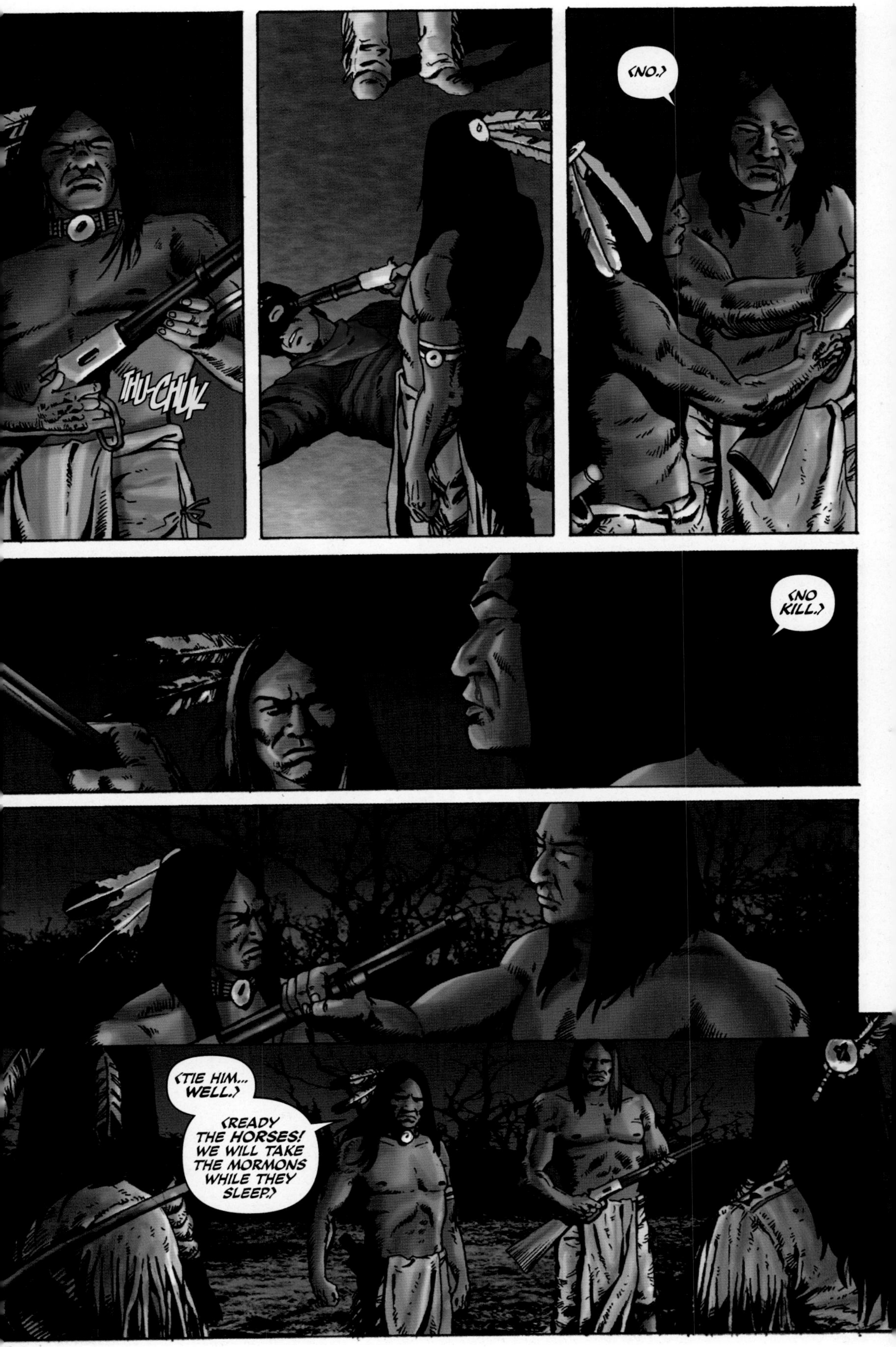
THU-CHUK
<NO.>
<NO KILL.>
<TIE HIM... WELL.>
<READY THE HORSES! WE WILL TAKE THE MORMONS WHILE THEY SLEEP.>

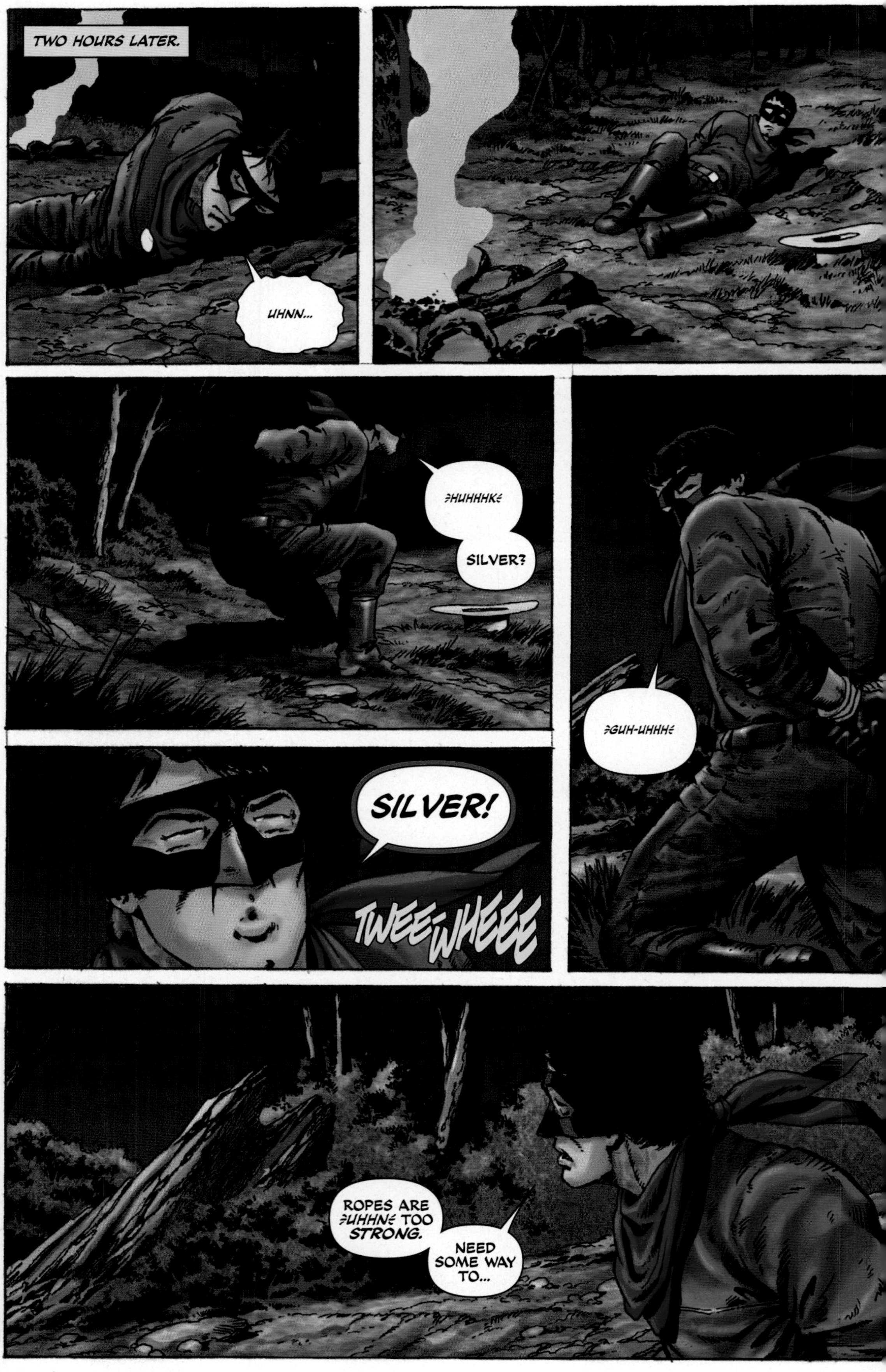
TWO HOURS LATER.
UHNN...
≠HUHHHK≠
SILVER?
SILVER!
TWEE-WHEEE
≠GUH-UHHH≠
ROPES ARE ≠UHHN≠ TOO STRONG.
NEED SOME WAY TO...

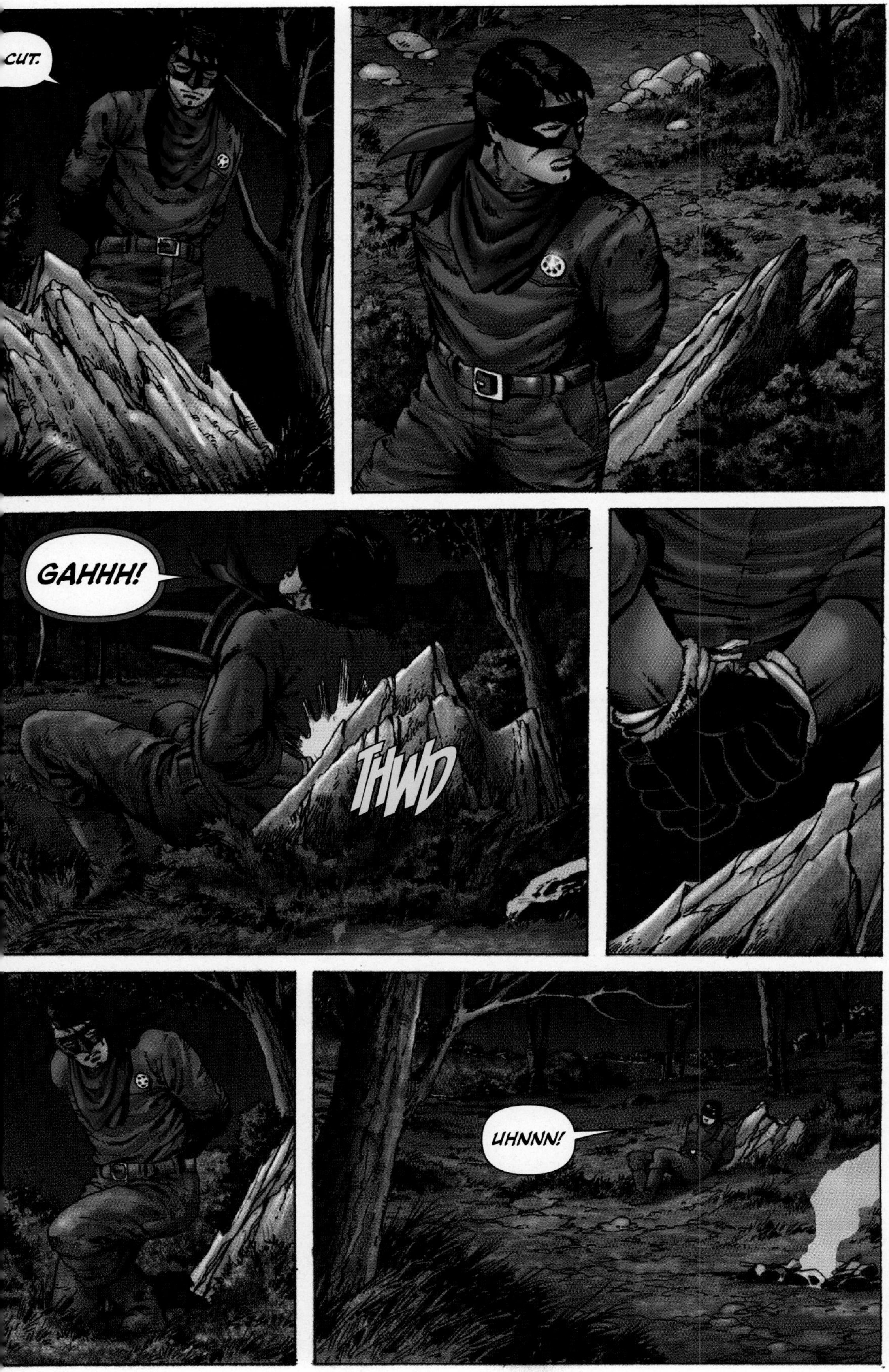
CUT.
GAHHH!
THWD
UHNNN!

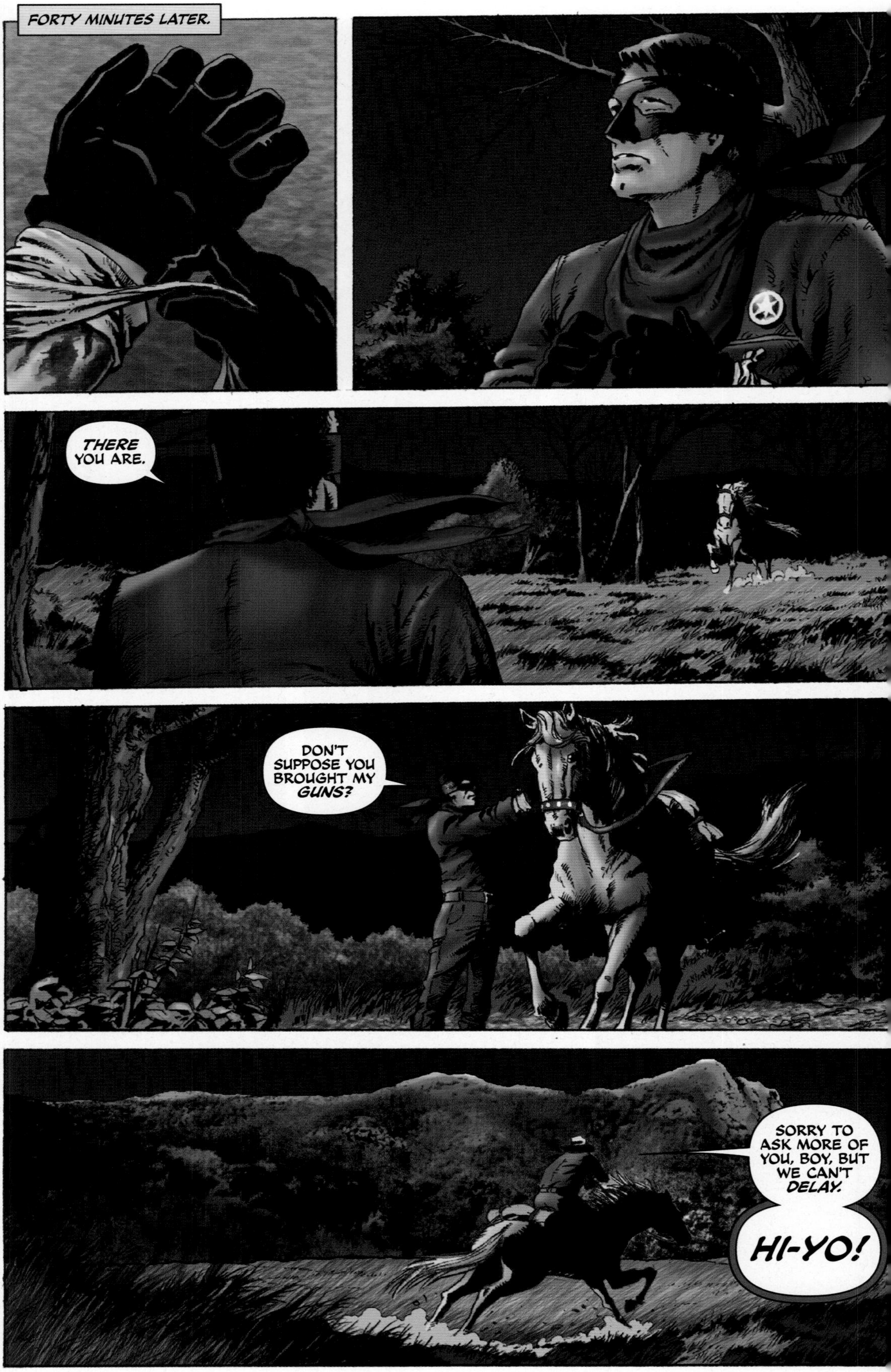
FORTY MINUTES LATER.
THERE YOU ARE.
DON'T SUPPOSE YOU BROUGHT MY GUNS?
SORRY TO ASK MORE OF YOU, BOY, BUT WE CAN'T DELAY.
HI-YO!

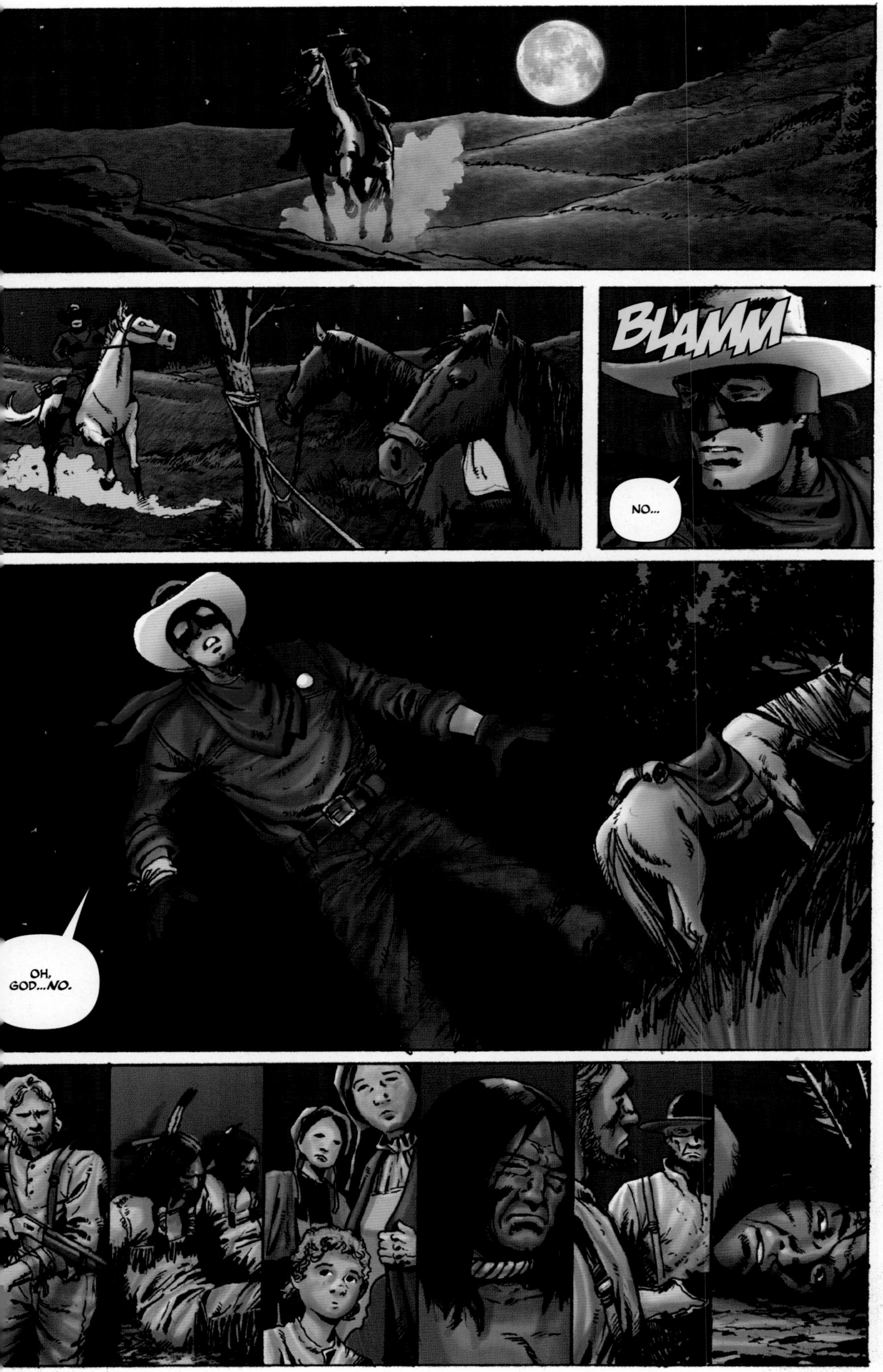
BLAMM
NO...
OH, GOD...NO.

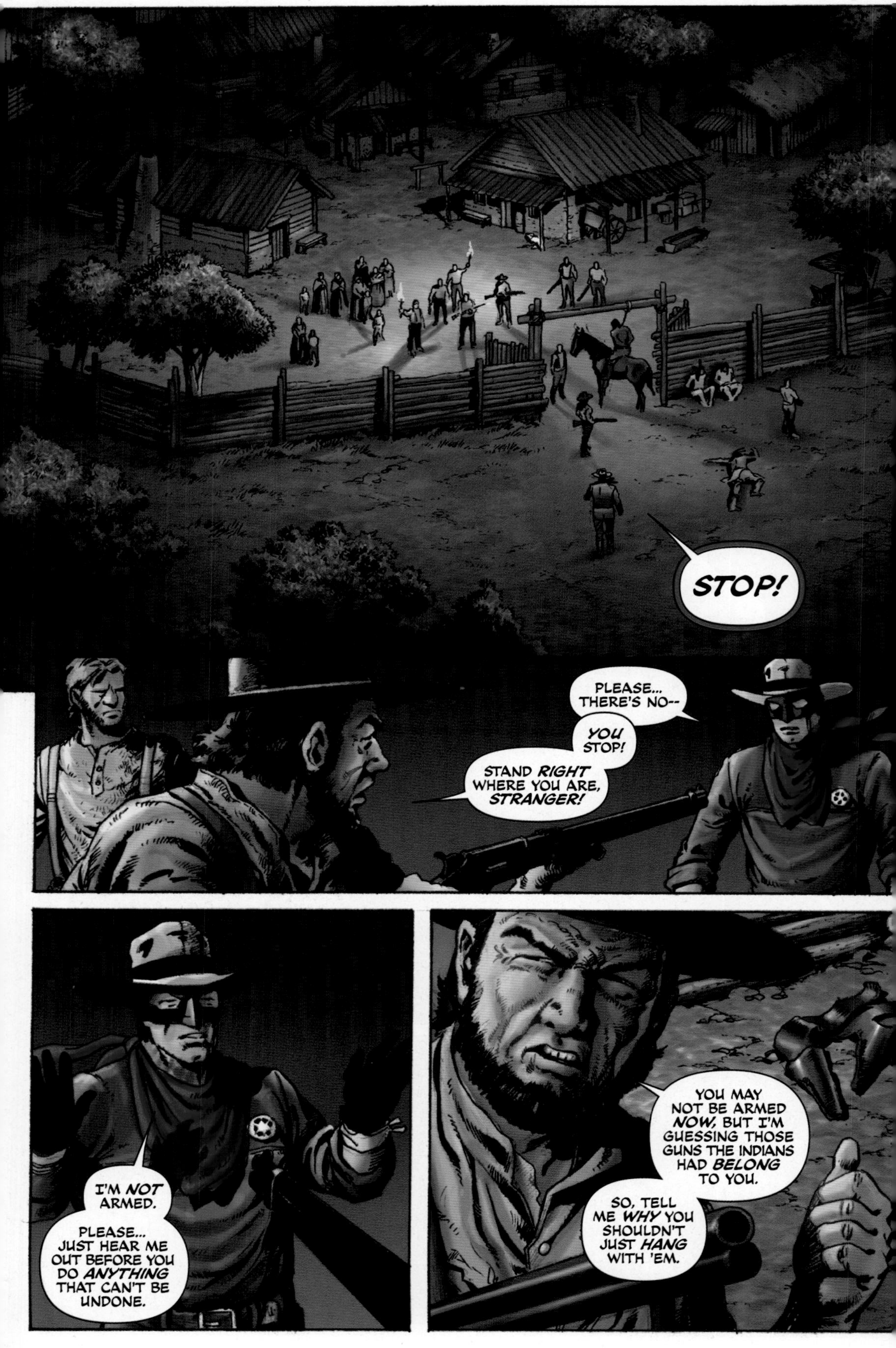
STOP!
PLEASE... THERE'S NO--
YOU STOP!
STAND RIGHT WHERE YOU ARE, STRANGER!
I'M NOT ARMED.
PLEASE... JUST HEAR ME OUT BEFORE YOU DO ANYTHING THAT CAN'T BE UNDONE.
YOU MAY NOT BE ARMED NOW, BUT I'M GUESSING THOSE GUNS THE INDIANS HAD BELONG TO YOU.
SO, TELL ME WHY YOU SHOULDN'T JUST HANG WITH 'EM.

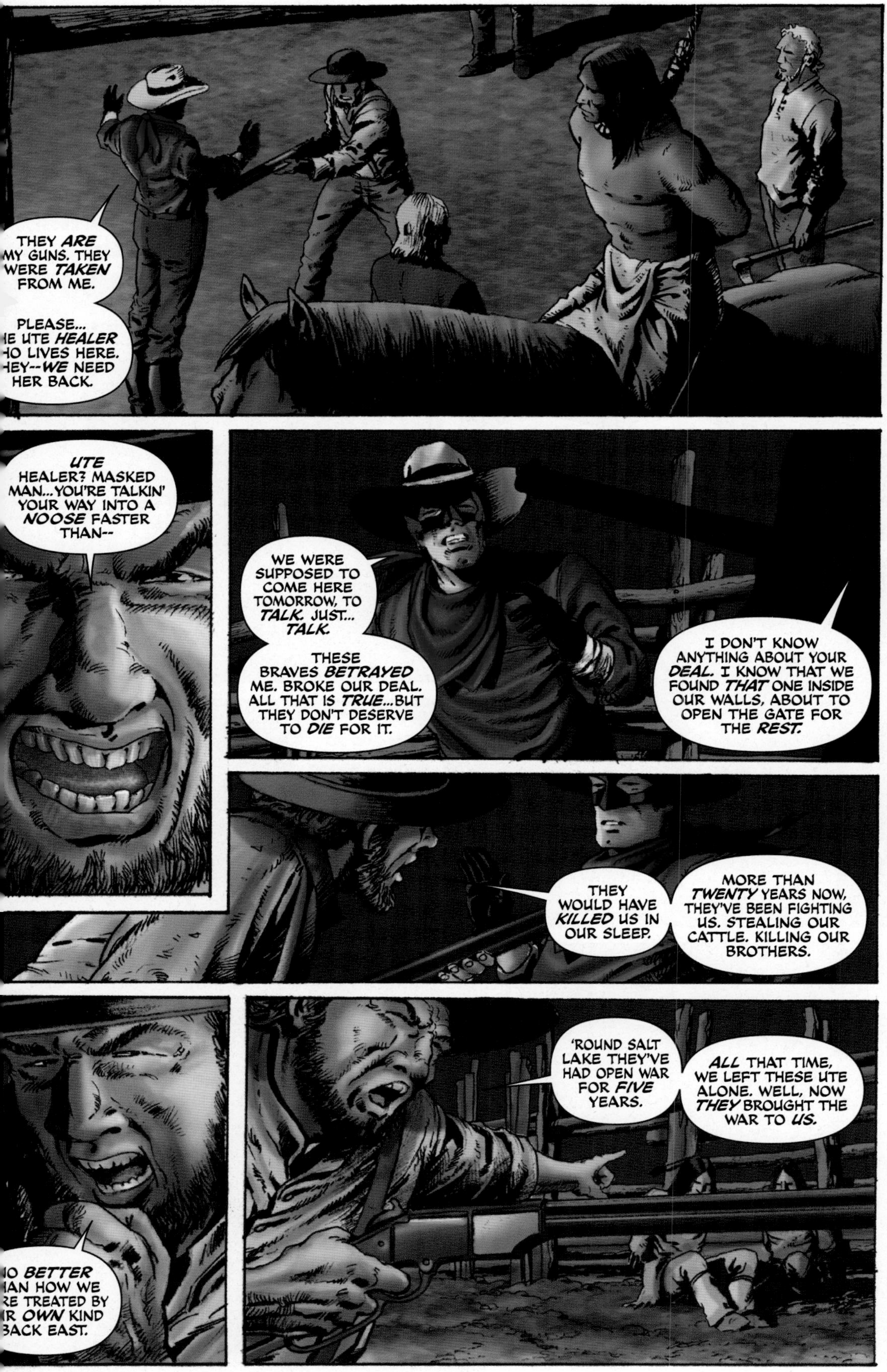

THEY ARE MY GUNS. THEY WERE TAKEN FROM ME.
PLEASE... IE UTE HEALER HO LIVES HERE. HEY--WE NEED HER BACK.
UTE HEALER? MASKED MAN...YOU'RE TALKIN' YOUR WAY INTO A NOOSE FASTER THAN--
WE WERE SUPPOSED TO COME HERE TOMORROW, TO TALK. JUST... TALK.
THESE BRAVES BETRAYED ME. BROKE OUR DEAL. ALL THAT IS TRUE...BUT THEY DON'T DESERVE TO DIE FOR IT.
I DON'T KNOW ANYTHING ABOUT YOUR DEAL. I KNOW THAT WE FOUND THAT ONE INSIDE OUR WALLS, ABOUT TO OPEN THE GATE FOR THE REST.
THEY WOULD HAVE KILLED US IN OUR SLEEP.
MORE THAN TWENTY YEARS NOW, THEY'VE BEEN FIGHTING US. STEALING OUR CATTLE. KILLING OUR BROTHERS.
'ROUND SALT LAKE THEY'VE HAD OPEN WAR FOR FIVE YEARS.
ALL THAT TIME, WE LEFT THESE UTE ALONE. WELL, NOW THEY BROUGHT THE WAR TO US.
IO BETTER IAN HOW WE RE TREATED BY IR OWN KIND BACK EAST.

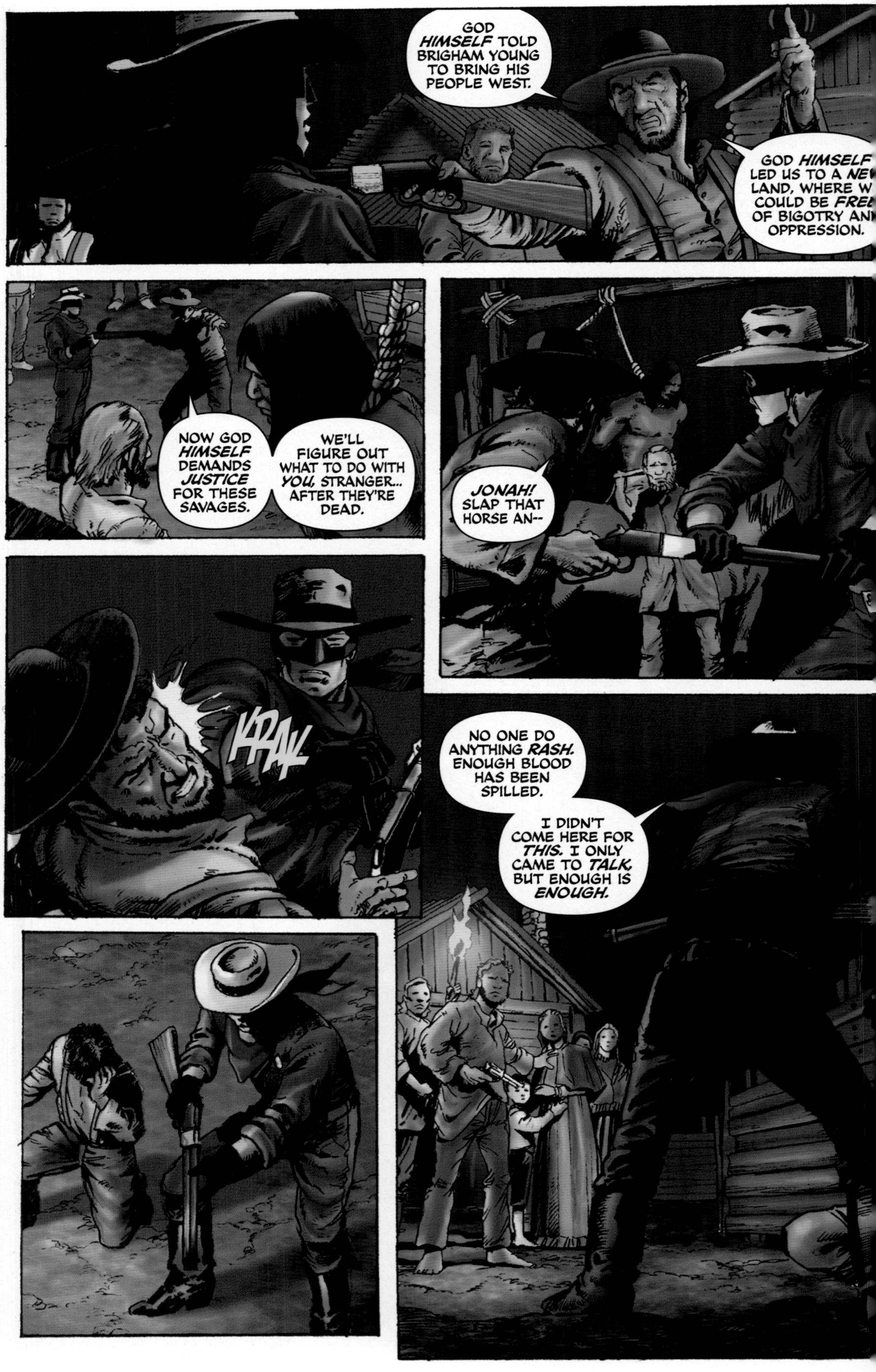
GOD HIMSELF TOLD BRIGHAM YOUNG TO BRING HIS PEOPLE WEST.
GOD HIMSELF LED US TO A NEW LAND, WHERE WE COULD BE FREE OF BIGOTRY AND OPPRESSION.
NOW GOD HIMSELF DEMANDS JUSTICE FOR THESE SAVAGES.
WE'LL FIGURE OUT WHAT TO DO WITH YOU, STRANGER... AFTER THEY'RE DEAD.
JONAH! SLAP THAT HORSE AN--
KRAK
NO ONE DO ANYTHING RASH. ENOUGH BLOOD HAS BEEN SPILLED.
I DIDN'T COME HERE FOR THIS. I ONLY CAME TO TALK, BUT ENOUGH IS ENOUGH.

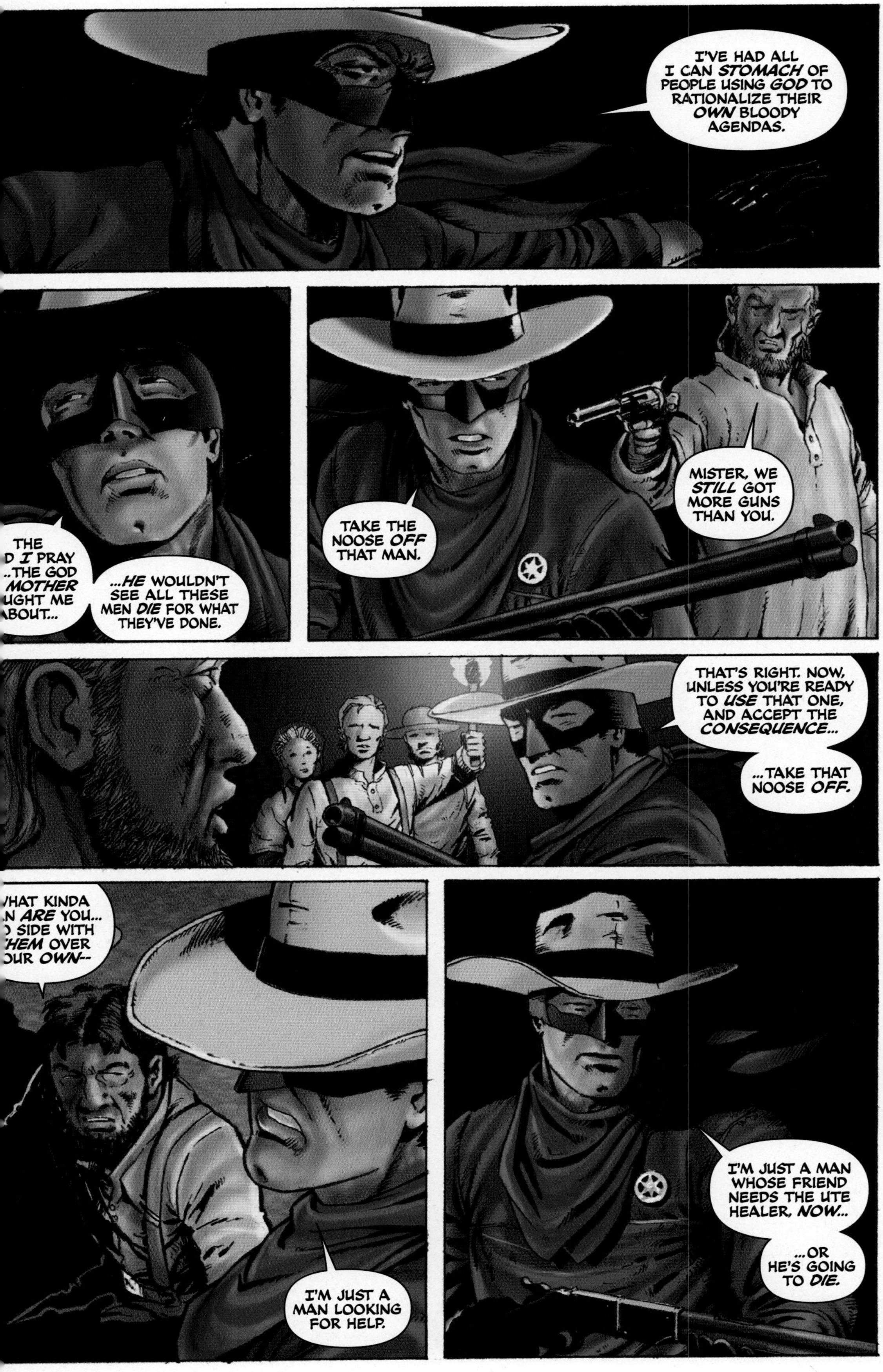
I'VE HAD ALL I CAN STOMACH OF PEOPLE USING GOD TO RATIONALIZE THEIR OWN BLOODY AGENDAS.
THE D I PRAY ..THE GOD MOTHER UGHT ME ABOUT...
...HE WOULDN'T SEE ALL THESE MEN DIE FOR WHAT THEY'VE DONE.
TAKE THE NOOSE OFF THAT MAN.
MISTER, WE STILL GOT MORE GUNS THAN YOU.
THAT'S RIGHT. NOW, UNLESS YOU'RE READY TO USE THAT ONE, AND ACCEPT THE CONSEQUENCE...
...TAKE THAT NOOSE OFF.
HAT KINDA N ARE YOU... SIDE WITH HEM OVER OUR OWN--
I'M JUST A MAN LOOKING FOR HELP.
I'M JUST A MAN WHOSE FRIEND NEEDS THE UTE HEALER, NOW...
...OR HE'S GOING TO DIE.

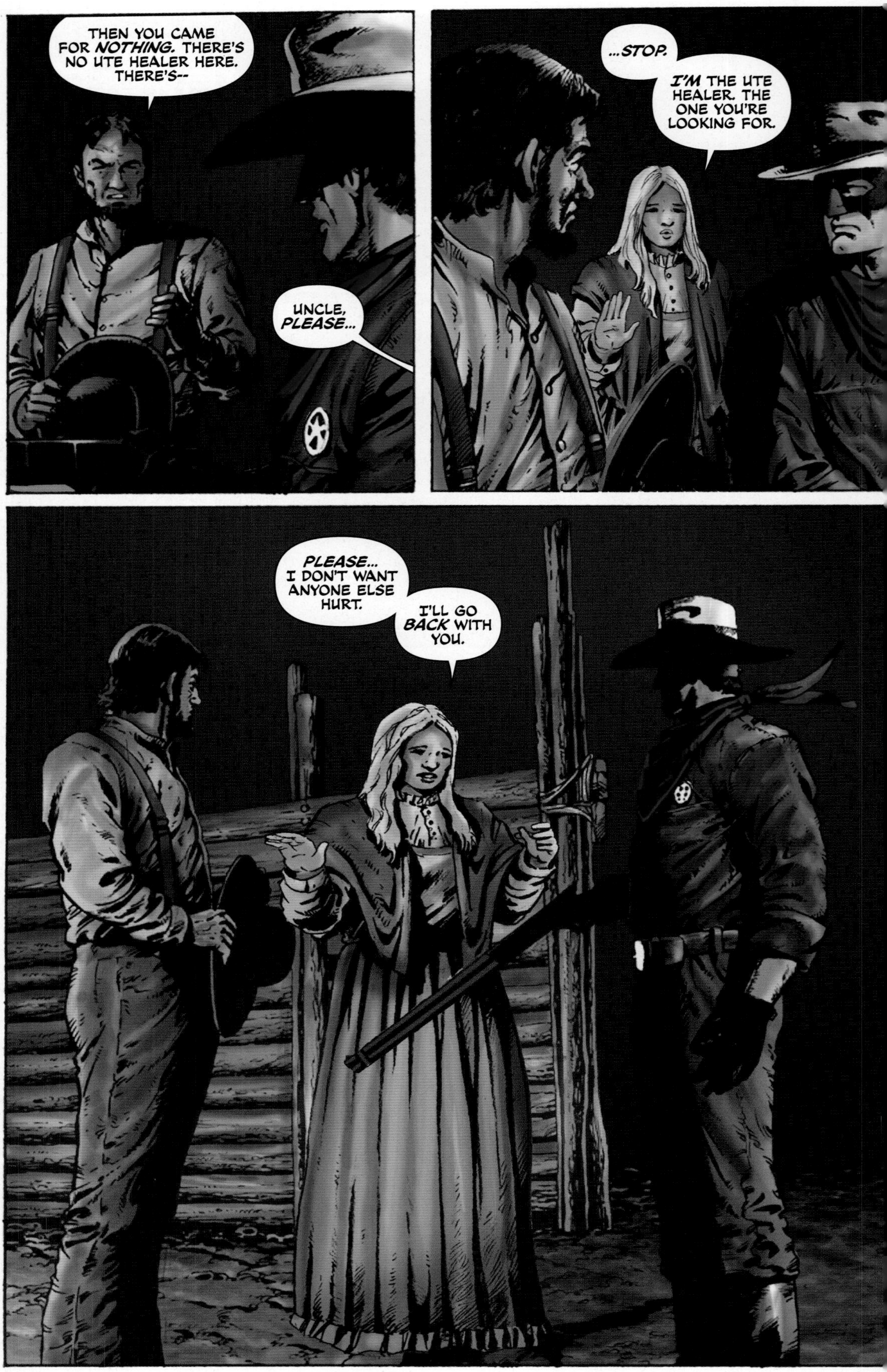

THEN YOU CAME FOR *NOTHING.* THERE'S NO UTE HEALER HERE. THERE'S--
UNCLE, *PLEASE...*
...*STOP.*
I'M THE UTE HEALER. THE ONE YOU'RE LOOKING FOR.
PLEASE... I DON'T WANT ANYONE ELSE HURT.
I'LL GO *BACK* WITH YOU.

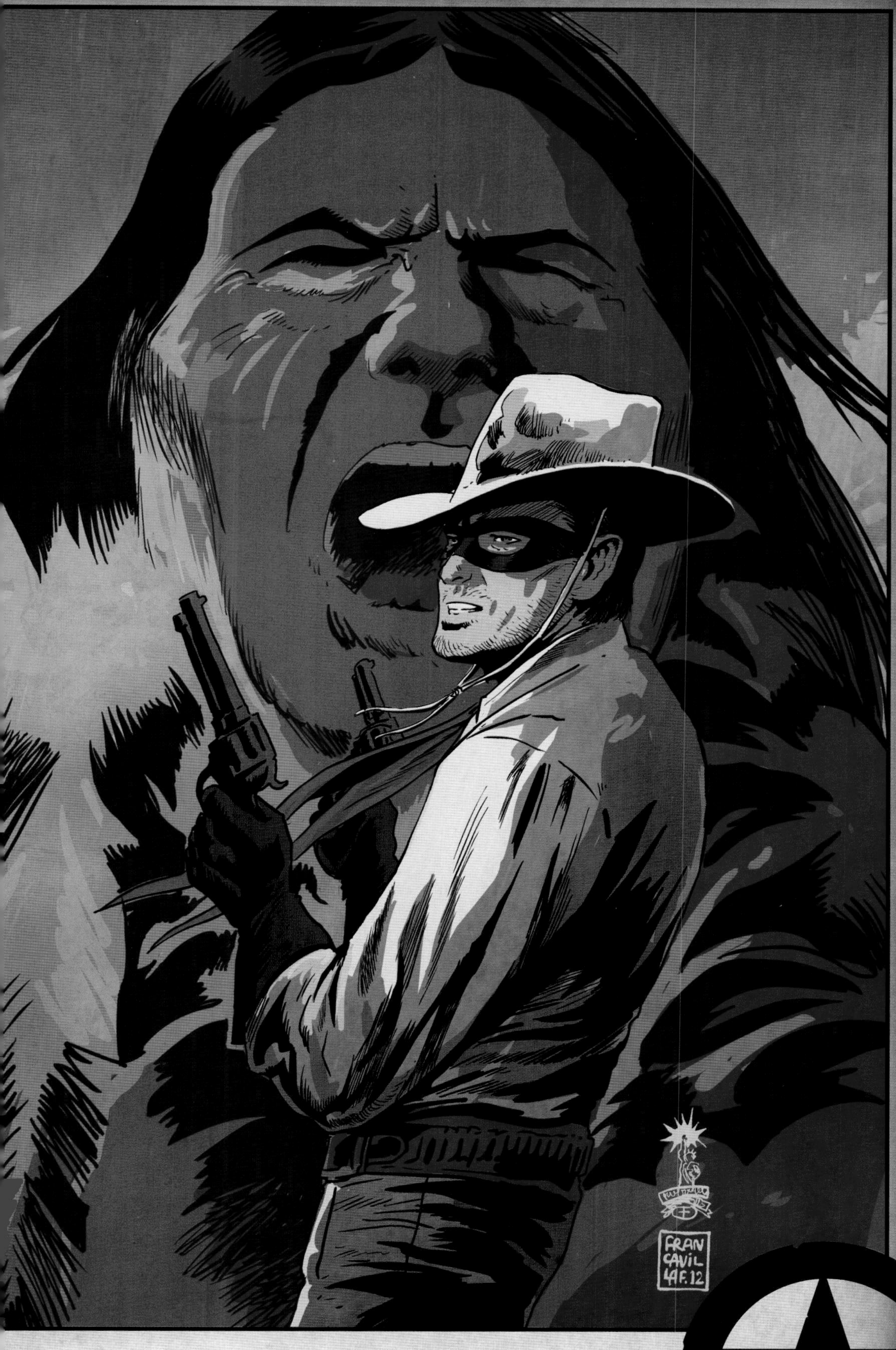
FRAN
CAVIL
LAF.12

COVER BY **FRANCESCO FRANCAVILLA**

12

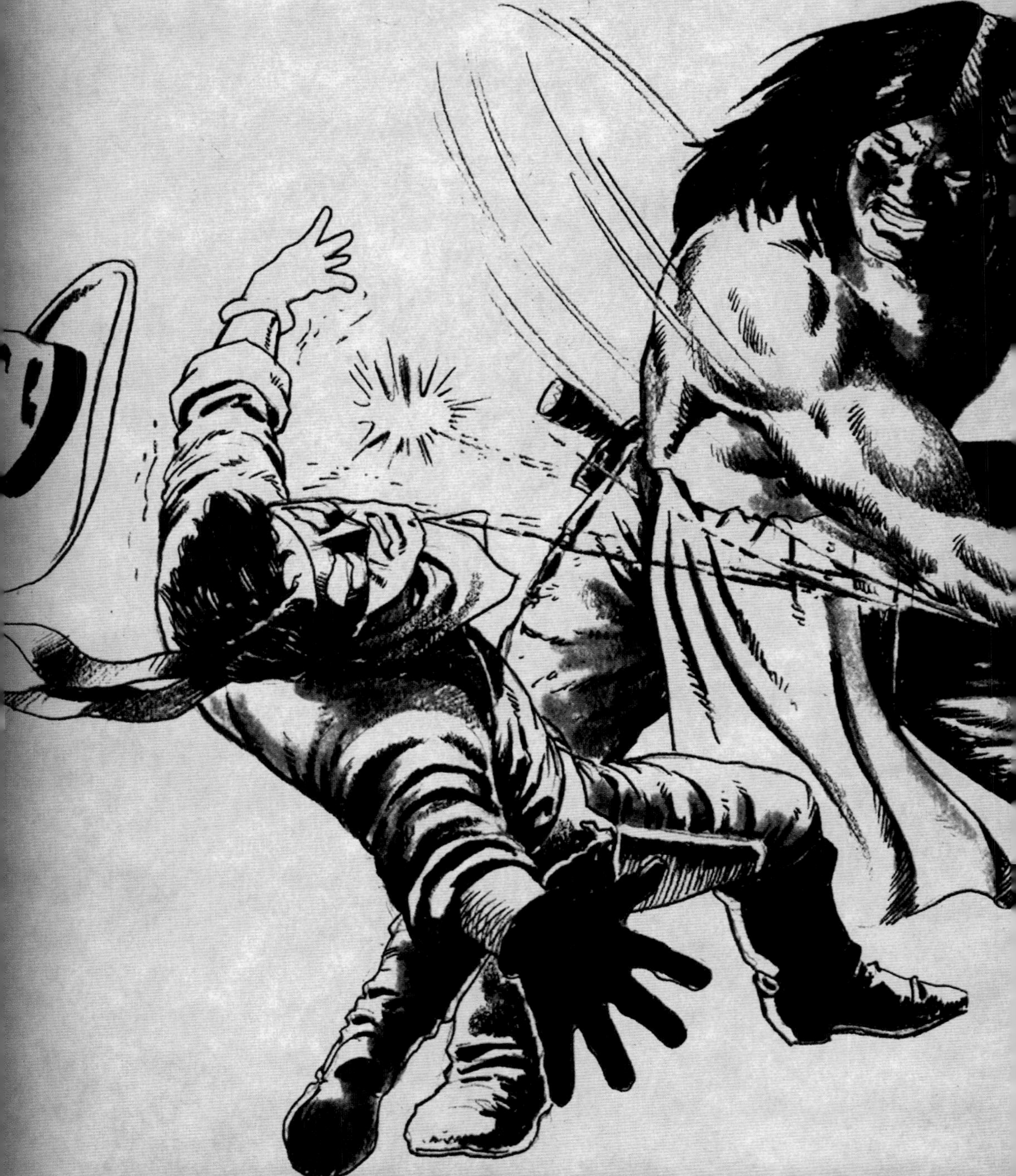

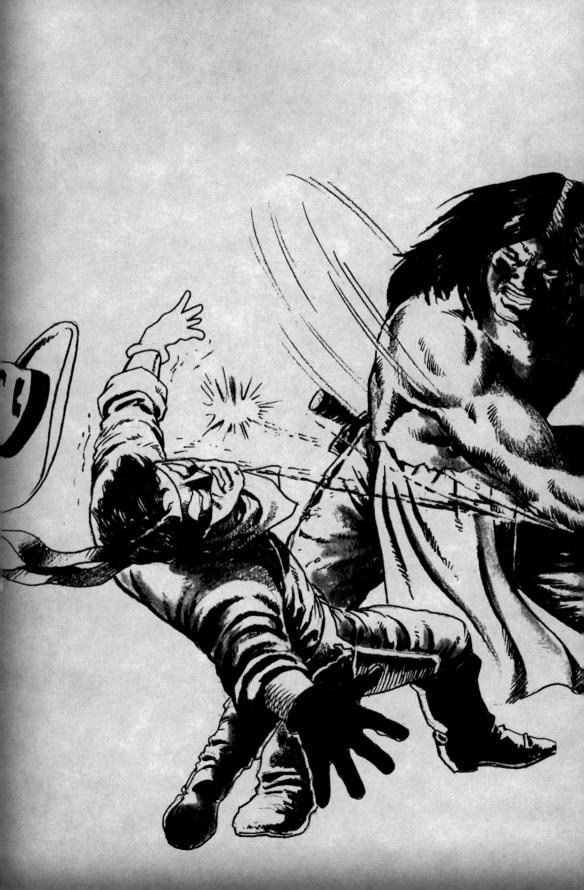

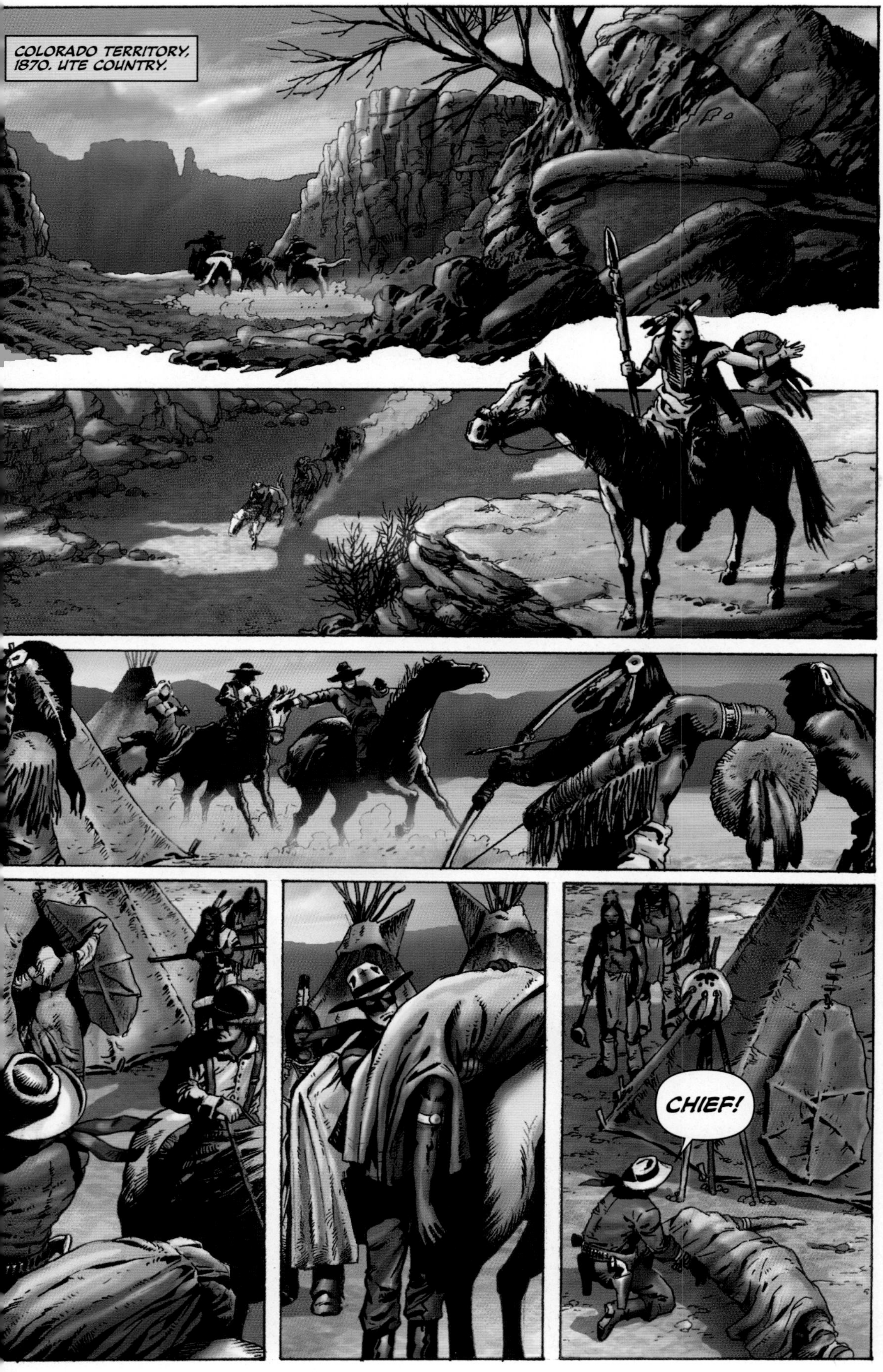
COLORADO TERRITORY, 1870. UTE COUNTRY.
CHIEF!

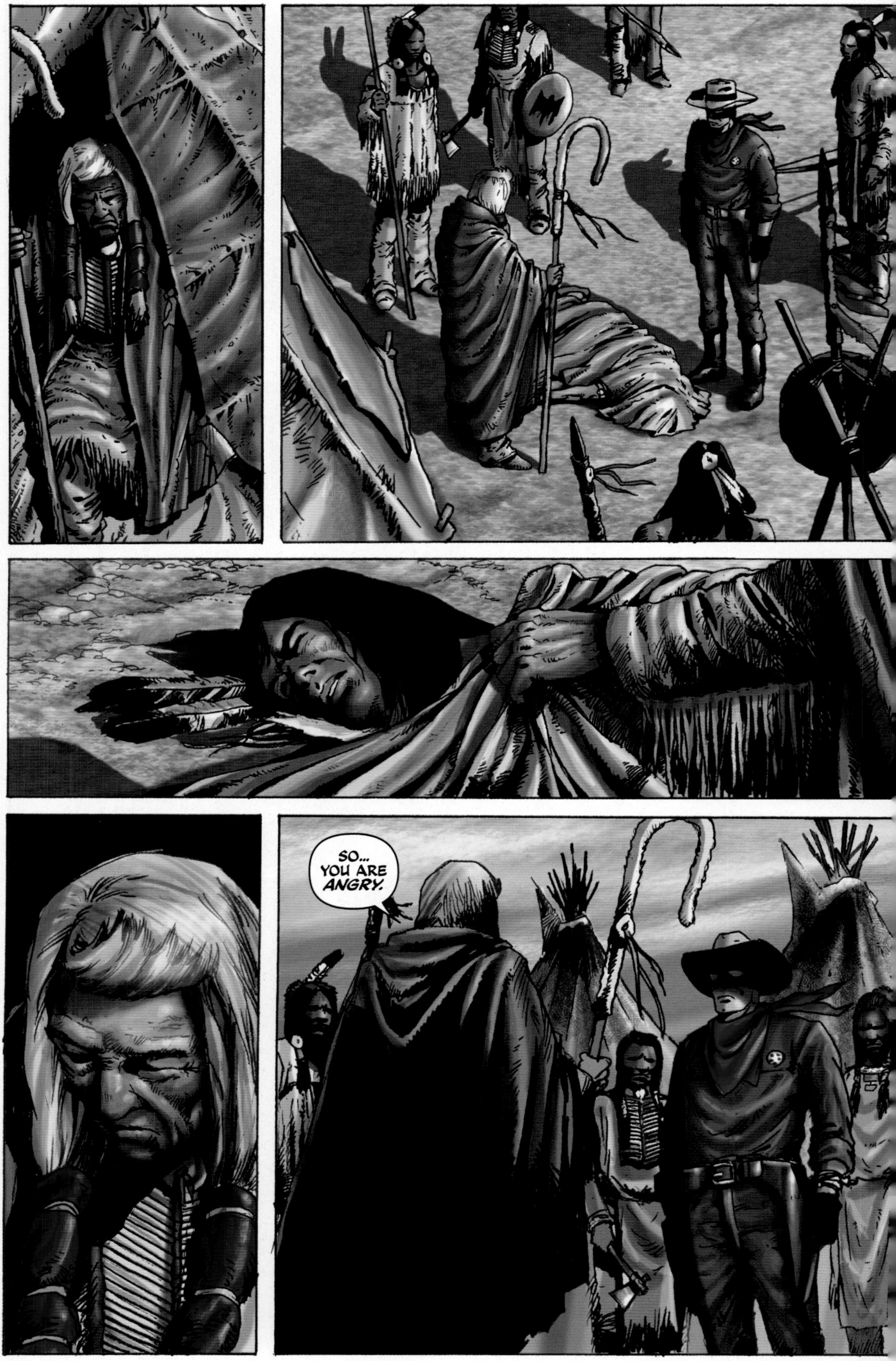
SO... YOU ARE ANGRY.

ANGRY?

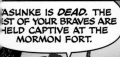

...ASUNKE IS *DEAD.* THE REST OF YOUR BRAVES ARE HELD CAPTIVE AT THE MORMON FORT.

YOU HAD ME *BETRAYED* AND LEFT FOR DEAD.

TONTO WAS NEARLY SACRIFICED AS PART OF YOUR PLAN.

HE MAY *STILL* DIE BECAUSE OF THE DELAY.

...L *THIS,* ...ND FOR ...HAT?

SO YOU COULD *STEAL* MY GUNS AND *KILL* A FEW MORE SETTLERS?

YES. I AM... ANGRY.

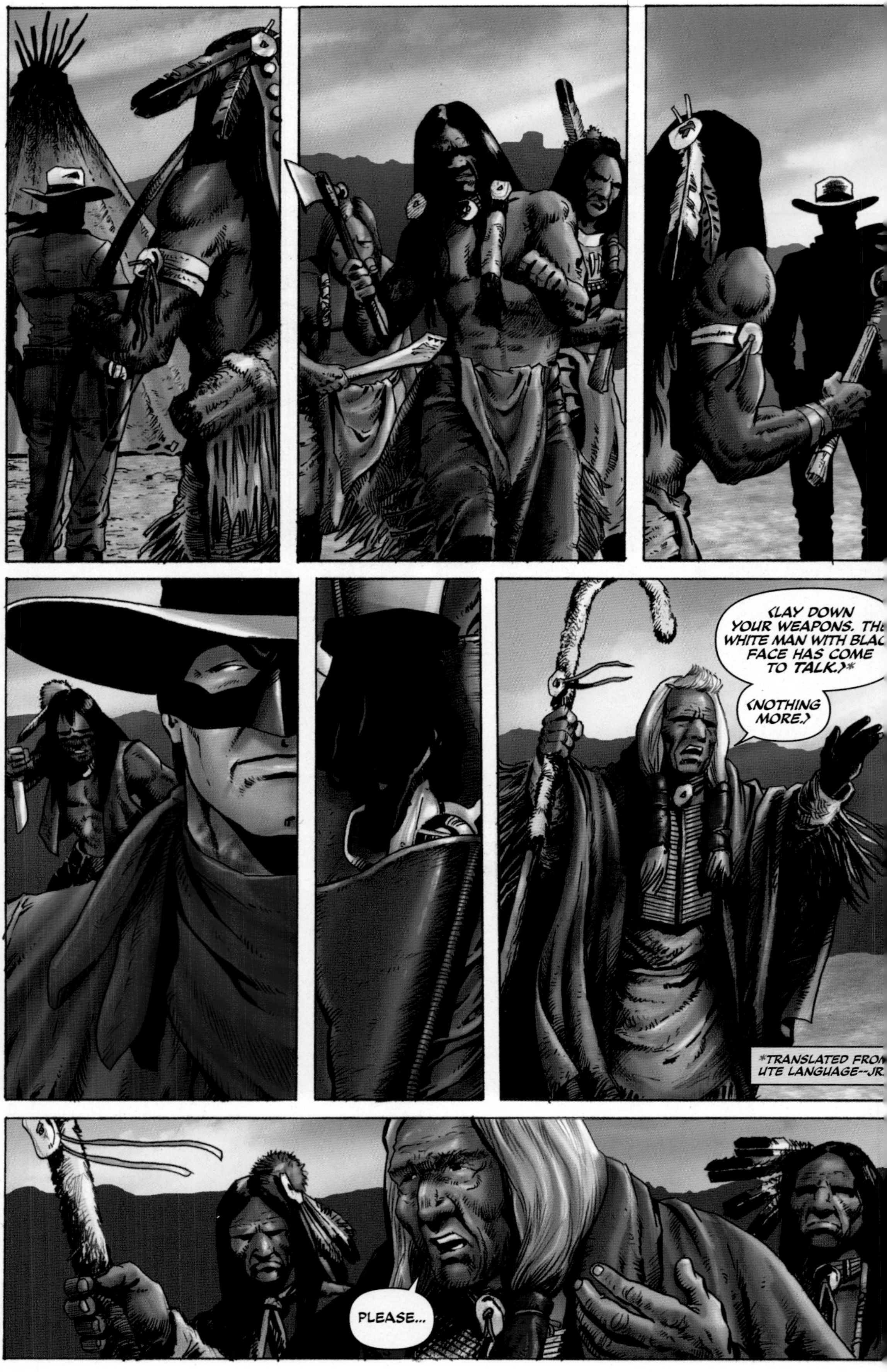
‹LAY DOWN YOUR WEAPONS. THE WHITE MAN WITH BLACK FACE HAS COME TO TALK.›*
‹NOTHING MORE.›
*TRANSLATED FROM UTE LANGUAGE--JR.
PLEASE...

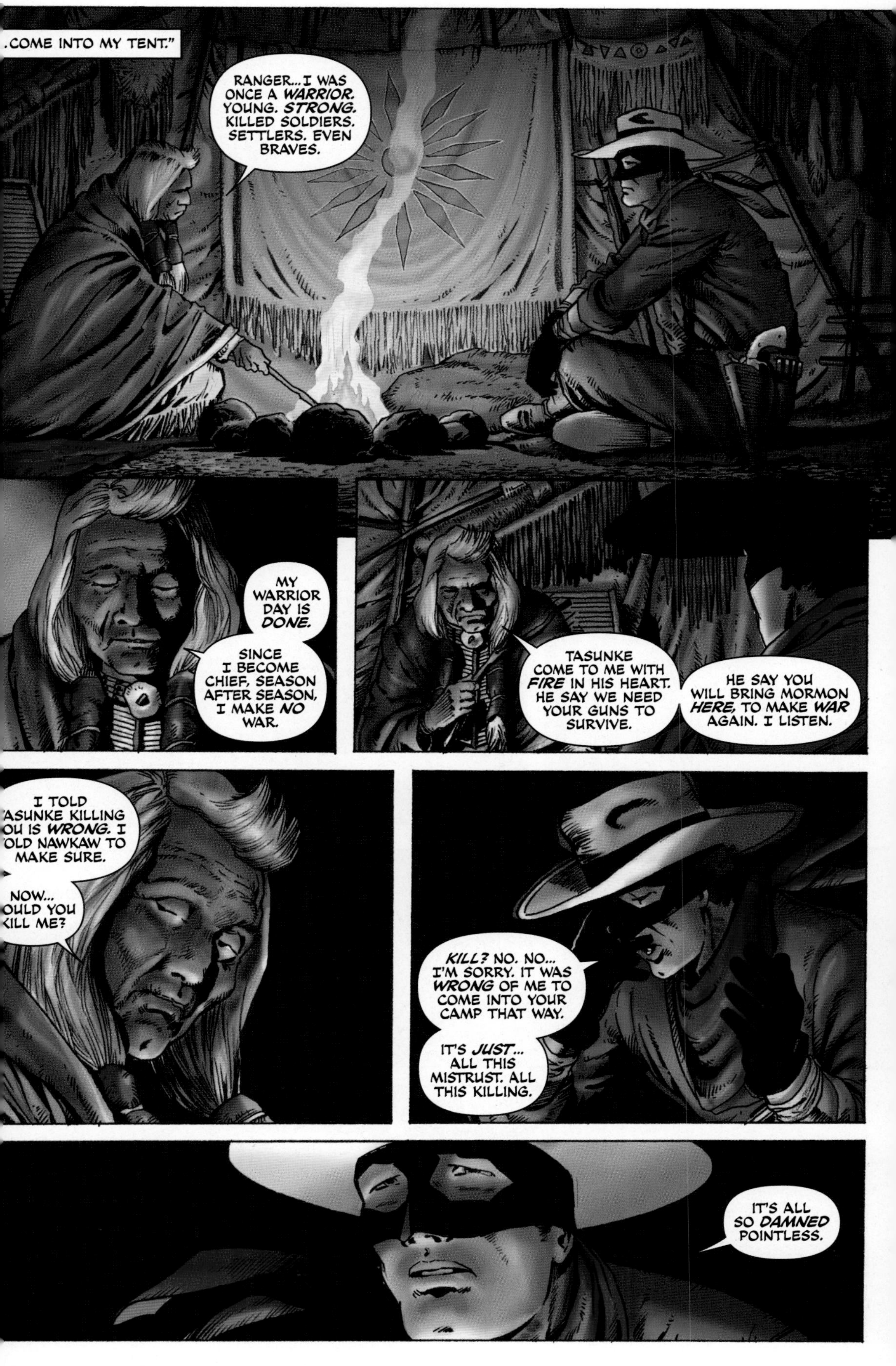

...COME INTO MY TENT."
RANGER...I WAS ONCE A *WARRIOR.* YOUNG. *STRONG.* KILLED SOLDIERS. SETTLERS. EVEN BRAVES.
MY WARRIOR DAY IS *DONE.*
SINCE I BECOME CHIEF, SEASON AFTER SEASON, I MAKE *NO* WAR.
TASUNKE COME TO ME WITH *FIRE* IN HIS HEART. HE SAY WE NEED YOUR GUNS TO SURVIVE.
HE SAY YOU WILL BRING MORMON *HERE,* TO MAKE *WAR* AGAIN. I LISTEN.
I TOLD TASUNKE KILLING YOU IS *WRONG.* I TOLD NAWKAW TO MAKE SURE.
NOW... WOULD YOU KILL ME?
KILL? NO. NO... I'M SORRY. IT WAS *WRONG* OF ME TO COME INTO YOUR CAMP THAT WAY.
IT'S *JUST*... ALL THIS MISTRUST. ALL THIS KILLING.
IT'S ALL SO *DAMNED* POINTLESS.

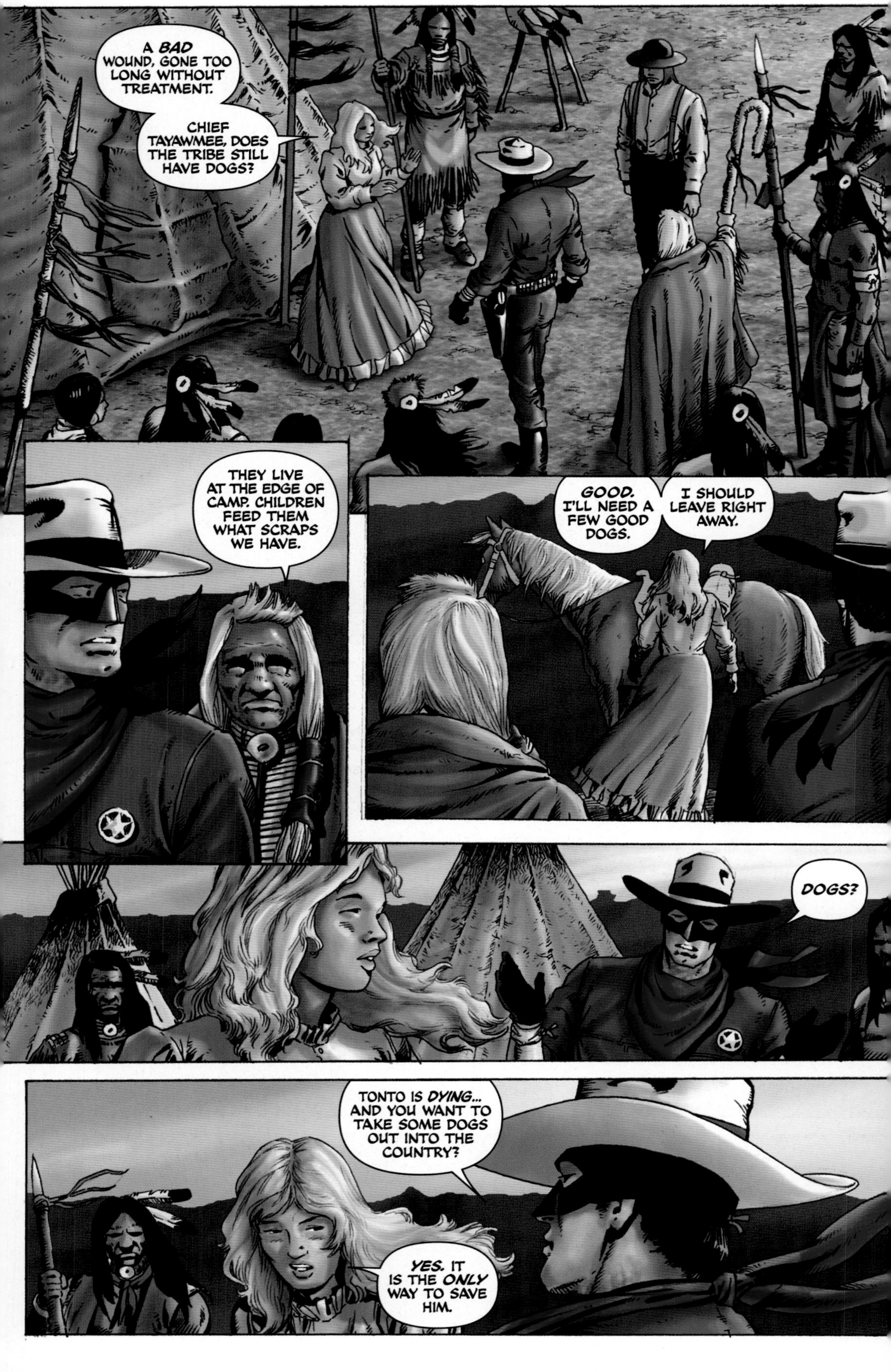
A BAD WOUND, GONE TOO LONG WITHOUT TREATMENT.
CHIEF TAYAWMEE, DOES THE TRIBE STILL HAVE DOGS?
THEY LIVE AT THE EDGE OF CAMP. CHILDREN FEED THEM WHAT SCRAPS WE HAVE.
GOOD. I'LL NEED A FEW GOOD DOGS.
I SHOULD LEAVE RIGHT AWAY.
DOGS?
TONTO IS DYING... AND YOU WANT TO TAKE SOME DOGS OUT INTO THE COUNTRY?
YES. IT IS THE ONLY WAY TO SAVE HIM.

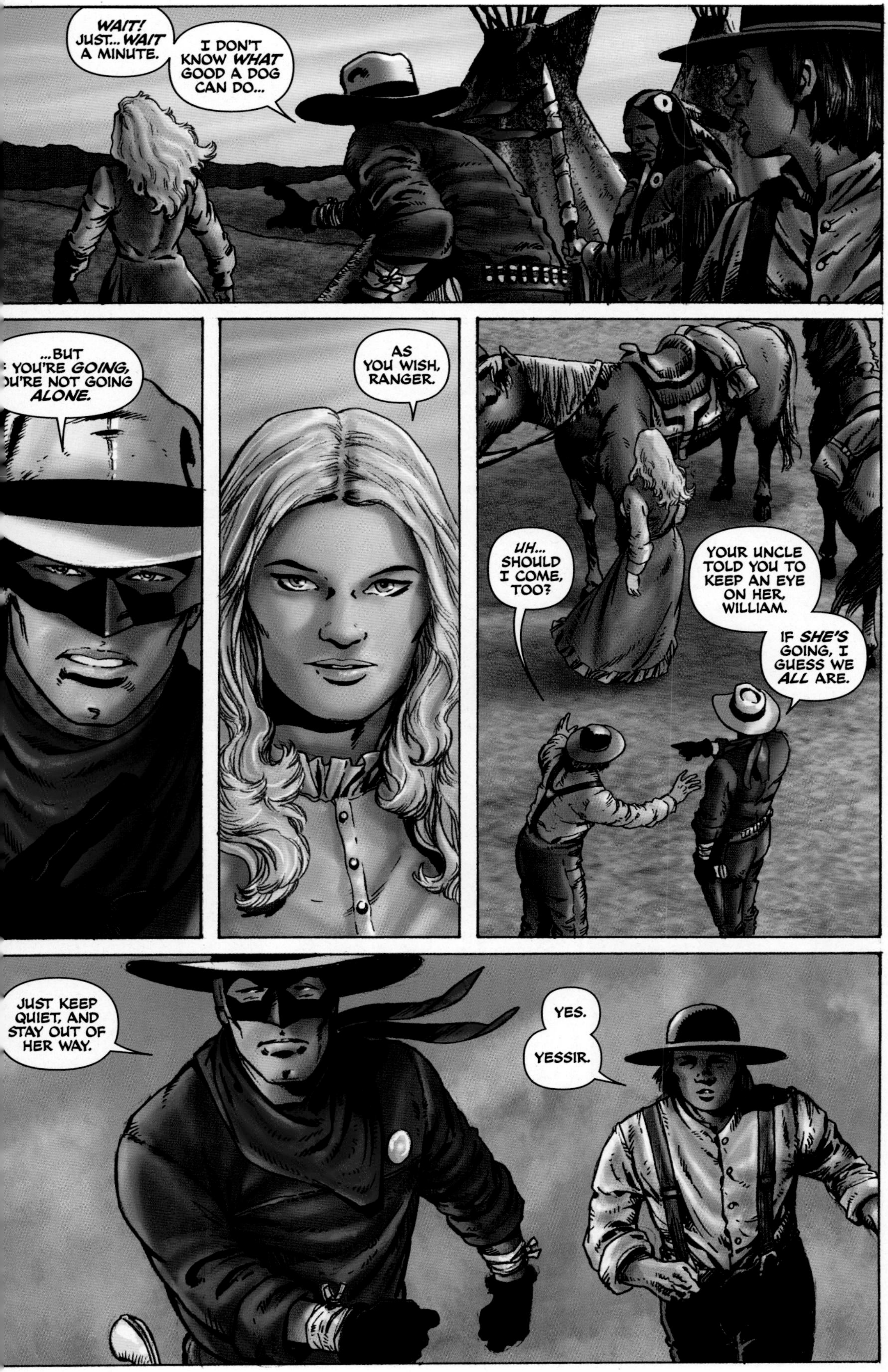
WAIT! JUST... WAIT A MINUTE.
I DON'T KNOW WHAT GOOD A DOG CAN DO...
...BUT IF YOU'RE GOING, YOU'RE NOT GOING ALONE.
AS YOU WISH, RANGER.
UH... SHOULD I COME, TOO?
YOUR UNCLE TOLD YOU TO KEEP AN EYE ON HER, WILLIAM.
IF SHE'S GOING, I GUESS WE ALL ARE.
JUST KEEP QUIET, AND STAY OUT OF HER WAY.
YES.
YESSIR.

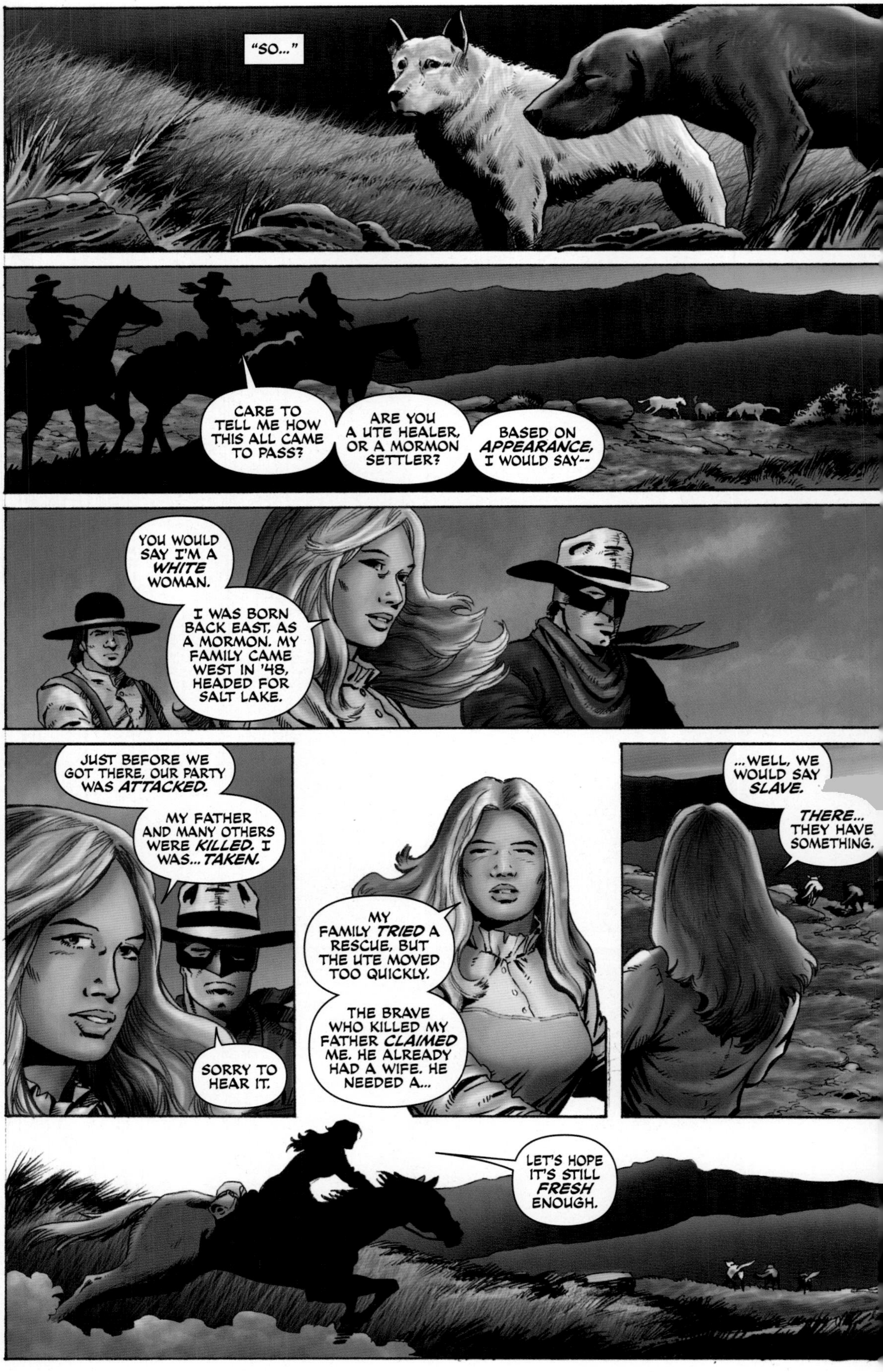
"SO..."
CARE TO TELL ME HOW THIS ALL CAME TO PASS?
ARE YOU A UTE HEALER, OR A MORMON SETTLER?
BASED ON *APPEARANCE,* I WOULD SAY--
YOU WOULD SAY I'M A *WHITE* WOMAN.
I WAS BORN BACK EAST, AS A MORMON. MY FAMILY CAME WEST IN '48, HEADED FOR SALT LAKE.
JUST BEFORE WE GOT THERE, OUR PARTY WAS *ATTACKED.*
MY FATHER AND MANY OTHERS WERE *KILLED.* I WAS... *TAKEN.*
SORRY TO HEAR IT.
MY FAMILY *TRIED* A RESCUE, BUT THE UTE MOVED TOO QUICKLY.
THE BRAVE WHO KILLED MY FATHER *CLAIMED* ME. HE ALREADY HAD A WIFE. HE NEEDED A...
...WELL, WE WOULD SAY *SLAVE.*
THERE... THEY HAVE SOMETHING.
LET'S HOPE IT'S STILL *FRESH* ENOUGH.

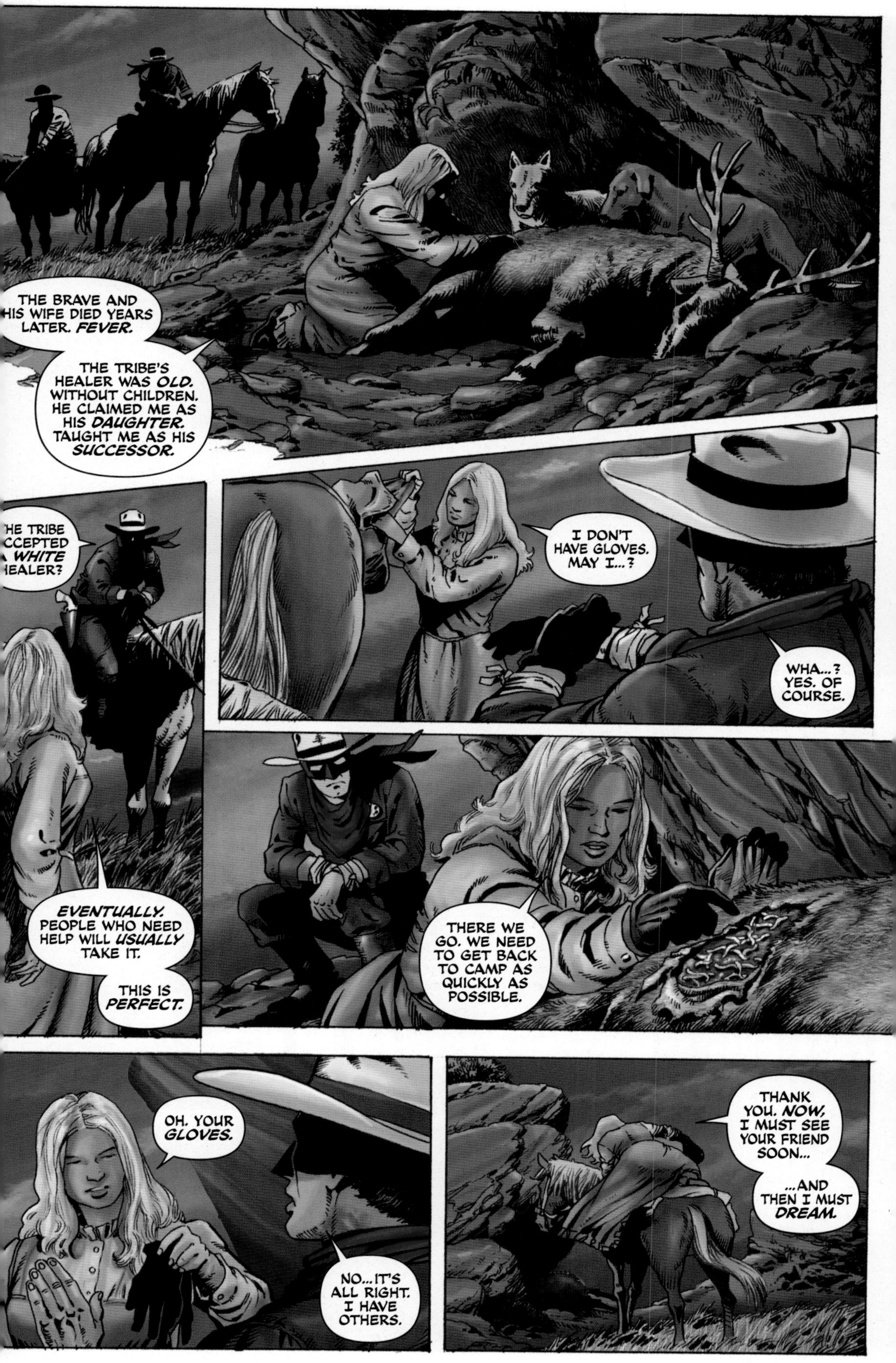
THE BRAVE AND HIS WIFE DIED YEARS LATER. *FEVER.*
THE TRIBE'S HEALER WAS *OLD.* WITHOUT CHILDREN. HE CLAIMED ME AS HIS *DAUGHTER.* TAUGHT ME AS HIS *SUCCESSOR.*
HE TRIBE CCEPTED *WHITE* EALER?
EVENTUALLY. PEOPLE WHO NEED HELP WILL *USUALLY* TAKE IT.
THIS IS *PERFECT.*
I DON'T HAVE GLOVES. MAY I...?
WHA...? YES. OF COURSE.
THERE WE GO. WE NEED TO GET BACK TO CAMP AS QUICKLY AS POSSIBLE.
OH. YOUR *GLOVES.*
NO...IT'S ALL RIGHT. I HAVE OTHERS.
THANK YOU. *NOW,* I MUST SEE YOUR FRIEND SOON...
...AND THEN I MUST *DREAM.*

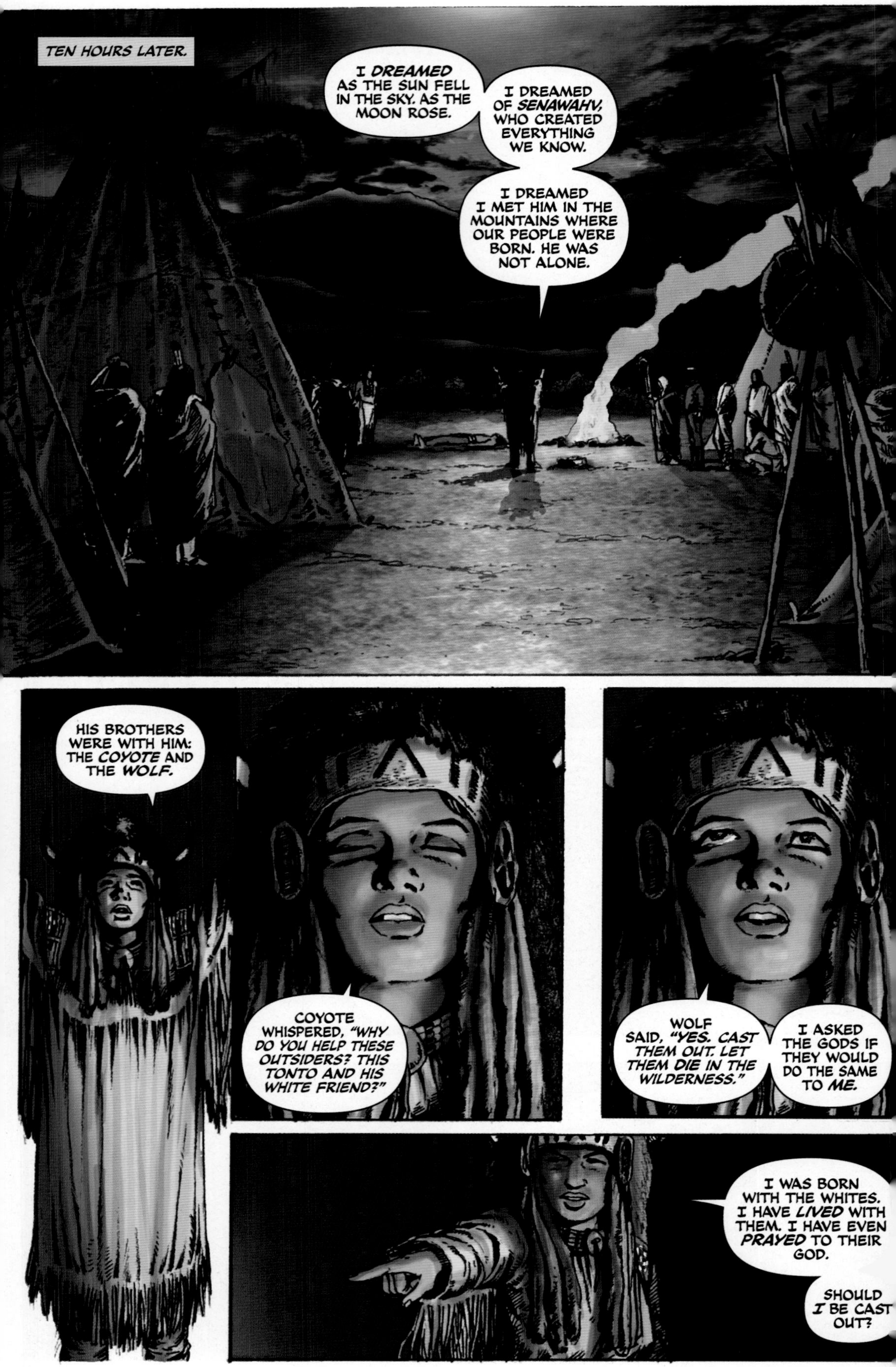
TEN HOURS LATER.
I DREAMED AS THE SUN FELL IN THE SKY. AS THE MOON ROSE.
I DREAMED OF SENAWAHV, WHO CREATED EVERYTHING WE KNOW.
I DREAMED I MET HIM IN THE MOUNTAINS WHERE OUR PEOPLE WERE BORN. HE WAS NOT ALONE.
HIS BROTHERS WERE WITH HIM: THE COYOTE AND THE WOLF.
COYOTE WHISPERED, "WHY DO YOU HELP THESE OUTSIDERS? THIS TONTO AND HIS WHITE FRIEND?"
WOLF SAID, "YES. CAST THEM OUT. LET THEM DIE IN THE WILDERNESS."
I ASKED THE GODS IF THEY WOULD DO THE SAME TO ME.
I WAS BORN WITH THE WHITES. I HAVE LIVED WITH THEM. I HAVE EVEN PRAYED TO THEIR GOD.
SHOULD I BE CAST OUT?

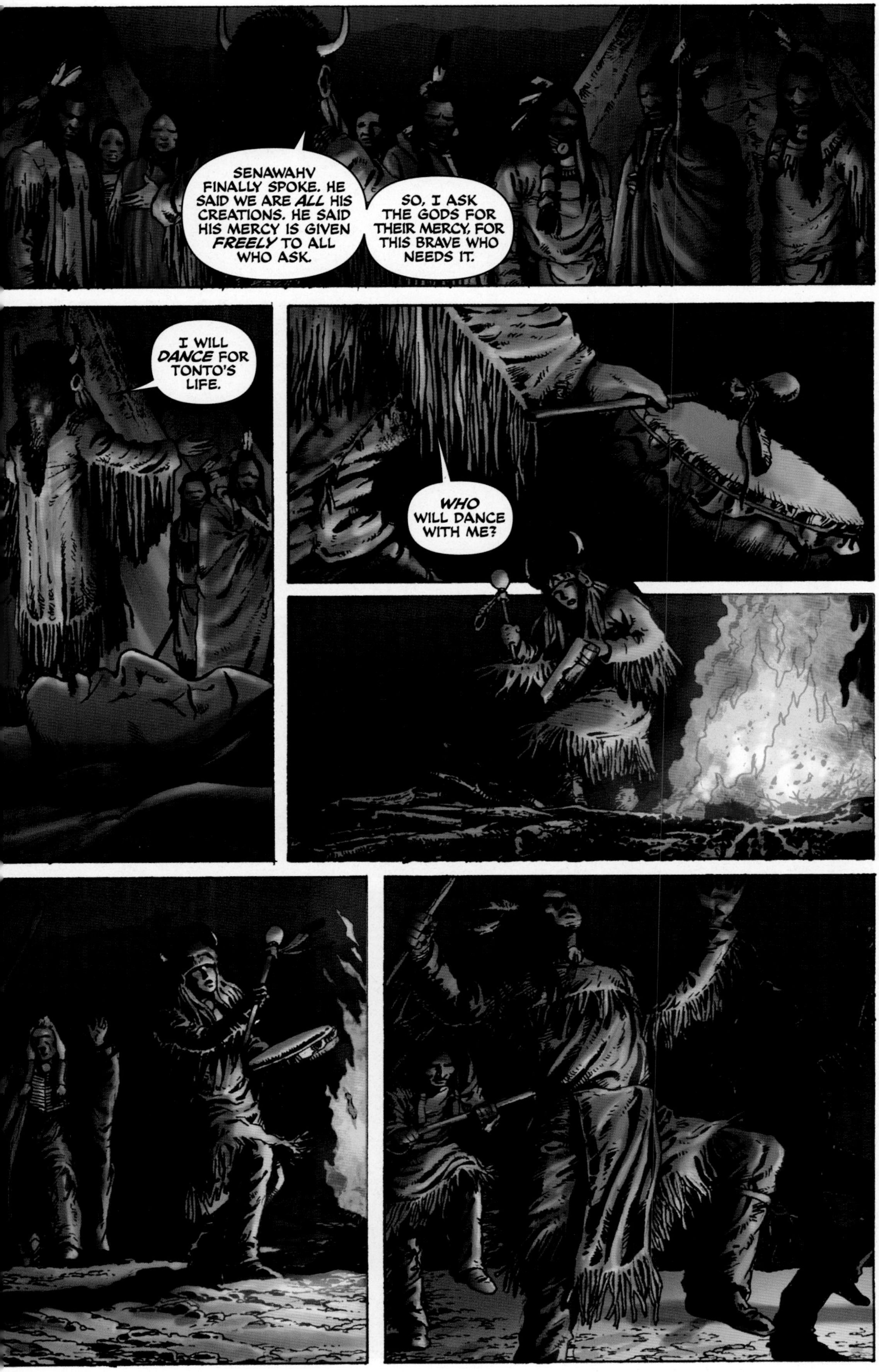
SENAWAHV FINALLY SPOKE. HE SAID WE ARE *ALL* HIS CREATIONS. HE SAID HIS MERCY IS GIVEN *FREELY* TO ALL WHO ASK.
SO, I ASK THE GODS FOR THEIR MERCY, FOR THIS BRAVE WHO NEEDS IT.
I WILL *DANCE* FOR TONTO'S LIFE.
WHO WILL DANCE WITH ME?

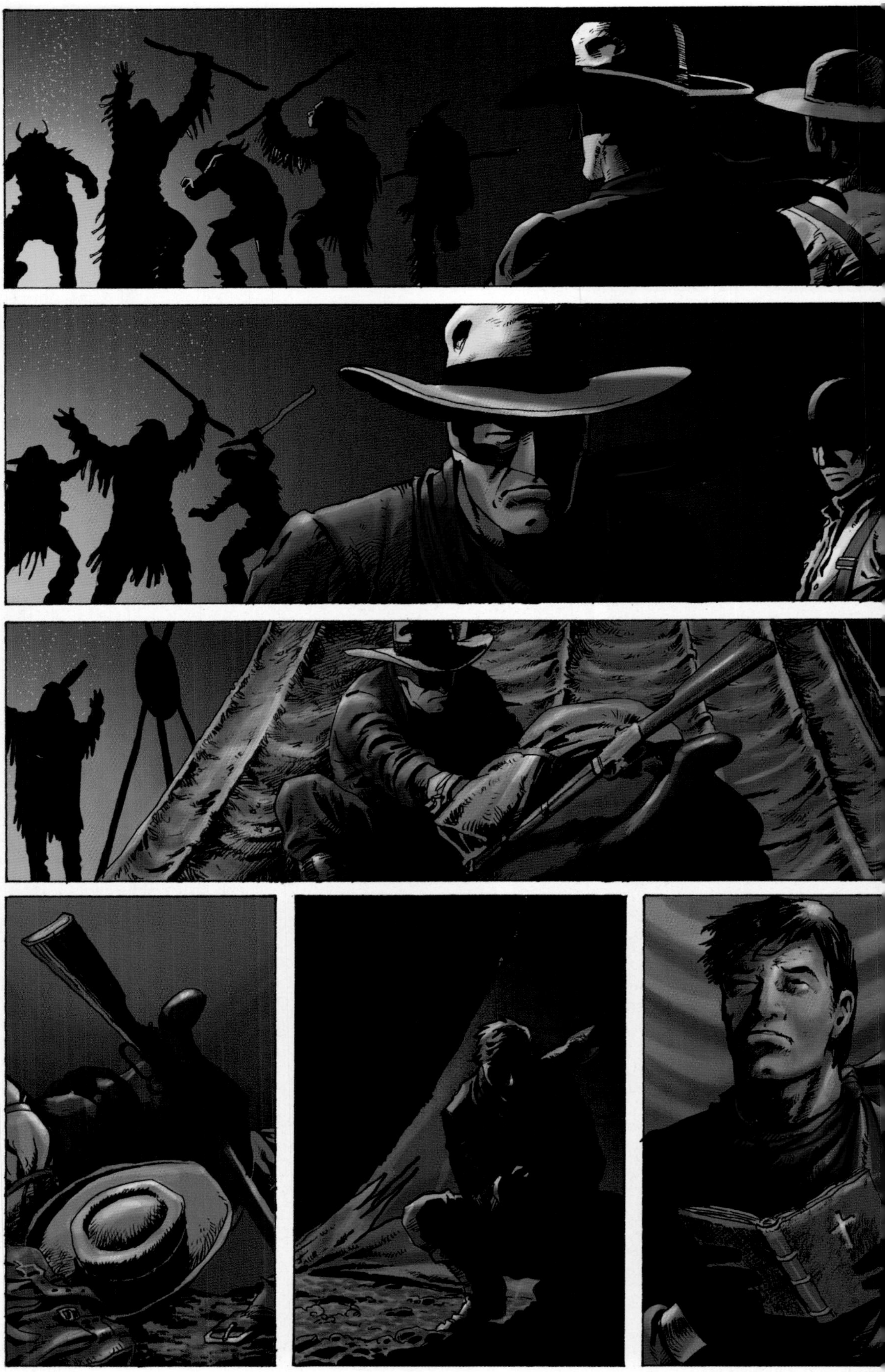

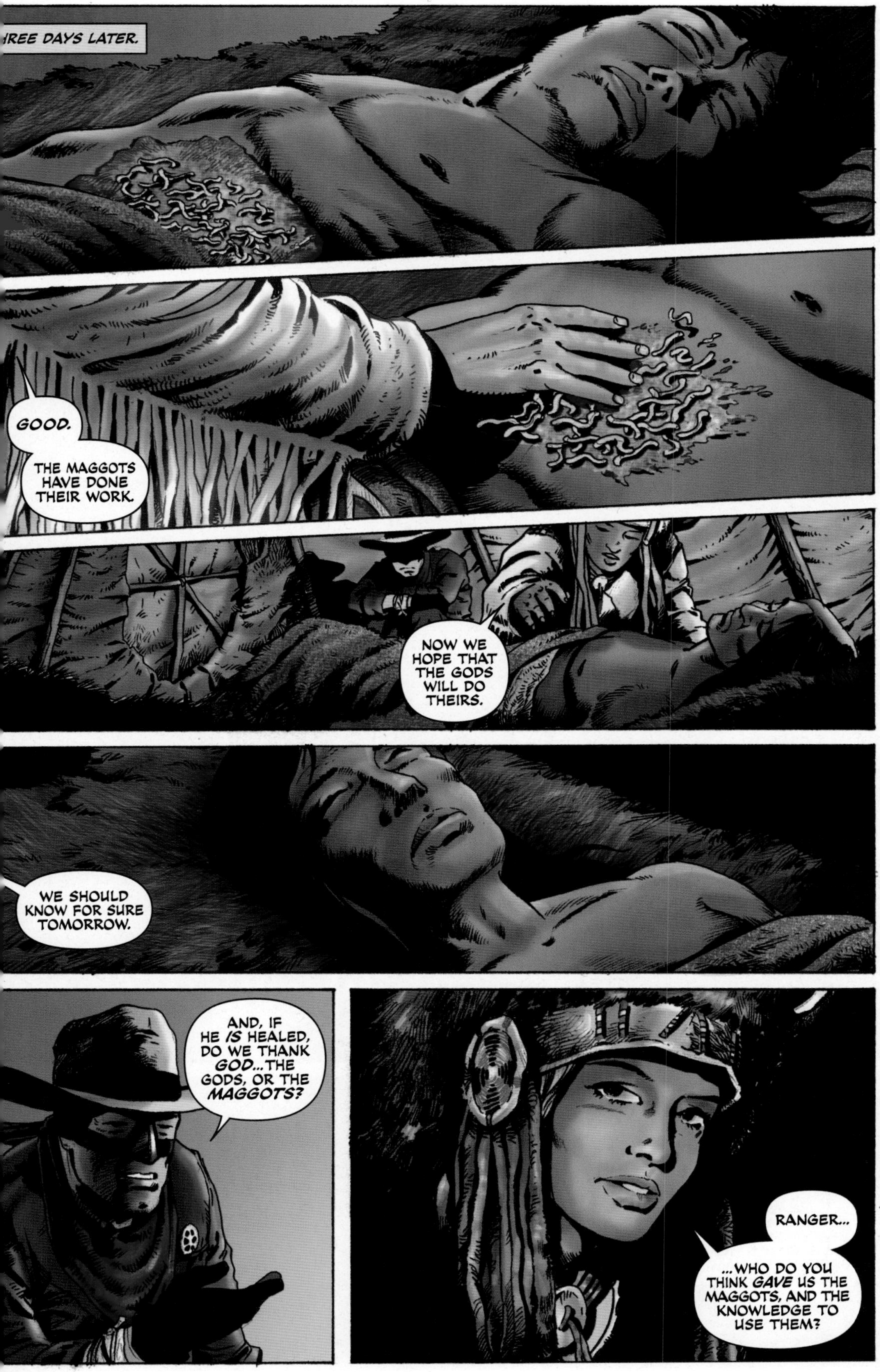
HREE DAYS LATER.
GOOD.
THE MAGGOTS HAVE DONE THEIR WORK.
NOW WE HOPE THAT THE GODS WILL DO THEIRS.
WE SHOULD KNOW FOR SURE TOMORROW.
AND, IF HE IS HEALED, DO WE THANK GOD...THE GODS, OR THE MAGGOTS?
RANGER...
...WHO DO YOU THINK GAVE US THE MAGGOTS, AND THE KNOWLEDGE TO USE THEM?

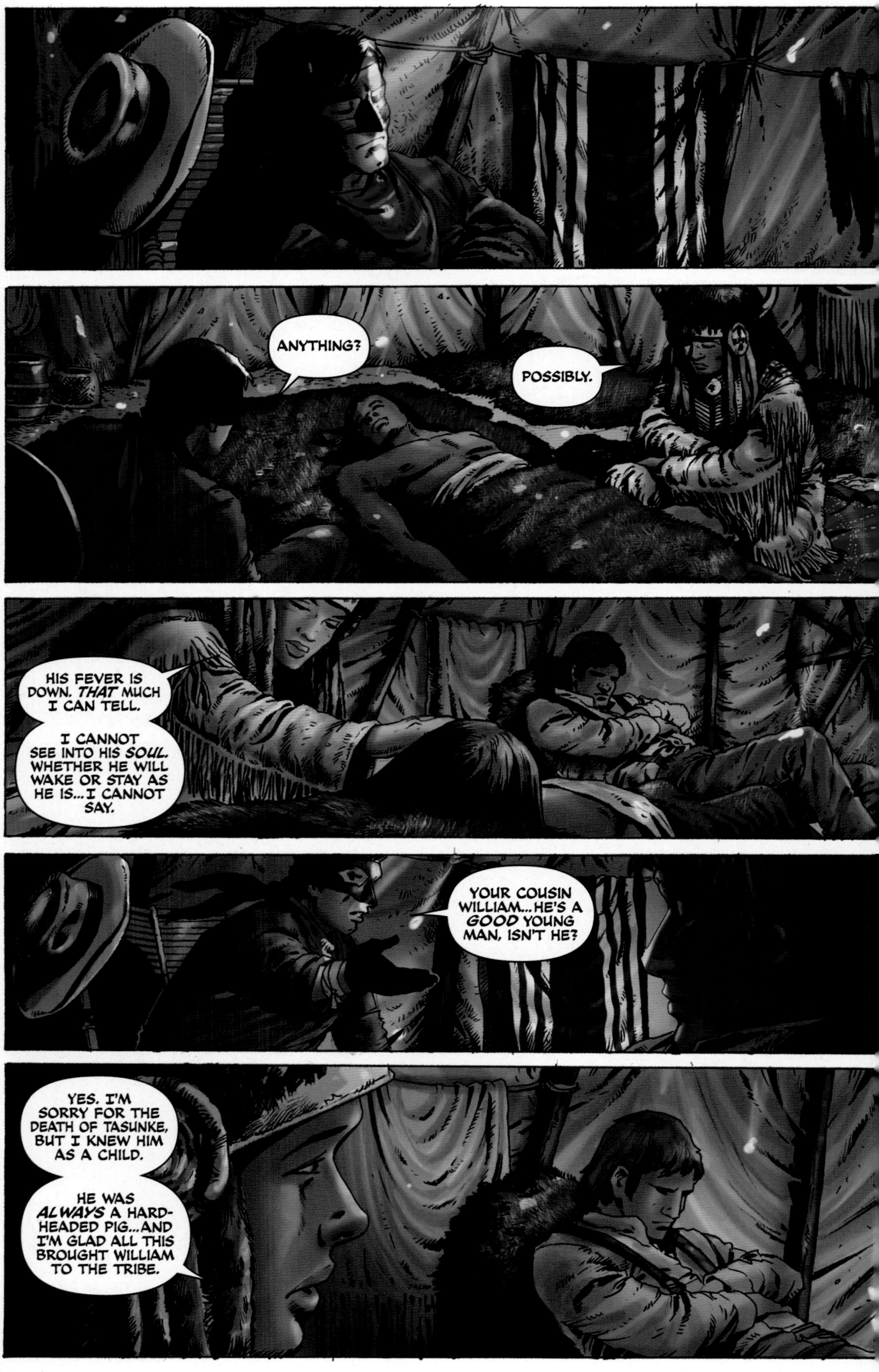
ANYTHING?
POSSIBLY.
HIS FEVER IS DOWN. *THAT* MUCH I CAN TELL.
I CANNOT SEE INTO HIS *SOUL.* WHETHER HE WILL WAKE OR STAY AS HE IS...I CANNOT SAY.
YOUR COUSIN WILLIAM...HE'S A *GOOD* YOUNG MAN, ISN'T HE?
YES. I'M SORRY FOR THE DEATH OF TASUNKE, BUT I KNEW HIM AS A CHILD.
HE WAS *ALWAYS* A HARD-HEADED PIG...AND I'M GLAD ALL THIS BROUGHT WILLIAM TO THE TRIBE.

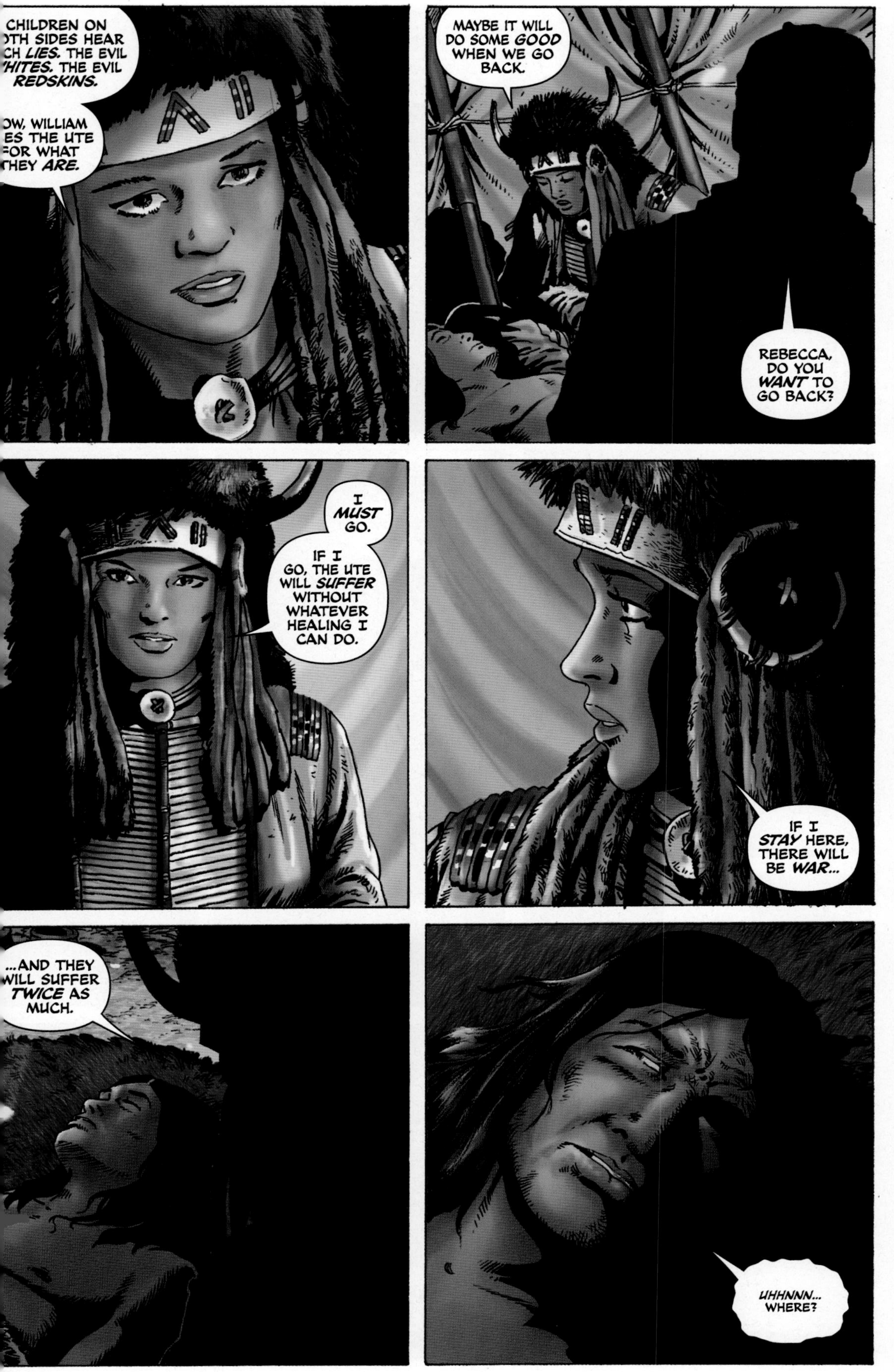

CHILDREN ON
OTH SIDES HEAR
CH LIES. THE EVIL
HITES. THE EVIL
REDSKINS.
OW, WILLIAM
ES THE UTE
FOR WHAT
THEY ARE.
MAYBE IT WILL DO SOME GOOD WHEN WE GO BACK.
REBECCA, DO YOU WANT TO GO BACK?
I MUST GO.
IF I GO, THE UTE WILL SUFFER WITHOUT WHATEVER HEALING I CAN DO.
IF I STAY HERE, THERE WILL BE WAR...
...AND THEY
WILL SUFFER
TWICE AS
MUCH.
UHHNNN... WHERE?

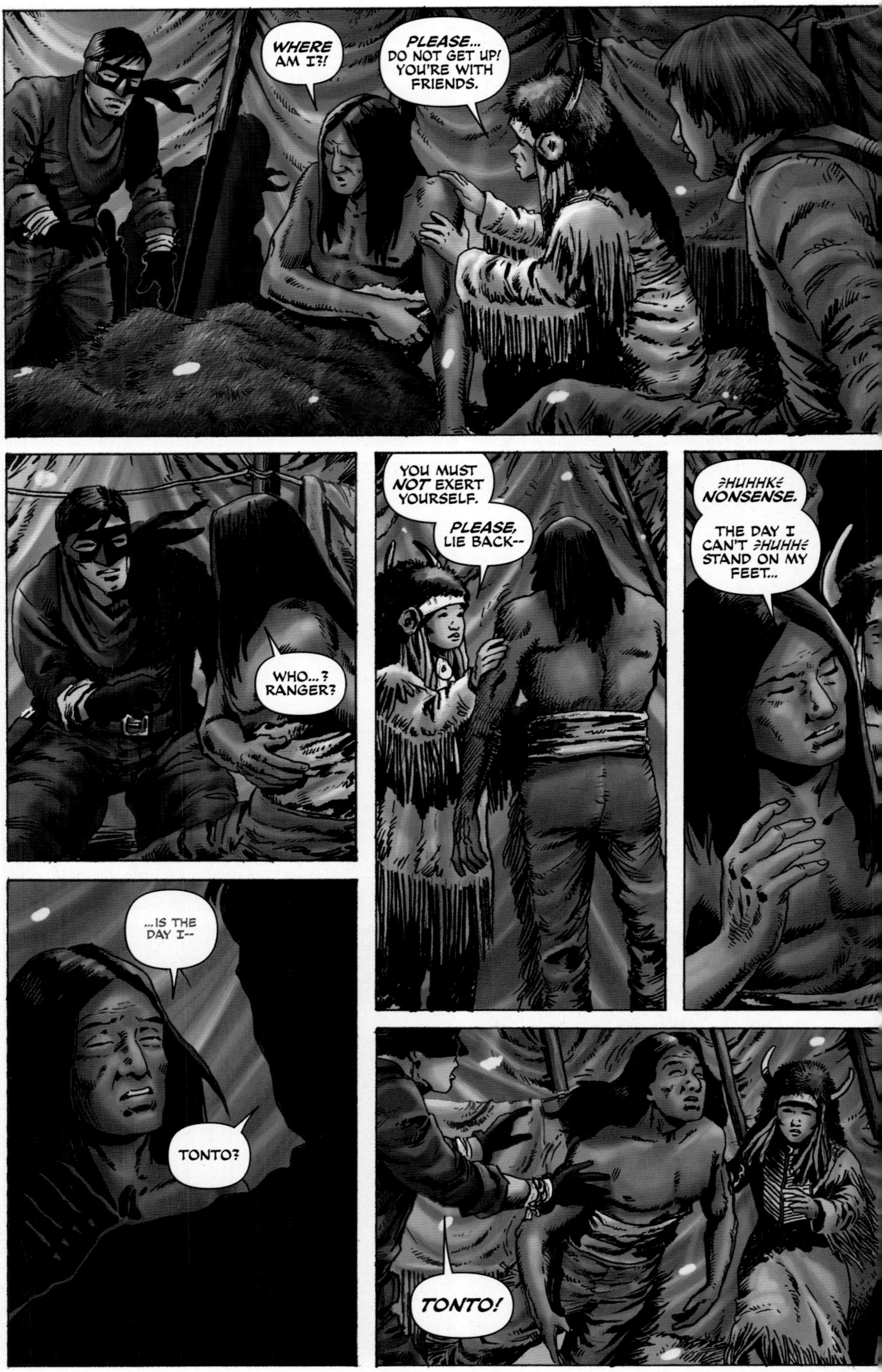
WHERE AM I?!
PLEASE... DO NOT GET UP! YOU'RE WITH FRIENDS.
WHO...? RANGER?
YOU MUST NOT EXERT YOURSELF.
PLEASE, LIE BACK--
HUHHK NONSENSE.
THE DAY I CAN'T *HUHH* STAND ON MY FEET...
...IS THE DAY I--
TONTO?
TONTO!

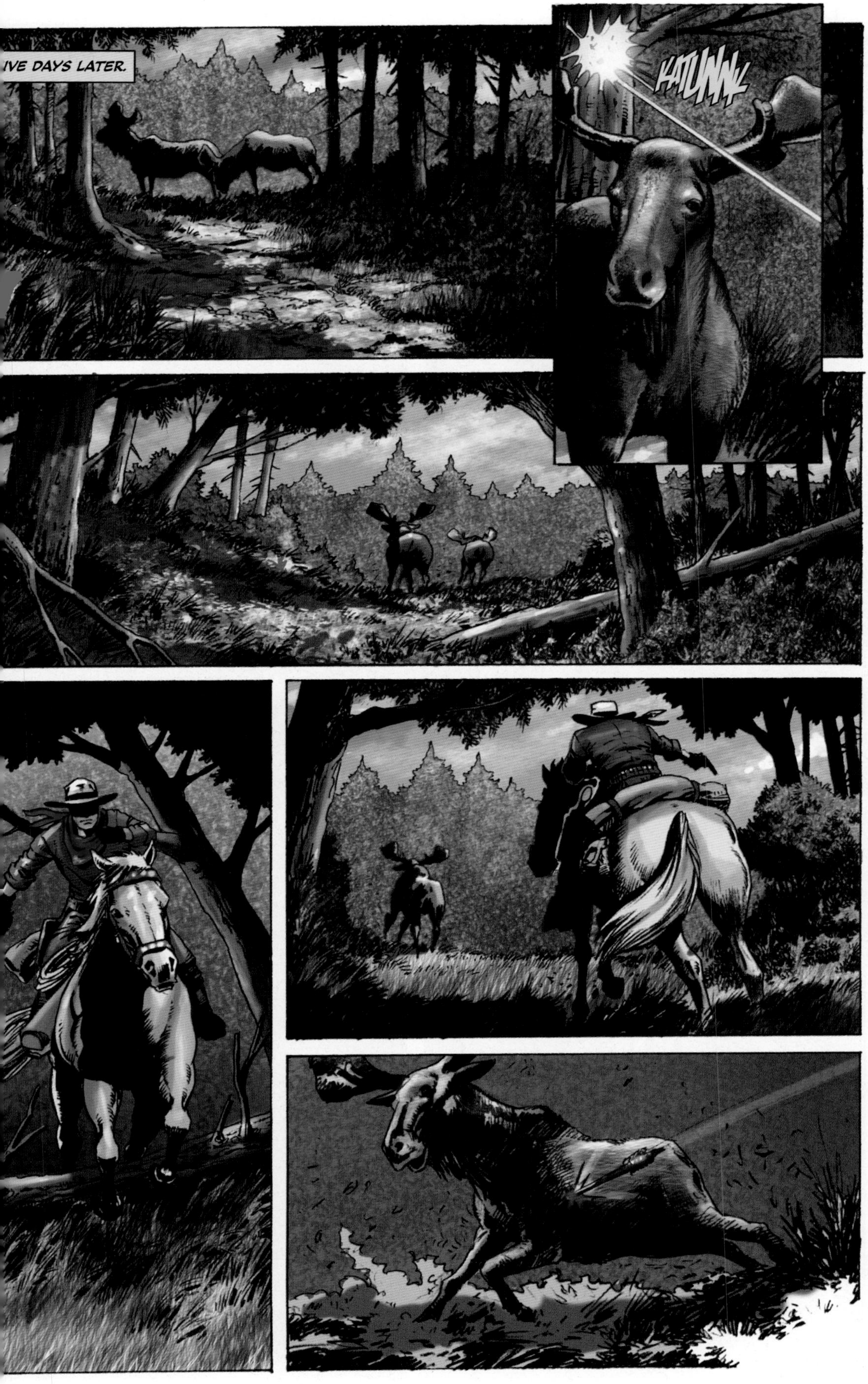
IVE DAYS LATER.
KATUNNK

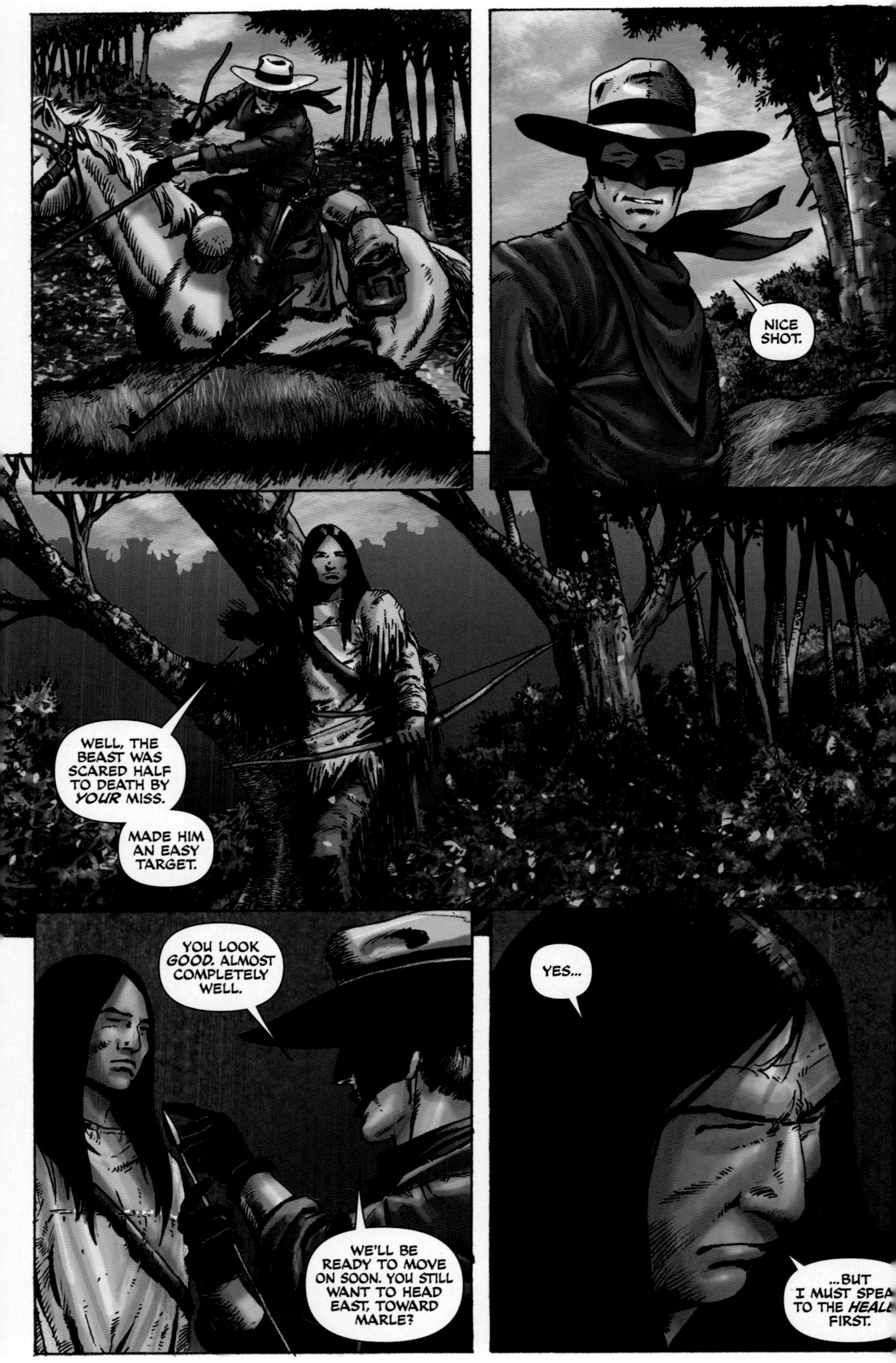
NICE SHOT.
WELL, THE BEAST WAS SCARED HALF TO DEATH BY *YOUR* MISS.
MADE HIM AN EASY TARGET.
YOU LOOK *GOOD.* ALMOST COMPLETELY WELL.
WE'LL BE READY TO MOVE ON SOON. YOU STILL WANT TO HEAD EAST, TOWARD MARLE?
YES...
...BUT I MUST SPEA TO THE *HEAL* FIRST.

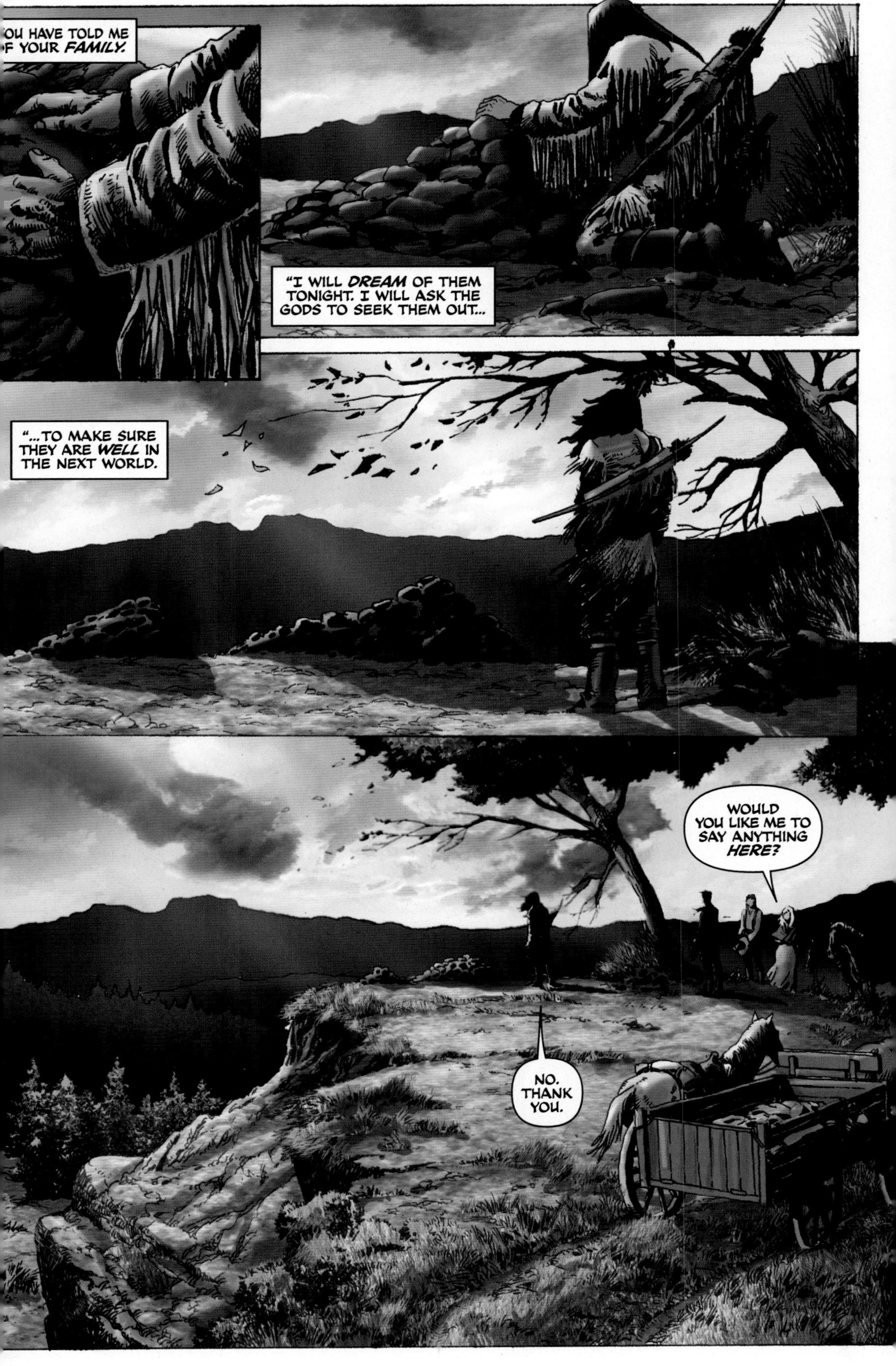
OU HAVE TOLD ME
F YOUR *FAMILY.*
"I WILL *DREAM* OF THEM TONIGHT. I WILL ASK THE GODS TO SEEK THEM OUT...
"...TO MAKE SURE THEY ARE *WELL* IN THE NEXT WORLD.
WOULD YOU LIKE ME TO SAY ANYTHING *HERE?*
NO. THANK YOU.

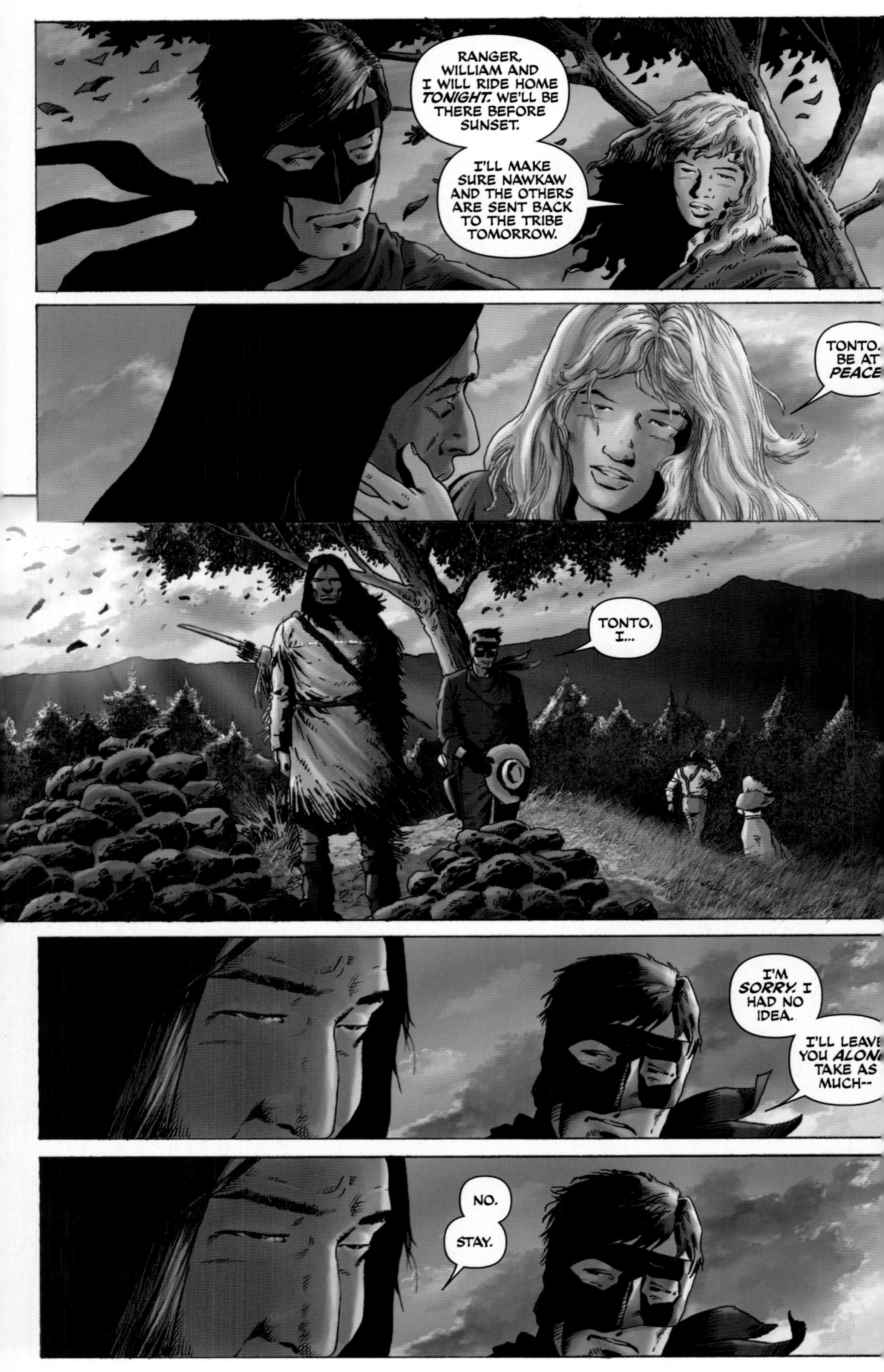
RANGER, WILLIAM AND I WILL RIDE HOME *TONIGHT.* WE'LL BE THERE BEFORE SUNSET.
I'LL MAKE SURE NAWKAW AND THE OTHERS ARE SENT BACK TO THE TRIBE TOMORROW.
TONTO. BE AT *PEACE*
TONTO, I...
I'M *SORRY.* I HAD NO IDEA.
I'LL LEAVE YOU *ALONE.* TAKE AS MUCH--
NO.
STAY.

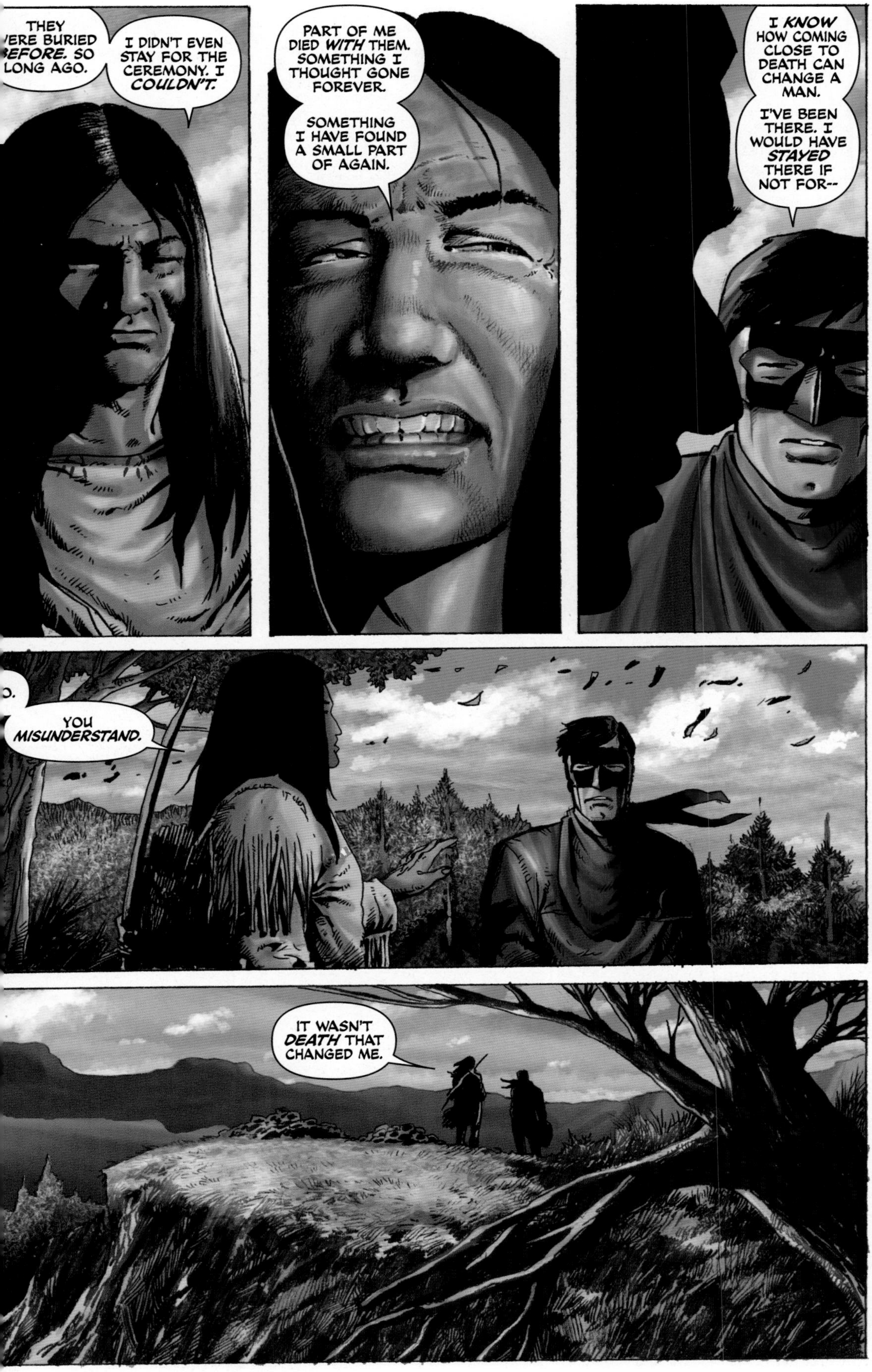
THEY WERE BURIED BEFORE. SO LONG AGO.
I DIDN'T EVEN STAY FOR THE CEREMONY. I COULDN'T.
PART OF ME DIED WITH THEM. SOMETHING I THOUGHT GONE FOREVER.
SOMETHING I HAVE FOUND A SMALL PART OF AGAIN.
I KNOW HOW COMING CLOSE TO DEATH CAN CHANGE A MAN.
I'VE BEEN THERE. I WOULD HAVE STAYED THERE IF NOT FOR--
YOU MISUNDERSTAND.
IT WASN'T DEATH THAT CHANGED ME.

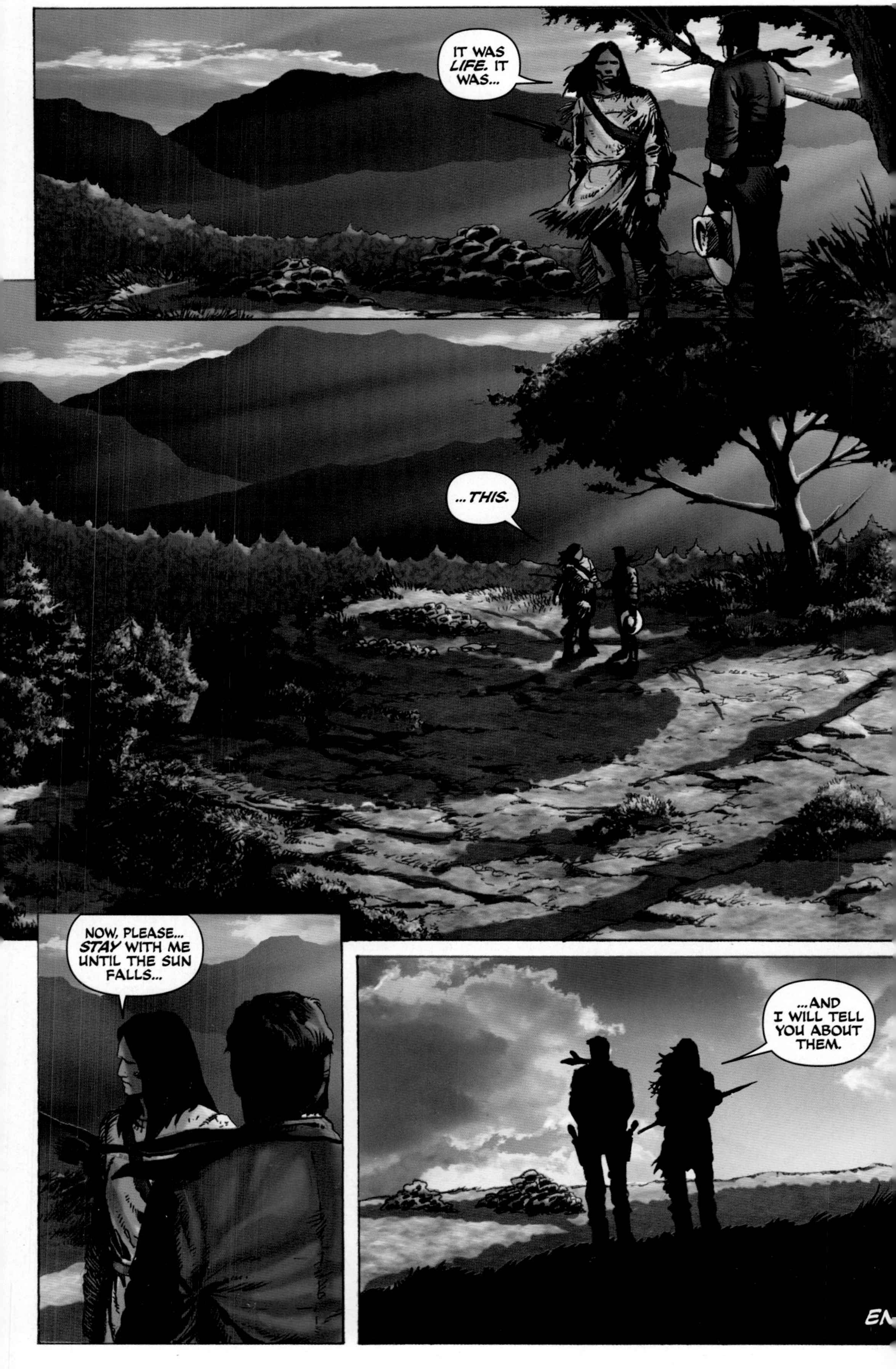
IT WAS LIFE. IT WAS...
...THIS.
NOW, PLEASE... STAY WITH ME UNTIL THE SUN FALLS...
...AND I WILL TELL YOU ABOUT THEM.